Kenneth Burke
Literature and Language
as Symbolic Action

To Tom,

A rare first edition (the second
edition will be even rarer), in
memory of all the long and intense
conversations that generated many of
the ideas contained herein. All the
best to you, Gwyn, and Ross.

Greig

Kenneth Burke

Literature and Language as Symbolic Action

Greig E. Henderson

THE UNIVERSITY OF GEORGIA PRESS
ATHENS AND LONDON

© 1988 by the University of Georgia Press
Athens, Georgia 30602
All rights reserved

Designed by Nighthawk Design
Set in 10.5 on 13 Sabon
The paper in this book meets the guidelines for
permanence and durability of the Committee on
Production Guidelines for Book Longevity of the
Council on Library Resources.

Printed in the United States of America

92 91 90 89 88   5 4 3 2 1

Library of Congress Cataloging in Publication Data

Henderson, Greig E.
   Kenneth Burke : literature and language as symbolic
action / Greig E. Henderson.
      p.   cm.
   Bibliography: p.
   Includes index.
   ISBN 0-8203-1037-9 (alk. paper)
   1. Burke, Kenneth, 1897–   —Knowledge—
Literature.   2. Literature—History and criticism—
Theory, etc.   3. Criticism—United States.   I. Title.
PS3503.U6134Z67   1988
801'.95'0924—dc19   88-1320
                                                 CIP

British Library Cataloging in Publication Data available

The epigraph, "Creation Myth," is from Kenneth Burke,
Collected Poems (Berkeley and Los Angeles: University
of California Press, 1968). Reprinted by permission of
the University of California Press.

To my parents

Creation Myth

In the beginning, there was universal Nothing.
Then Nothing said No to itself and thereby begat
    Something,
Which called itself Yes.

Then No and Yes, cohabiting, begat Maybe.
Next all three, in a ménage à trois, begat Guilt.

And Guilt was of many names:
Mine, Thine, Yours, Ours, His, Hers, Its, Theirs—
    and Order.

In time things so came to pass
That two of its names, Guilt and Order,
Honoring their great progenitors, Yes, No, and Maybe,
Begat History.

Finally, History fell a-dreaming
And dreamed about Language—

(And that brings us to critics-who-write-critiques-
    of-critical-criticism.)
                                    KENNETH BURKE

Contents

Acknowledgments

I would like to thank Bill Rueckert for his helpful and insightful criticism, Bob Greene for his direction and supervision of my initial explorations of Burke, my wife, Erica, for her assistance and support, and Leonard and Edith Steinberg for their expert proofreading. I would also like to thank Kenneth Burke, whose attitudes toward language, life, literature, and method remain an inspiration.

Abbreviations

Kenneth Burke
Literature and Language
as Symbolic Action

Introduction

THE PIVOTAL IDEA that animates all of Kenneth Burke's critical theory and practice is embodied in his contention that "the ultimate metaphor for discussing the universe and man's relations to it must be the poetic or dramatic metaphor."[1] According to Burke, "dramatism" is a method of analysis that "invites one to consider the matter of motives in a perspective that, being developed from the analysis of drama, treats language and thought primarily as modes of action."[2] "Poetry, or any verbal act, is to be considered as 'symbolic action.' "[3] Burke's idea of dramatism, then, applies to both literature and language. Its very definition, in fact, goes a long way toward breaking down any absolute distinctions between the literary and ordinary uses of language.

In the preface to the first edition of his landmark study—*Kenneth Burke and the Drama of Human Relations*—William H. Rueckert notes that when one confronts Burke's

> monolithic dramatistic system . . . at least two kinds of basic studies can be undertaken. . . . The first kind is a more or less chronological, developmental study which presents as organic the development through stages to the final synthesis. . . . The second kind begins where the first one ends: its organization would come from the system it-self. . . . A wonderful kind of simultaneity and coherence would be achieved in this way, for the beginning and middle works could be seen, not as *culminating* in dramatism, but in *terms* of dramatism.[4]

In contemporary parlance, Rueckert's is a distinction between diachronic and synchronic modes of analysis. The diachronic undertakes to construct the historical evolution of a system of thought, whereas the synchronic undertakes to describe the system as an existing whole without respect to its history. Rueckert opts for the first mode of analysis, and his illuminating study of Burke attests to the efficacy of his approach. In this study I opt mainly for the second, though I do not believe that the diachronic and synchronic approaches are mutually exclusive. As Frank Lentricchia points out in "Reading History with Kenneth Burke," "there is never any question of choosing between them, never any question of segregating them as if the interpreting subject . . . could master the process of reading. . . . Like interpretation, history is never synchrony or diachrony . . . it is both."[5]

Nevertheless, my approach to Burke is more synchronic than diachronic; I address certain key themes that recur throughout Burke's work and examine them in contexts that often extend beyond their original scope. I do not achieve, however, anything resembling that "wonderful kind of simultaneity and coherence" Rueckert speaks of, primarily because I do not believe that it exists. In Burke's writings there is a perceptible and sometimes disturbing discontinuity between dramatism—the idea that literature and language are to be considered as symbolic action—and logology—the idea that words about God (theology) bear a strong resemblance to words about words (logology) and that "the close study of theology and its forms will provide us with a good insight into the nature of language itself as a motive."[6] It is true that one must see logology in *terms* of dramatism, but one must also recognize the diachronic differences between them. From the time of *The Rhetoric of Religion* (1961) and afterward, logology, a language-centered view of reality, tends to prevail. Logology converts methodological priority—the heuristic method of treating communication as primary to all categories of experience and of adopting the poetic perspective of man as communicant, a dramatistic method first developed in *Permanence and Change* (1935)—into ontological priority—the logological view that language is the source and origin of all value because it affords the peculiar possibility of the negative, the possibility of saying "no" to "thou shalt not," a view that finds its ultimate expression in *The Rhetoric of Religion*. The relationship between dramatism and logology is extremely complex, and it will be dealt with in detail in the fourth chapter. My point here is that a purely synchronic approach to the dialectic of ideas in Burke's writings will not suffice; there are real contradictions and disharmonies to be grappled with. One banishes historical considerations at the cost of misrepresentation.

In the first chapter of this study, I argue that Burke's dramatistic theory of literature is able to integrate two modes of critical analysis—the intrinsic mode, which tends to construe literature as a self-enclosed universe of discourse, and the extrinsic mode, which tends to construe literature as reducible to some other frame of reference. Symbolic action is part of the conceptual apparatus that makes this intrinsic/extrinsic merger possible. Throughout his writings Burke refuses to essentialize literary discourse by making it a unique kind of language and is always attuned to the dialectical relationship between literary productions and their sociohistorical contexts. "Whatever 'free play' there may be in esthetic enterprise," he writes, "it is held down by the gravitational pull of historical necessities; the poetic forms are symbolic structures designed to equip us for confronting given historical and personal situations."[7] In order to show how Burke manages to yoke together formalist and sociological approaches to literature, I consider his relationship to both New Criticism and Marxist Criticism, giving in the process an embryonic account of his dramatistic theory of literature and a conceptual framework for further discussion.

In the second chapter I show how Burke's critical terms function when deployed to analyze texts from various genres. The implicit claim is that theoretical abstraction has validity only to the degree that it can meet the exigencies of practical criticism, for the value of a literary theory resides in its generating new insights, not in its converting what any intelligent reading would yield into abstruse technical terms. First, I make my own application of Burke's ideas to a poem; second, I examine his own analyses of *Julius Caesar, Antony and Cleopatra, Coriolanus, A Passage to India,* and *A Portrait of the Artist as a Young Man.*

In the third chapter I place dramatism into a broader philosophical context by considering three other orientations toward language—positivism, structuralism, and deconstruction. I contend that the strength of dramatism resides in its recognition of the necessarily ambiguous transaction between the system of signs and the context of situation. As Burke puts it: "Words are aspects of a much wider communicative context, most of which is not verbal at all. Yet words also have a nature peculiarly their own. And when discussing them as modes of action, we must consider both this nature as words in themselves *and* the nature they get from the nonverbal scenes that support their acts" (*PLF,* xvii).

In the fourth chapter I spell out the connection between dramatism and logology, arguing that Burke's logological thesis, which establishes an analogy between discourse about God and discourse about discourse, runs the risk of leading one into an intrinsic fallacy. By stressing the built-in deductive aspects of any nomenclature (the closed complex of mutual implications that makes for what Burke calls a tautological cycle of terms), logology tends to downplay the importance of the nonverbal scenes that support verbal acts.

In the fifth chapter I show how logology functions when deployed to analyze "Burnt Norton." Logological analysis is particularly effective in dealing with works that, like the *Four Quartets,* are essentially religious and philosophical in subject matter. Burke's ideas about the perfectionism implicit in religious discourse, the rhetoric of the ineffable, the oxymoron as the master trope of mysticism, and the temporizing of essence (the spinning out into narrative of a series of logical relationships) help to illuminate aspects of Eliot's rhetorical strategy in "Burnt Norton."

In the final section I examine the ethical implications of Burke's lifelong commitment to the view that literature is equipment for living, that "art is the dial on which the fundamental psychological processes of *all* living are recorded" (*ATH,* 202). Dramatism is more than just a theory of literature and language; it is also a moral vision. Against the scientific and technological psychoses that dominate our culture, dramatism makes its humanistic counterstatement.

In our own historical moment it is painfully obvious that what Burke said more than fifty years ago still holds.

> Meaning or symbolism becomes a central concern precisely at that stage when a given system of meanings is falling into decay. In periods of firmly established meanings, one does not *study* them, one uses them: One frames his acts in accordance with them. . . . For in the last analysis, men do not communicate by a neutral vocabulary. In the pro-

foundest human sense, one communicates by a *weighted* vocabulary in which the weightings are shared by his group as a whole. (*PC,* 162)

And perhaps this is the most important message to derive from studying Kenneth Burke: that words are agents of power; that they are value-laden, ideologically motivated, and morally and emotionally weighted instruments of persuasion and representation; that the semantic ideal of neutral naming is part of a hegemonic discourse that negates the sociohistorical individual by effacing him; and that the most morally bankrupt of all things is to be the neutral namer or the disinterested specialist, what Socrates calls in Plato's *Phaedrus* the nonlover. It is at the peril of inanition that one divorces literature from the social, cultural, and political matrix that gives it life and meaning.

One

The Intrinsic/Extrinsic Merger

MORE THAN SIXTY years ago I. A. Richards entitled the first chapter of his *Principles of Literary Criticism* "The Chaos of Critical Theories." Despite the magnitude of subsequent theoretical activity, that chaos has not been resolved into any semblance of cosmos. Thus to propose in the spirit of clarity a distinction that would divide a plurality of critical approaches into two opposed orientations—intrinsic and extrinsic—is equivocal from the outset. The distinction is elaborated only to be destroyed, for neither the intrinsic nor the extrinsic can be isolated in its elemental purity. Both are dialectical concepts; each must be defined in terms of the other. Hence, as Burke would put it, they are susceptible to endless transformations—symbolic mergers and divisions. At an ultimate level, text and context are not categorically separable. Nonetheless, this distinction is not as self-defeating as it might seem, for "what we want is *not terms that avoid ambiguities,* but *terms that reveal clearly the strategic points at which ambiguities necessarily arise*" (*GM,* xviii).

By "intrinsic" I mean what Burke calls the "implicit or explicit 'equations' . . . in any work considered as one particular structure of terms, or symbol system" (*PLF,* viii). In general, an intrinsic approach tends to construe either the text itself or the entire literary system of which it is a part as a self-enclosed universe of discourse, reflecting the whole post-Saussurian tendency to construe language as a system of structures with no substantive content and only a complex, fluctuating, and inherently problematic referential function.

By "extrinsic" I mean those aspects of reality that permeate the literary system and are the main concerns of biography, psychology, history, sociology, philosophy, and so on. In general, an extrinsic approach tends to construe literature as reducible to some other frame of reference, whether it be that of psychoanalysis, dialectical materialism, or whatever. Such an approach assumes the ontological priority of context over text.[1]

Even expressed in such an abstract way, this distinction is familiar enough. In the intrinsic category one might place Russian Formalism, New Criticism, and Structuralism. In the extrinsic category one might place Freudian, Marxist, sociological, historical, moral, phenomenological, mythological, and archetypal criticism. (These lists are by no means exhaustive, and any number of permutations and combinations is possible.) Yet even this preliminary grouping might seem arbitrary. There is no doubt, for example, that certain archetypal critics would consider their approach intrinsic. They would argue that archetypes emerge from within the total form of literature itself and that the archetypal core of a text is a deep structure intrinsic to that text's primary signification. From this point of view, the structuralist attempt to view the text as a linguistic system would be regarded as merely the application of a metaphor, the imposition of an extrinsic model. Moreover, deconstructionist critics, with their insistence on the heterogeneity of the individual text and their accompanying emphasis on the marginal and supplementary, undermine any possibility of distinguishing the intrinsic from the extrinsic. If the text has no boundaries and occupies an intertextual space outside of which nothing shall fall ("*il n'y a pas de hors-texte*"), then such a distinction is by definition indeterminate and undecidable. These are murky waters but further discussion of the deconstructionist project will be deferred until the third chapter. For in the context of twentieth-century criticism up to deconstruction, the predominant critical orientation has been so decidedly toward the intrinsic that the extrinsic has had status primarily as a pejorative term.

The intrinsic orientation involves a cluster of interrelated images and ideas. The literary work is conceived of as an autonomous object of some description, whether it be a verbal icon, a well-wrought urn, a spatial form, a linguistic artifact, or whatever. It is a verbal construct, a language complex, a semiological system, a system of norms, a structure of determination, a synchronic whole, or an organic unity. It is neosymbolist, self-sustaining, self-referential, internally coherent, holistic, and nonmimetic. One must approach the work ontologically, battering the object but committing neither the intentional nor affective fallacies. One must be on the lookout for irony, paradox, ambivalence, ambiguity, tension, estrangement, defamiliarization, foregrounding, the baring of the device, the absorption of content into form or quantity into quality, the bracketing of the referent, and so on. Obviously, this accumulation of detail could be extended indefinitely and would demand more than a sheer enumeration of characteristic terms in order to have historical validity. But it is not my intention to give an account of the intrinsic approach in its full complexity. I want merely to give an indication of the kind of vocabulary of critical terms such an approach has generated.

M. H. Abrams conveniently summarizes the intrinsic orientation, using the word "objective" to epitomize it. "The 'objective orientation,' which on principle regards the work of art in isolation from all these external points of reference, analyzes it as a self-sufficient entity constituted by its parts in their internal relations, and sets out to judge it solely by criteria intrinsic to its own mode of being."[2] He also points out a crucial implication of this critical stance. "Poetic statement and poetic truth are utterly diverse from scientific statement and scientific truth, in that a poem is an object-in-itself, a self-contained universe of discourse, of which we cannot demand that it be true to nature, but only, that it be true to itself."[3] Thus the poetic and scientific functions of language are clearly distinguished.

I. A. Richards's conception of poetry as pseudostatement is symptomatic of this dichotomous view of the functions of language, and his statement of the matter is at the center of the Anglo-American tradition of the intrinsic. As early as 1923 Richards and Ogden note in *The Meaning of Meaning* that "very much poetry consists of statements, symbolic arrangements capable of truth or falsity, which are not used for the sake of their truth or falsity but for the sake of the attitudes which their acceptance will evoke. . . . Any symbolic function that the words may have is instrumental only and subordinate to the evocative function."[4] In *Poetries and Sciences* Richards further develops this distinction by using the term "pseudo-statement" to define an utterance in which the evocative function is dominant and the term "state-

ment" to define an utterance in which the symbolic function is dominant. According to him, "A pseudo-statement is justified entirely by
its effect in releasing or organizing our impulses and attitudes. . . . A
statement, on the other hand, is justified by its truth, that is its correspondence, in a highly technical sense, with the fact to which it
points."[5] Hence an utterance "may be used for the sake of the *reference,* true or false, which it causes. This is the *scientific* use of language. But it may also be used for the sake of the effects in emotion
and attitude produced by the reference it occasions. This is the *emotive* use of language."[6]

Science, therefore, yields us a body of undistorted references whose
criteria for legitimacy are empirical verifiability and correspondence
to objective reality, whereas literature yields us a body of distorted
references whose criteria for legitimacy are coherence, convincingness,
and sincerity. As science organizes the external realm of reference, so
poetry organizes the internal realm of impulse and attitude.

I shall not consider the extent to which Richards's position is a
strategic response to a determinate historical moment, a moment during which the encroachment of scientism seemed a threat to humanistic endeavor and religious belief. It is sufficient to note that the development of an intrinsic mode of criticism has coincided with what
Richards calls the "amazing swiftness" with which "science has
opened out field after field of possible reference" (*PLC,* 265). It is one
way of guaranteeing the autonomy of the privileged object of study.

Not all critics of the intrinsic orientation, however, would find
Richards's version of the emotive/referential distinction acceptable;
even Richards himself qualifies it in later writings. In *The Structure of
Complex Words,* for example, William Empson seeks to refute simple-
minded critical distinctions between the emotive and cognitive uses of
words. His purpose is to trace both the interconnections and distinctions between the various intellectual and emotional meanings a given
word may possess in a given context, by providing "more elaborate
machinery to disentangle the Emotive from the Cognitive part of poetical language."[7] W. K. Wimsatt and Monroe Beardsley also provide
more elaborate machinery for disentanglement, noting that "a large
and obvious area of emotive *import* depends directly upon descriptive
meaning" and that "a great deal of emotive *import* which does not
depend thus directly on descriptive *meaning* does depend on descriptive *suggestion.*"[8]

Moreover, the emotive/referential distinction is implicitly present in many critical writings where the terms themselves are not explicitly used. Ransom's distinction between structure—the argument of a poem—and texture—its rich particularity—is a case in point. Even though he is critical of Richards's "characteristic rejection of the cognitive" and reliance on psychological explanation, he posits a sharp discontinuity between scientific and poetic uses of language.[9] According to Ransom science is pure structure without any texture because it deals with the logical apprehension of universals, whereas texture in a poem, what he also calls local irrelevance, "things in their thinginess," happily impedes argument because poetry deals primarily with the imaginative apprehension of particulars.[10] It is true that, unlike Richards, Ransom does give poetry some cognitive status—poetry gives us "knowledge by images"—but he is as emphatic as Richards about keeping science separate.[11] "The sciences deal almost entirely with structures, which are scientific structures, but poetic structures differ radically from these, and it is that difference which defines them. The ontological materials are different, and are such as to fall outside the possible range of science."[12]

In a similar vein, Cleanth Brooks also keeps the two realms separate. His statement that "the language of poetry is the language of paradox" is followed soon after with the observation that "it is the scientist whose truth requires a language purged of every trace of paradox."[13]

Even where the distinction is vehemently denied, its omnipresence is intensely felt. Yvor Winters's polemic against "qualitative progression" (a term he borrows from Kenneth Burke, who defines it as "a bold juxtaposition of one quality created by another, an association in ideas which, if not logical, is nevertheless emotionally right"),[14] against, in other words, the building of poetry out of the suggestive, evocative, and emotive aspects of language, and his concomitant insistence that a poem be implicitly rational, that it supply an adequate motive for the emotion produced, underscores the pervasiveness of the view he is opposing. "The concept represented by the word," Winters writes, "motivates the feeling which the word communicates. . . . The relationship in the poem, between rational statement and feeling, is . . . that of motive to emotion."[15] For him there should be no distinction between scientific and poetic language as far as referentiality is concerned. What he calls pseudoreference, grammatical coherence without rational coherence, is anathema to him. Poetry should have paraphrasable content.

On the basis of these examples it would seem that however much these critics differ in perceiving the implications of the emotive/referential distinction, there is no denying that the distinction is at the center of the ideology of the intrinsic.

In the continental tradition the distinction expresses itself in terms of a poetic/ordinary language dichotomy—"the belief that literature is formally and functionally distinct from other kinds of utterances and the concomitant belief that literature is linguistically autonomous."[16] That is, "poetry is not merely a specialized part of everyday language, but constitutes a total linguistic system in its own right."[17] According to the Prague School, for example, "in its social role language must be specified according to its relation to extralinguistic reality. It has either a communicative function, that is, it is directed toward the signified, or a poetic function, that is, it is directed toward the sign itself."[18] What both traditions have in common, then, is the assumption that poetic language is qualitatively different from other kinds of language. While they use different terms to define this difference, their conclusions are not incompatible.

It is much more difficult to isolate the extrinsic orientation since it comprehends a diversity of approaches. As a pejorative term, however, it usually stands for vulgar reductionism of some type—the view of literature as wish-fulfillment or fantasy-gratification, or the view of literature as an unequivocal expression of class interests. Earlier in the century its status as a pejorative term was understandable—the excesses of genetic criticism, especially in their historicist and biographical varieties, are well documented—but now that the more sophisticated practitioners of extrinsic criticism manage to avoid the pitfalls of deterministic circularity the whole issue must be reassessed. Moreover, many intrinsic approaches, committed to the irrelevancy of the extrinsic on ideological grounds, simply disguise all notions of intention, motive, and background by converting them into textual attributes. The uniqueness of Kenneth Burke's approach resides in its ability to integrate intrinsic and extrinsic modes of criticism through the theory of symbolic action.

Norman Holland is an example of a sophisticated practitioner of extrinsic criticism. He openly admits that a poem has *both* a "nucleus

of fantasy *and* the central meaning regular explication points out."
According to him, the critic should focus on the "process of transformation from fantasy to intellectual significance."[19] That he says "conscious meaning is a *transformation* of the unconscious fantasy" is significant.[20] It shows the extent to which he yokes extrinsic and intrinsic
aspects together. While there is no doubt that he ascribes ontological
priority to the unconscious fantasy—the psychoanalytic context of the
poetic act—he does not downplay the role of "the strategy of the
poem . . . in pressing the unconscious fantasy towards meaning."[21]

With a similar sensitivity to both the extrinsic and intrinsic, Fredric
Jameson speaks of

> the essential movement of all dialectical criticism, which is to reconcile
> the inner and the outer, the intrinsic and the extrinsic, the existential
> and the historical, to allow us to feel our way within a single determi-
> nate form or moment of history at the same time that we stand outside
> of it, in judgment on it as well, transcending that sterile and static op-
> position between formalism and a sociological or historical use of liter-
> ature between which we have been so often asked to choose.[22]

Jameson is concerned with "the influence of a given social raw material, not only on the content, but on the very form of the works themselves" (*MF*, 165). The dialectical interaction of work and background, "this fact of sheer interrelationship, is prior to any of the
conceptual categories, such as causality, reflection, or analogy, subsequently evolved to explain it" (*MF*, 6). For him, as for Burke, the
literary work is not simply a passive reflection of an objective situation; it is a dynamic and strategic response, something that transforms
a subject matter that is itself historically fluid and analyzable as a
determinate moment only after the fact. While there is no doubt that
Jameson ascribes ontological priority to the material infrastructure—
the subtext of social, economic, and historical forces—he does not
downplay the role of the strategy of the work in transforming these
forces into an ideological superstructure.

Jameson's description of the relationship between text and context
as dialectical implies the Burkean point that although literature necessarily arises out of a particular social context, it is not reducible to
that context in terms of a one-to-one correspondence between cause
and effect. For social reality does not cause a particular kind of literary

response; it merely sets limitations upon the possibilities of response. It is possible, for example, that "the work of art 'reflects' society and is historical to the degree that it *refuses* the social, and represents the last refuge of individual subjectivity from the historical forces that threaten to crush it" (*MF*, 34–35). That is, the historicity of any moment in time is just as much the upsurge of the potential as the actual, of the latent as the emergent, and it is captured as much by repression as by expression, by reaction as by revolution, by acceptance as by rejection, by evasion as by confrontation, by nostalgic regression as by utopian projection. A text is always a strategic response to historical reality, and while it must reflect that reality in some manner, if only through conspicuous neglect, its type of response may only be prophesied after the event.

It is true, of course, that as a Marxist Jameson favors the kind of ideological analysis that dissolves "the illusion of reification . . . back into the reality of human action" (*MF*, 296). He would agree with Brecht that historical conditions must not be seen as mysterious powers but as human action,[23] and that the critical attitude begins when we see our own epoch in historical terms.[24] As Brecht points out, dialectical materialism aspires to being a scientific method. "In order to unearth society's laws of motion this method treats social institutions as processes, and traces out all their inconsistencies. It regards nothing as existing except insofar as it changes; in other words, is in disharmony with itself. This also goes for those human feelings, opinions, and attitudes through which at any time the form of men's life together finds its expression."[25]

The alienation effect, which Brecht heralds as the supreme dramatic technique, defamiliarizes the present in order to divest it of any aura of permanence.[26] This effect is designed to make us aware that objects and institutions, which seem natural to us because of their familiarity, are in reality historical. Because they are the products of change, they become in their turn changeable. Similarly, Utopian projection, which envisages a future society different from the present one, can also expose the alterability of the present. The apparently static is in fact dynamic.

Much of what Jameson and Brecht say is also to be found in Burke's writings, save for their ascribing ontological priority to context over text. For Burke, the transaction between text and context is essentially ambiguous because there is no neutral viewpoint, no extralinguistic perspective from which to distinguish the priority of either. But, as the following excerpt from *Counter-Statement* indicates, the margin of overlap is significant.

> In one sense, art or ideas do "reflect" a situation, since they are a way of dealing with a situation. When a man solves a problem, however, we should hardly say that his solution is "caused" by the problem to be solved. The problem may limit somewhat the *nature* of his solution, but the problem can remain unsolved forever unless he *adds* the solution. Similarly, the particular ways of feeling and seeing which the thinker or artist develops to cope with a situation, the vocabulary they bring into prominence, the special kinds of intellectual and emotional adjustment which their works make possible by the discovery of appropriate symbols for encompassing the situation, the kinds of action they stimulate by their attitudes toward the situation, are not "caused" by the situation which they are designed to handle. The theory of economic causation seemed to rest upon the assumption that there is only one possible aesthetic response to a given situation, and that this situation is solely an economic one. (*CS*, 80–81)

As Burke puts it in *Attitudes Toward History,* "whatever 'free play' there may be in esthetic enterprise, it is held down by the gravitational pull of historical necessities; the poetic forms are symbolic structures designed to equip us for confronting given historical or personal situations" (*ATH,* 57).

Burke identifies two opposing views of the relationship between art and society—the censorship principle and the lightning rod principle. He sees Plato's *Republic* as paradigmatic of the former and Aristotle's *Poetics* as paradigmatic of the latter. "Censorship," he writes, "implies a one-to-one relation between expression and society," between a given aesthetic stimulus and a given behavioral response (*CS,* xii). Plato believes that martial music will engender martial attitudes, and since he finds certain kinds of attitudes desirable for the ideal state (militarism is one of them), he believes that there is a need for the state to control the kinds of aesthetic stimuli to be made available to the citizenry.

> In contrast with this strongly "totalitarian" view of art and thinking, there is a more complex "liberal" view. "Purification," in this scheme, is got by the draining-off of dangerous charges, as lightning rods are designed, not to "suppress" danger, but to draw it into harmless channels.

I take this to be the principle implicit in Aristotle's view of tragedy, his somewhat homeopathic notion that we are cleansed of emotional tensions by kinds of art deliberately designed to affect us with these tensions under controlled conditions. (*CS*, 112)

A homeopathic remedy seeks to "*attenuate* a risk (to control by chan-nelization)" whereas an allopathic remedy seeks to "*abolish* it (to con-trol by elimination)" (*ATH*, 45n).

Burke, of course, opts for the lightning rod principle. The upshot of this commitment is that "no categorical distinction can possibly be made between 'effective' and 'ineffective' art. The most fanciful, 'un-real,' romance may stimulate by implication the same attitudes to-wards our environment as a piece of withering satire attempts ex-plicitly" (*CS*, 90). Nostalgia for remembered plenitude, alienation from present reality, or projection toward future plenitude are all ca-pable of functioning as revolutionary stimuli. "People have gone too long with the glib psychoanalytic assumption that an art of 'escape' promotes acquiescence. It may, as easily, assist a reader to clarify his dislike of the environment in which he is placed" (*CS*, 119).

The large part of Kenneth Burke's criticism is directed against what Jameson calls "that sterile and static opposition between formalism and a sociological or historical use of literature." As Burke himself puts it: "Words are aspects of a much wider communicative context, most of which is not verbal at all. Yet words also have a nature pecu-liarly their own. And when discussing them as modes of action, we must consider *both* this nature as words in themselves *and* the nature they get from the nonverbal scenes that support their acts" (*PLF*, xvii). It follows from the above that

the search for the intrinsic, demanding in its logical completion a com-plete divorce of relations with contextual impurities, would seem to require in the end such a view of "pure" or "separate" forms subsisting without admixture of "matter." That is, the subsistence of the poem must be discussed without reference to any individuating principle drawn from some extrinsic source, which would function as "matter" in being *scenic* to the poem as act. (*GM*, 484n)

Such a search for the intrinsic is, in Burke's view, fundamentally misguided.

What Burke constructs, then, is a theory of language and literature capable of encompassing both intrinsic and extrinsic aspects without being reducible to either of them. Dramatism is his name for the theory, and "symbolic action" is part of the conceptual apparatus that makes an intrinsic/extrinsic merger possible. "Dramatism," Burke writes,

> is built about the systematic view of language as a species of "symbolic action." While not slighting the great importance of terminology in the communicating of *knowledge,* which in turn shapes our concepts of "reality," Dramatism is a method of terministic analysis (and a corresponding critique of terminology) designed to show that the most direct route to the study of human relations and human motives is via a methodic inquiry into the cycle or cluster of terms and their functions implicit in the key term, "act." "Act" is thus a terministic center from which many related considerations can be shown to "radiate," as though it were a "god-term" from which a whole universe of terms is "derived." The study of language from this point of view comes to a focus in a philosophy of language (and of "symbolicity" in general) offered as proper basis for a general definition of man, with corresponding attitudes toward the problem of human relations.[27]

In *A Grammar of Motives* Burke systematically fleshes out his idea of dramatism, but I shall postpone consideration of this until chapters 3 and 4. In brief, however,

> dramatism centers in observations of this sort: For there to be an *act,* there must be an *agent.* Similarly, there must be a *scene* in which the agent acts. To act in a scene, the agent must employ some means, or *agency.* And there cannot be an act, in the full sense of the term, unless there is a *purpose.* (That is, if a support happens to give way and one falls, such motion on the agent's part is not an act, but an accident.) In *A Grammar of Motives,* I specifically labeled these five terms (act, scene, agent, agency, purpose) the Dramatistic pentad—and the aim was to show how the functions which they designate operate in the imputing of motives. The pattern is incipiently a hexad, in connection with the . . . analysis of *attitude* (as an ambiguous term for *incipient* action). (*D,* 332)

Dramatism, then, approaches human reality in terms of *action* rather than *knowledge,* viewing language as "primarily a species of action, or attitudinizing, rather than an instrument of definition" (*D,*

335). Whereas a "scientistic" approach to the nature of language "begins with questions of *naming, or definition,*" a "dramatistic" approach begins with the attitudinal or hortatory: "attitudinal as with expressions of complaint, fear, gratitude, and such; hortatory as with commands or requests" (*LASA,* 44). "The dramatistic view of language, in terms of 'symbolic action,' is exercised about the necessarily *suasive* nature of even the most unemotional scientific nomenclatures" (*LASA,* 45).

Burke's theory hinges on a distinction between linguistic action and nonlinguistic motion. "Action," Burke writes, "is a term for the kind of behavior possible to a typically symbol-using animal (such as man) in contrast with the extrasymbolic or nonsymbolic operations of nature (rotating of the earth, for instance, or the growth and decay of vegetation)" (*D,* 335). "That is, the social sphere is considered in terms of situations and acts, in contrast with the physical sphere, which is considered in mechanistic terms, idealized as a flat cause-and-effect or stimulus-response relationship" (*PLF,* 103). The relation between these realms or spheres is as problematic as the relation between text and context, and I shall discuss the philosophic implications of Burke's dualism later. For present purposes, the virtue of regarding language dramatistically is that it orients one to both the intrinsic and extrinsic aspects of symbolic action. For as Burke reflects, "the dramatistic perspective . . . points equally towards a concern with 'internal structure' and towards a concern with 'act-scene relationships'" (*GM,* 482).

Because of the ambiguity built into the transaction between text and context, there arises a need for mediation. Symbolic action is the principle of mediation between the two realms of linguistic action and nonlinguistic motion. From the dialectical point of view, in its dual nature as symbolic in the sense of not actual and symbolic in the Ricardian sense of pointing to an implicit referent, symbolic action is an ambiguously middle term bringing these two realms together. For language, Burke argues, is symbolic action, and "words are a mediatory realm, that joins us with wordless nature while at the same time standing between us and wordless nature" (*ATH,* 373).

The role of symbolic action as mediator is connected with at least two other claims, both of which will be elaborated later. First, that literature is not linguistically autonomous, that its language is not different in essence from language at large. This claim involves a re-valuation of the significance of rhetoric and an argument against sim-pleminded distinctions between the scientific or referential use of lan-guage and the poetic or emotive use of language. Second, that intrinsic and extrinsic are not mutually exclusive for the simple reason that they are dialectical concepts and require an opposite to define them. The virtue of dramatistic criticism is that it neither valorizes the anti-referential text nor views the sociohistorical ground of the text as some mere inert given. Dramatism emphasizes the necessarily ambigu-ous transaction between the system of signs and the frame of refer-ence.

Throughout his writings Burke consistently maintains that "the ul-timate metaphor for discussing the universe and man's relations to it must be the poetic or dramatic metaphor" (PC, 263). His charac-teristic regarding of "the poem as act" is central to dramatism, for through the lens of the metaphor of drama we regard "language and thought primarily as modes of action" rather than as means of convey-ing information (GM, xxii). We are thus oriented to the contextual liquidity of verbal expression rather than to its semantic or ideological rigidity.[28] Burke is very much attuned to dialectic, which he defines as "the employment of the possibilities of linguistic transformation" (GM, 402). Dialectical transcendence and dramatic catharsis are re-lated in that both are agents of transformation—the one on the idea-tional or conceptual level, the other on the bodily or emotional level. The attitudinal is the ambiguously middle level that combines them both. For language is symbolic action, the dancing of an attitude, and the image itself neatly combines the physical and mental aspects. The mental play of attitudes is likened to the ritual gesturing of dance, which cuts a living form in time.

The difference between dramatic catharsis and dialectical transcen-dence is that whereas "catharsis involves fundamentally purgation by the imitation of victimage" (LASA, 186), transcendence involves "the building of a terministic bridge whereby one realm is transcended by being viewed in terms of a realm 'beyond' it" (LASA, 187). But be-cause both involve formal development they both give us modes of transformation—victimage and symbolic sacrifice in drama, the treat-ing of contingent things in terms of a beyond in dialectic. The inter-weaving of notions of guilt, redemption, hierarchy, and victimage in

Burke's theory of language, literature, and human relations is complicated but must remain unexplored for the time being.

The orientation toward the contextual liquidity of verbal expression implicit in Burke's idea of dramatism is analogous to Richards's rejection of the "Proper Meaning Superstition"—"the common
belief . . . that a word has a meaning of its own (ideally, only one)
independent of and controlling its use and the purpose for which it
should be uttered."[29] In *The Philosophy of Rhetoric* Richards contends that such a view is committed to the mistaken proposition that
meaning is context-neutral. He proposes as an alternative the context
theorem of meaning. "Freud taught us that a dream may mean a
dozen different things; he has persuaded us that some symbols are, as
he says, 'over-determined' and mean many different selections from
among their causes. This theorem goes further, and regards all discourse—outside the technicalities of science—as over-determined, as
having multiplicity of meaning" (*PR,* 38–39).

Richards's theorem emphasizes "the interinanimation of words" in
a text, claiming that "the senses of an author's words . . . are resul-
tants which we arrive at only through the interplay of the interpreta-
tive possibilities of the whole utterance" (*PR,* 55). We must attempt to
decipher the "systematic ambiguity or transference patterns" (*PR,* 73),
the dialectical possibilities of linguistic transformation.

For Richards, "metaphor is the omnipresent principle of language"
(*PR,* 92). It is in fact language's constitutive form.[30] "Fundamentally
it is a borrowing between the intercourse of *thoughts,* a transaction
between contexts. *Thought* is metaphoric, and proceeds by comparison, and the metaphors of language derive therefrom" (*PR,* 94).
Richards goes on to say that "the co-presence of vehicle and tenor
results in a meaning (to be clearly distinguished from the tenor) which
is not attainable without their interaction." Against the traditional
view of metaphor as embellishment, he argues that "vehicle and tenor
in cooperation give meaning of more varied powers than can be as-
cribed to either" (*PR,* 100).

Richards's definition of metaphor as a transaction between contexts
is akin to Burke's definition of it as perspective by incongruity. Perspective by incongruity, Burke writes, "would liquidate belief in the absolute truth of concepts by reminding us that the mixed dead metaphors
of abstract thought are metaphors nonetheless" (*ATH,* 229). It is "a

method for gauging situations by verbal 'atom cracking.' That is, a word belongs to a certain category—and by rational planning you wrench it loose and metaphorically apply it to a different category" (*ATH*, 308).[31] This, as Burke points out, is similar to the methodology of the pun, "though it links hitherto unlinked words by rational criteria instead of tonal criteria" (*ATH*, 309). Of supreme importance is the fact that "'perspective by incongruity' makes for a *dramatic* vocabulary, with weighting and counter-weighting, in contrast with the liberal ideal of *neutral* naming in the characterization of processes. . . . The neutral idea prompts one to forget that terms are *characters,* that an essay is an *attenuated* play. . . . Names are shorthand designations for certain fields and methods of action" (*ATH*, 311–12).

Perspective by incongruity is a defamiliarizing strategy akin to Brecht's alienation effect. Its political genius resides in its ability to co-opt the hegemonic vocabulary of the dominant class—the ideology of the status quo that converts the historical into the natural—and to transform it into a counterstatement, a rhetoric of social change. By allowing us to translate back and forth between conceptual schemes that are traditionally kept apart, perspective by incongruity is both a methodological device for giving us a handle on the bewildering diversity of interpretations with which we are bombarded and a rhetorical technique for subverting a given hegemonic discourse from within by transvaluating its symbols of authority. This I shall discuss in detail in the third chapter.

The important point for now is that for both Richards and Burke what Empson calls ambiguity ("any verbal nuance, however slight, which gives room for alternative reactions to the same piece of language")[32] is the essence of language. Richards, of course, exempts the "technicalities of science," showing the vestiges of his referential/emotive distinction. Burke, however, who defines man as the symbol-using animal, regards all discourse as over-determined.

The problem with the referential/emotive or the scientific/poetic distinction is that it draws the lines at the wrong places; it makes a difference of kind out of one of degree. In "Semantic and Poetic Meaning," Burke's "rhetorical defense of rhetoric," he claims that there is

no basic opposition between the ideals of semantic and poetic meaning. . . . They are different rather than antithetical in their ultimate realistic aims. . . . [But] semantic meaning, that may be considered as a partial aspect of poetic meaning, tends to become instead the *opposite* of poetic meaning, so that a mere graded series, comprising a more-than and less-than, changes instead to a blunt battle between poetry and anti-poetry, "Poetry vs. science." (*PLF,* 138)

Burke defines the difference between the semantic and poetic ideals thus:

> The semantic ideal envisions a vocabulary that *avoids* drama. The poetic ideal envisions a vocabulary that *goes through* drama. In their ideal *moral act* by attaining a perspective *atop all the conflict of attitudes.*
>
> The first would try to *cut away,* to *abstract,* all emotional factors that complicate the objective clarity of meaning. The second would try to derive its vision from the maximum *heaping up* of all these emotional factors, playing them off against one another, inviting them to reinforce and contradict one another, and seeking to make this active participation itself a major ingredient of the vision. (*PLF,* 147)

As usual, the issue involves the role of drama.

> The semantic ideal envisions a vocabulary that *avoids* drama. The poetic ideal envisions a vocabulary that *goes through* drama. In their ideal completion, they have a certain superficial resemblance, in that both are "beyond good and evil." But the first seeks to attain this end by programmatic elimination of a weighted vocabulary at the start (the neutralization of names containing attitudes, emotional predisposition); and the second would attain the same end by exposure to the *maximum profusion* of weightings. The first would be aside from the battle, stressing the role of the observer, whose observations it is hoped define situations with sufficient realistic accuracy to prepare an adequate *chart* for action; the second would contend, by implication, that true knowledge can only be attained through the battle, stressing the role of the participant, who in the course of his participation, it is hoped, will define situations with sufficient realistic accuracy to prepare an *image* for action. (*PLF,* 149–50)

Burke concludes that "the controversy does not resolve itself into an opposition between poetry as metaphorical and semantics as nonmetaphorical. Every perspective requires a metaphor, implicit or explicit, for its organizational base . . . and semantics as a perspective cannot skirt this necessity" (*PLF,* 152n).

Burke's conclusion finds some support in contemporary philosophy of science. In *The Structure of Scientific Revolutions,* for example, Thomas Kuhn traces the historical succession of paradigmatic metaphors in science. He argues that no current attempt to achieve a neutral observation language has yet come close to a generally applicable language of pure percepts.

> And those attempts that come closest . . . from the start they presuppose a paradigm, taken either from a current scientific theory or from some fraction of everyday discourse, and they then try to eliminate from it all non-logical and non-perceptual terms. But their result is a language that . . . embodies a host of expectations about nature and fails to function the moment these expectations are violated. . . . No language . . . can produce mere neutral and objective reports on "the given."[33]

"Even while guarding against the misguidance of metaphor on one level," Burke suggests, "we are simply forcing the covert operation of metaphorical thought to a deeper level. . . . It is precisely through metaphor that our perspectives, or analogical extensions, are made— a world without metaphor would be a world without purpose" (*PC,* 194). On the one hand the referential or literal is the opposite of the rhetorical or figural, but on the other hand any putatively literal expression is also a metaphor whose figurative status has been forgotten. At its deepest level all discourse—even scientific discourse—is already metaphorical.

I have quoted copiously so that Burke might make his rhetorical defense of rhetoric in full splendor. I am not implying that this defense should be regarded as a surrogate for detailed argumentation. Moreover, the formative role of metaphor in any conceptual system will be especially relevant when we come to consider Burke's own central metaphor—the linguistic or dramatic one—to which he ascribes methodological, if not ontological, priority. These matters, along with the general matter of what Burke variously calls nomenclatures, terministic screens, or vocabularies of motives, will be discussed in the third chapter.

For the moment it is pertinent to note that Burke's regarding of literature as symbolic action works toward seeing the text not as an object but as a system of relations. He replaces the static model of the text with a dynamic one. Accordingly, the text is seen as a fluid process with respect to its system of internal relations (that is, its intrinsic aspects—the interinanimation of words and the transaction between contexts within the system), its intertextuality[34] (that is, its relation to the system of literature and language as a whole, how as a text it relates to other texts), and its extrinsic function as a strategic response to reality (that is, its relation to an external context, a context of situation). In practice, of course, these three components are not categorically separable.

Burke distinguishes the two senses in which a word has a context thus: "There is the context of the other words among which it is used in a sentence (or, by extension, in an article or book or entire universe of discourse). And there is the nonverbal or extra-verbal context (what the anthropologist Malinowski has called 'context of situation'), the circumstances involving many elements that are not verbal."[35] With regard to internal context it is useful to recall what Saussure points out—namely, that "the signs of units of meaning tend to form two different general kinds of relationships: the syntagmatic and the associative. . . . The syntagma is a horizontal grouping, a succession of meaning-units or words in time. . . . At the same time, however, the word . . . carries in itself another, we might call it a vertical, dimension."[36]

We might analogically extend this distinction to the analysis of literature, for if ambiguity is the essence of language then there must be some principle of contextual relevance such that the ambiguities proliferated by author or critic are not just products of ingenuity. Overstress on the horizontal grouping of terms, on, in other words, their function in a diachronic sequence of contributing to a univocal meaning, tends toward semantic rigidity, whereas overstress on the vertical dimension of any given term, on, in other words, the synchronic whole of implications and possibilities it conjures up, tends toward random associationism and dissolution of meaning.[37]

The problem of contextual relevance, however, is more easily described than remedied, for indeterminacy of meaning seems to be a central if paradoxical feature of all symbol systems. As deconstructionist theory persistently reminds us, meaning is context-bound but contexts (both intraverbal and extraverbal) are infinitely extendable.

Moreover, the relationship between the literal and the figurative is permanently unstable, giving rise to a fundamental undecidability as to whether a given part of a discourse should be read literally or figuratively. These difficulties cannot be explained away, though the real question, as I shall try to make clear in the third chapter, is whether indeterminacy of meaning is as threatening as it seems to be and whether it merits being inflated into an all-embracing linguistic nihilism.

My claim that Burke's dramatism works toward seeing the text not as an object but as a system of relations might initially seem to contradict those passages elsewhere in his corpus where Burke considers the work of art to be internally synecdochic, its parts being consubstantially related. Substance, one might think, is a static concept. For Burke, however, substance is dialectical. Hence the concept of substance is endowed with an unresolvable ambiguity, stemming from the fact that, as Spinoza observes, all determination is negation. Burke makes the point explicitly in a key passage from *A Grammar of Motives*.

> Dialectically considered (that is, "dramatistically" considered) men are not only *in nature*. The cultural accretions made possible by the language motive become a "second nature" with them. Here again we confront the ambiguities of substance, since symbolic communication is not merely an external instrument, but also intrinsic to men as agents. Its motivational properties characterize both "the human situation" and what men are "in themselves."
>
> Whereas there is an implicit irony in other notions of substance, with dialectic substance the irony is explicit. For it derives its character from the systematic contemplation of the antinomies attendant upon the fact that we necessarily define a thing in terms of something else. "Dialectic substance" would thus be the over-all category of dramatism, which treats of human motives in terms of verbal action. (*GM*, 33)

For Burke this is "an *inevitable* paradox of definition"—"to *define*, or *determine* a thing, is to mark its boundaries, hence to use terms that possess, implicitly at least, contextual reference" (*GM*, 24). The paradox of substance has implications for notions of the intrinsic and extrinsic in literary criticism.

> Historicists who deal with art in terms of its background are continually suffering from the paradox of contextual definition, as their

opponents accuse them of slighting the work of art in its esthetic aspects; and on the other hand, critics who would center their attention upon the work "in itself" must wince when it is made apparent that their inquiries, in ignoring contextual relevance, frustrate our desire to see the products of artistic creation treated in terms of [their cultural, sociohistorical, and biographical contexts]. (*GM*, 26)

The point is neither to banish substance terms nor to banish talk of intrinsic and extrinsic, but to be aware of their equivocal nature and to find a way of talking about literature that does justice to what it is in itself and to how it relates to other things. As Burke reflects, "banishing the term 'substance' doesn't banish its functions; it merely conceals them" (*GM*, 21).

In considering the relationship between intrinsic and extrinsic, Burke wants to clarify three quite different procedures.

In the cause of method, one must not confuse three quite different procedures: (1) Saying *only* what could be said about a work, considered in itself; (2) saying all that might be said about the work in terms of its relation to the author, his times, etc.; (3) while meeting tests of the first sort (discussing the work intrinsically, as a poem) also making observations of the second sort (concerning its possible relation to nonpoetic elements, such as author or background). (*LASA*, 41)

He argues subsequently that intrinsic and extrinsic should go together, that there should be a movement from symbolic action in particular (the poem as poem, "internal terministic relationships as such" [*LASA*, 368]) to symbolic action in general (the poem as the product of an author in an environmental scene, "the terms' possible direct or indirect reference to a universe of discourse beyond their internal relations to one another" [*LASA*, 368]).

In the preface to *The Philosophy of Literary Form* Burke asserts that "a work is composed of implicit or explicit equations (assumptions of 'what equals what'), in any work considered as one particular structure of terms, or symbol system" (*PLF*, viii). His use of the term "equations" is deliberately vague. It can comprehend Aristotelian topics, Freudian associations, images, symbols, metaphors, or simply terms in general. Along with identifications or equations (what equals what), there are also dissociations or agons (what versus what). And this apposition and opposition of terms unfolds in a certain way, making for dramatic resolution and dialectical transformation (what leads to what). According to Burke, then, intrinsic analysis should take at least three factors into account: associative clusters, dramatic alignments, and narrative progressions.

If critical analysis operates on the first level, the critic is focusing on "poems in particular," on "intrinsic, internal development from-what, through-what, to-what" (*PLF,* 10). Second, there is the "analysis of the relationship between literary 'strategies' and extra-literary 'situations'" (*PLF,* 9). "The situation-strategy design says in effect: the poet is not poetizing in the middle of nowhere; though his poem may be viewed purely within itself ('in terms of' its internal consistency), it is also the act of an agent in a non-literary scene; but by the nature of the notation, it survives the *particulars* of the scene in which it was originally enacted" (*PLF,* ix).

We thus get "the two modes of literary substance (the substance of a literary act as placed upon a scene, and the substance of the act within itself)" (*PLF,* xviii). Somewhere within these two modes the role of the poem's place in the corpus of the poet falls— "the problem of the 'lexical' meaning of a term (its public meaning as defined in a dictionary) and the special connotations that may surround it in one particular poet's nomenclature" (*PLF,* xii). The issue is intrinsic in that one can regard all the works of the author as one self-enclosed system, but it also is extrinsic in that one can regard all the other works, aside from the particular work under scrutiny, as external to that work's particular symbol system.

The third level that Burke identifies involves "symbolic action in general." On this level the aim is to "identify the substance of a particular literary act with a theory of literary action in general." Burke calls this "dialectical criticism," "dramatic criticism methodized" (*PLF,* xx). Since it attends to the problems of both internal structure and act-scene relationships, dialectical criticism is the desideratum.

Burke thinks of poetry, which in his extended sense of the term comprises "any work of critical or imaginative cast," as

> the adopting of various strategies for the encompassing of situations. These strategies size up the situations, name their structure and outstanding ingredients, and name them in a way that contains an attitude

towards them. . . . The situations are real; the strategies for handling them have public content; and in so far as situations overlap from individual to individual, or from one historical period to another, the strategies possess universal relevance. (*PLF,* 1)

He divides the poem into three components:

dream (the unconscious or subconscious factors in a poem) . . .
prayer (the communicative functions of a poem, which leads us into the many considerations of form, since the poet's inducements can lead us to participate in his poem only in so far as his work has a public, or communicative structure) . . .
chart (the realistic sizing-up of situations that is sometimes explicit, sometimes implicit, in poetic strategies). (*PLF,* 5–6)

The dream component involves the psychological, archetypal, and mythic elements embedded in a text. As Burke suggests, "we should take Freud's key terms, 'condensation' and 'displacement,' as overall categories for the analysis of the poem as dream" (*PLF,* 277). Events have a tendency to become synecdochic representatives of other events. Condensation, the image as more than itself—a combining of several images or ideas in one, works along the associative, or vertical, axis of meaning; whereas displacement, the image as other than itself, works along the syntagmatic, or horizontal, axis of meaning. For Burke the unconscious is structured like a language, and the critic is its cryptologist.

The prayer component involves the rhetorical and communicative functions of a text, its nature as "addressed," and the kinds of identifications and dissociations it encourages, the structure of motives it realizes and implies. Rhetoric deals with the arousal and fulfillment of expectations, the inducing of attitudes and actions. The prayer component is connected with the view that "form" is "the psychology of the audience," "the creation of an appetite in the mind of the auditor, and the adequate satisfying of that appetite" (*CS,* 31).

Prayer would enter the Freudian picture in so far as it concerns the optative. But prayer does not stop at that. Prayer is also an act of communion. Hence, the concept of prayer, as extended to cover also secular forms of petition, moves us into the corresponding area of communication in general. We might say that, whereas the expressionistic emphasis reveals the ways in which the poet, with an attitude, embodies it in appropriate gesture, communication deals with the choice of gesture for the inducement of corresponding attitudes. Sensory imagery has this same function, inviting the reader to make himself over in the image of the imagery. (*PLF,* 281)

Burke treats the rhetorical function of art more thoroughly in his *Rhetoric of Motives,* [38] where he shows the inextricability of persuasion and identification (the latter he includes in his notion of consubstantiality—the identifying of one's own substance with something larger and more comprehensive). Moreover, he extends the usage of the term "rhetoric" so that it might include unconscious factors of appeal as well.

The chart component involves the poem's relationship to an objective situation.

> The ideal magic is that in which our assertions (or verbal decrees) as to the nature of a situation come closest to a correct gauging of the situation as it actually is. Only a *completely accurate* chart would dissolve magic, by making the structure of names identical with the structure named. This latter is the kind of chart that Spinoza, in his doctrine of the "adequate idea," selected as the goal of philosophy, uniting free will and determinism, since the "So be it" is identical with the "It must be so" and the "It is so." A completely adequate chart would, of course, be possible only to an infinite, omniscient mind. (*PLF,* 7)

According to Spinoza, freedom is the recognition of necessity, for, as Burke points out, he thought that "through the cultivation of 'adequate ideas,' one could transform the passives (of human bondage) into the actives (of human freedom)" (*GM,* 139). Given the human condition as Burke sees it, however, the adequate idea is something to be striven toward but never fully realized. Human life is a dialectic of the upward way, a striving toward a better life and toward better, more adequate, ideas. Adequate ideas are not supreme fictions, imaginative concords that the mind constructs for consolation and compensation; they are realistic strategies for encompassing real situations. It is I. A. Richards's continual overstressing of the compensatory and therapeutic aspects of symbolic action that Burke finds wrongheaded.

Burke notes that Richards "proposes that we become adept in accepting the many pseudo-statements of poetry and using them purely for their value as mental prophylactics" (*PC,* 252). Richards's proposition is problematical from two standpoints. First, it restricts fictiveness to the realm of poetry and religion, making again that false disjunction between the poetic and semantic ideals. Since our encounter with the world is necessarily ethical in that our behavior and attitudes project and embody values, "all universe-building is ethical universe-building" (*PC,* 256). Second, it ignores the revisions made necessary by the recalcitrance of reality. "For the interpretations themselves must be altered as the universe displays various orders of recalcitrance" (*PC,* 256). In short, Richards's proposition downplays both the prayer and chart components of poetic action. Burke makes his objection explicit. "The symbolic act is the *dancing of an attitude* (a point that Richards has brought out, though I should want to revise his position to the extent of noting that in Richards's doctrines the attitude is pictured as too sparse in realistic content)" (*PLF,* 9).

Richards defines attitudes as "imaginal or incipient activities or tendencies to actions" (*PLC,* 112). The function of poetry is to organize these attitudes and impulses, converting "a welter of responses" into a "systematized complex response" (*PLC,* 183) and thus creating in the reader "a balanced poise, stable through its power of inclusion, not through the power of its exclusions" (*PLC,* 248). For Richards, then, this equilibrium of synaesthesis is the vibrant poise of a completely coordinated individual, whose harmonized attitudes are "imaginal" rather than "stimulative." He is poised, but not to act.

According to Burke, this is an inadequate account of the matter because "the concept of *incipient* acts is ambiguous. As an attitude can be the *substitute* for an act, it can likewise be the *first step towards* an act" (*GM,* 236). The incipient may be either substitutive or introductory. Richards errs in consistently seeing it as substitutive, thereby overstressing the dream component and seeing symbolic action as merely compensatory or therapeutic. Burke argues that

> the attitude is essentially ambiguous, as an attitude of sympathy may either lead to an act of sympathy or may serve as substitute for an act of sympathy. It is thus "potentially" two different kinds of acts. . . . The realm of the incipient, or attitudinal, is the realm of "symbolic action"

par excellence; for symbolic action has the same ambiguous potentialities of action (when tested by norms of overt, practical action). Here
is the area of thought wherein actual conflicts can be transcended, with
results sometimes fatal, sometimes felicitous. (*GM*, 243)

The problem with Richards's approach is that it ignores the persuasive
and realistic aspects of the poem. It also reveals, as Frank Lentricchia
points out in *After the New Criticism*, the self-defeating modernist
tendency to view reality and truth as hostile and impoverished, as an
inhuman chaos that threatens to overwhelm the individual's capacity
for constructive thought and action. According to Richards and his
followers, fictions are heuristic devices that temporarily redeem us
from our state of alienated subjectivity and are validated only by our
skeptical self-consciousness, by our beleaguered and world-weary ac-
knowledgment that they are mere pseudostatements whose fictive status must always be borne in mind. "What serenity," Lentricchia rhetorically asks, "can we purchase from a self-consciousness of the
impotence of fantasy in the face of truth?"[39] What comfort can come
from "constructing a starkly agonistic image of the self's confrontation with its world"?[40]

We are now in a better position to understand what Burke means
when he says that "poetry, or any verbal act, is to be considered as
'symbolic action'" (*PLF*, 8). Symbolic action has at least three dimensions. First, on the level of dream, it is symptomatic action and plays a
compensatory or therapeutic role. It has an author-regarding element
and is expressive, either directly or indirectly, of his psyche, of the
pattern of his identifications and dissociations. In this sense symbolic
action is more substitutive than introductory; catharsis for the author
may be the act of self-expression itself.

Second, on the level of prayer, the emphasis falls on *action*. In this
sense symbolic action is more introductory than substitutive. It has an
audience-regarding element and induces attitudes and actions, yet insofar as it does not result in overt, practical action the residuum of
substitution remains. As Lentricchia points out in *Criticism and Social Change*, Burke is always sensitive to the fact that "form is a relationship of manipulation between a text and an audience," that "the
definition of text, and textuality, must include the factor of its reception," and that "reception is always firmly planted in the historical

world."[41] Communication exists in the margin of overlap between the writer's experience and the reader's. For Burke, meaning has a dual nature. On the level of dream it is primarily the product of an author and the property of a text, whereas on the level of prayer it is primarily the response and interpretation of a reader.

Third, on the level of chart, the emphasis falls on *symbolic* in the Ricardian sense of pointing to an implicit referent, of being symbolic of something; symbolic action has a reality-regarding element. "The Symbol is the verbal parallel to a pattern of experience" (*CS*, 152) and has realistic content insofar as it accurately encompasses the situation and adequates itself to reality. The encompassment or adequation, of course, is necessarily imperfect, given that we have no nonsymbolic or nonlinguistic access to the structure of reality. For Burke this recognition is not demoralizing because even if representation cannot be ontologically anchored in some transcendental signified or objective frame of reference, it is nonetheless socially powerful and rhetorically effective; it does its work in the world and subserves a realistic function.

In later writings Burke ramifies the dream/prayer/chart triad of "The Philosophy of Literary Form" into a fourfold division: grammar (chart), rhetoric (prayer), poetics or symbolic (dream), and ethics (self and social portraiture).

The grammatical he associates with Cicero's first office of the orator—to teach or inform.[42] Its realm comprises logic, dialectic, knowledge, information, external reference, and objective reality. As Burke suggests in *A Grammar of Motives*, the grammatical is a series of blanks to be filled out when one imputes motive to action, and any statement of motives involves the dramatistic pentad of act (what was done), agent (who did the act and under what subjective conditions), scene (the environment in which the act took place, the extrinsic causal factors that determined it), agency (how the act was done, what intruments were used), and purpose (why the act was done, its ultimate motive or final cause). The grammatical blanks offer opportunities for "*disposition* and *transposition*" (*GM*, 402), and dialectic explores the combinatory possibilities. Different philosophical systems emphasize different parts of the pentad: realism emphasizes act, idealism emphasizes agent, materialism emphasizes scene, pragmatism emphasizes agency, and mysticism emphasizes purpose. The combinatory possibilities, of course, are endless, but Burke's point is that any statement of motives must deal with the five terms he has isolated even if it would collapse one into the other. It must be remembered, however, that in striving toward adequate ideas, "charts of meaning are not 'right' or 'wrong'— they are relative approximations to the truth" (*PLF*, 108).

The rhetorical Burke associates with Cicero's third office—to move or bend. Rhetoric regards symbolic action as audience-directed discourse, focusing upon its nature as communication, persuasion, exhortation, address, prayer, petition, and inducement to action.

> In contrast to dialectic's exploration of verbal forms, Burke sees rhetoric's function as the overcoming of estrangement. Human beings are alienated from each other by differences of ethnic and social background, level of education, race, sex, age, economic class, etc. When language is used to overcome these differences, to foster cooperation and establish community, we are in the realm of rhetoric—and since all language use to varying degrees involves this end, all language use has a rhetorical dimension.[43]

To the classical notion of rhetoric as persuasion, Burke adds the dramatistic notion of rhetoric as identification, by which he means the inducement to identify one's own substance with something more comprehensive. (He also adds the notion of unconscious factors of appeal, as we shall see in regard to the suasive function of imagery in "The Rhetoric of Hitler's 'Battle.'") For Burke, dialectic and rhetoric "are counterparts because to identify is to share substance with something or someone, the study of substance (or motivational essence) being the affair of dialectic, the study of tactics for achieving identification (or consubstantiality) being the affair of rhetoric."[44]

Although rhetoric involves the formation of identity and the establishment and maintenance of affiliation and community, it is predicated upon division and difference. Utopia requires no rhetoric, and if identification and consubstantiality were really possible, there would be no need to proclaim them. Moreover, as I mentioned earlier, the concept of substance is itself endowed with an unresolvable ambiguity, stemming from the fact that all determination is negation, that we necessarily define a thing in terms of something else. Tragedy, whose dramatic catharsis is achieved through the imitation of victimage, of-

fers fertile ground for Burke's speculations about the rhetoric of identification and the paradox of substance.

The symbolic Burke associates with Cicero's second office—to
please or entertain. Poetics regards symbolic action as sheer linguistic
exercising, as the use and enjoyment of a faculty that only we symbol-
using animals possess. The symbolic, then, involves the architectonic
or developmental motive, the pleasure we derive from experiencing the
narrative unfolding and resolution of associative clusters and dramatic
alignments, what Burke calls elsewhere the labyrinthine internal consistency of the text.

In this way Burke subtilizes the dream/prayer/chart triad, and to
this triad he adds the realm of ethics or self-portraiture. This realm
comprises the ethical proscriptions of a given social order (its "thou
shalt not's") and the kind of identity a personality builds up through
the ensemble of social roles it incorporates. As Burke points out, "the
so-called 'I' is merely a unique combination of partially conflicting
'corporate we's' " (*ATH,* 246). The character of a work always reflects
the magic of the social order, for it is a portrait of both self and society.
"The words of the poet are not puppets, but acts. They are a function
of him, and he is a function of them. They are a function of society,
and he is a function of society" (*ATH,* 336).

Portraiture involves what Aristotle calls ethos, the character of the
speaker, and what Wayne Booth calls the "implied author," the com-
posite picture of the author that emerges from the total form of the
work itself, from the grammatical, rhetorical, symbolical, and ethical
choices that make the work the kind of thing that it is.[45]

All told, then, we have symbolic action as designation (the grammatical), communication (the rhetorical), expression (the symbolical),
and portraiture (the ethical). Vis-à-vis drama in general and tragedy in
particular, it is easy to see that insofar as ethics involves the "sym-
bolizing of guilt, redemption, hierarchy, mortification, victimage, 'catharsis,' "[46] it overlaps with rhetoric, "the ways in which the members
of a group promote social cohesion by acting rhetorically upon themselves and one another" (*RM,* xiv).

These dimensions and components of symbolic action, of course,
are not categorically separable. "Since the work of art is a synthesis,
summing up a myriad of social and personal factors at once, an analysis of it necessarily radiates in all directions at once" (*ATH,* 199). The

symbolic act of synthesis lends itself to infinite conceptual analysis and demands a theory of multiple causation rather than a reductive schema. This is why Burke admits that his

> general approach to the poem might be called "pragmatic" in this sense: It assumes that a poem's structure is to be described most accurately by thinking always of the poem's function. It assumes that the poem is designed to "do something" for the poet and his readers, and that we can make the most relevant observations about its design by considering the poem as the embodiment of this act. (*PLF*, 89–90)

Structure and function are not antithetical.

> The main point is to note *what the poem's equational structure is*. This is a statement about its *form*. But to guide our observations about the form itself, we seek to discover the *functions* which the structure serves. This takes us into a discussion of purpose, strategy, the symbolic act. . . . At every point, the content is functional—hence, statements about a poem's "subject," as we conceive it, will also be statements about the poem's "form." (*PLF*, 101–2)

Burke blithely commits what Wimsatt and Beardsley call the affective fallacy. For him, however, it is not a question of confusing what a poem is with what a poem does, but one of equating them. According to Burke, form is function—what a poem is is what a poem does.

Burke's pragmatic approach, as Lentricchia observes, entails a "deliberate vulgarization of literature to mean any use of language that has the effect of shaping and controlling attitudes and behavior."[47] Such vulgarization has the consequence, memorably enunciated by R. P. Blackmur, that Burke's "method could be applied with equal fruitfulness to Shakespeare, Dashiell Hammett, or Marie Corelli." "When I got through wincing," Burke replied, "I had to admit that Blackmur was right. . . . As a matter of fact I'll go a step further and maintain: You can't properly put Marie Corelli and Shakespeare apart until you have first put them together. First genus, then differentia" (*PLF*, 302). Burke proceeds to point out that "in typical contemporary specialization, we have been getting the Philosophy of the Bin. Each of these mental localities has had its own peculiar way of life, its own values, even its own special idiom for seeing, thinking, and 'proving'"

(*PLF,* 303). Burke's dramatistic theory of symbolic action is an attempt to provide "a reintegrative point of view" (*PLF,* 304).

A case in point is his brilliant essay "The Rhetoric of Hitler's 'Battle'" (1939), wherein he brings his full critical arsenal to bear on *Mein Kampf.* Burke sees Nazism, with its projective device of the scapegoat ("the 'curative' unification by a fictitious devil function" [*PLF,* 218]) and its ritual of rebirth (the compensatory doctrine of inborn superiority whereby the Aryan is born again into the purity of his ancestral blood), as the materialization and perversion of a religious pattern. He examines Hitler's use of sexual symbolism, of the imagery of blood, pollution, and disease, and of the rhetoric of identification and dissociation, focusing on the dialectical relationship between the literary strategy and the extraliterary situation. *Mein Kampf* provides "a noneconomic interpretation of economic ills" (*PLF,* 204). This interpretation appeals, Burke goes on to say, because it supplies "a 'world view' for people who had previously seen the world but piecemeal" and is thus "the *bad* filling of a good need" (*PLF,* 218).

It is worth examining this essay in some detail, for in my view it is an exemplary illustration of how literary criticism can perform a vital social and political role. Admittedly, "The Rhetoric of Hitler's 'Battle'" is not literary criticism per se (little of Burke's work is), but its focus on how imagery and ideas reinforce each other demonstrates how the categories of literary analysis can contribute to historical understanding.

The occasion of the essay is the appearance of *Mein Kampf* in unexpurgated translation. Burke starts by noting that it is insufficient merely to make "vandalistic comments" about Hitler's book. Such righteous indignation, however justified, contributes "more to our gratification than to our enlightenment." He suggests that we should "try also to discover what kind of 'medicine' this medicine-man has concocted, that we may know, with greater accuracy, exactly what to guard against. . . . Hitler found a panacea, a 'cure for what ails you,' a 'snakeoil,' that made such sinister unifying possible within his own nation. . . . This book is the well of Nazi magic; crude magic, but effective" (*PLF,* 192–93). This metaphor of the writer as medicine man recurs throughout Burke's writings, for he always acknowledges that symbolic action has its attendant dangers; every writer dispenses medicine, and all medicine is potentially poison. As he puts it in another essay, "The poet is, indeed, a 'medicine man.' But the situations for which he offers his stylistic medicine may be very real ones. . . . The poet, in his pious or tragic role, would immunize us by stylistically infecting us with the disease. As we move towards the impious response, on the other hand, we get an 'allopathic' strategy of cure. We get the recourse to 'antidote'" (*PLF*, 64–65).

Hitler's thought and behavior constitute the quintessence of the impious response and the allopathic cure. Through the workings of symbolic action, Hitler is able to convert his own psychotic dream into a secular prayer that successfully exhorts others to follow his chart for political action. That is, an obsessive pattern of identifications and dissociations becomes an effective mechanism for persuading others to make themselves over in the image of its imagery and ultimately provides a vehicle for the exercise of political power. That Hitler's representations were ontologically unanchored and obscenely false did not matter at all; their consequences were invidiously real.

Burke contends that Hitler's book revolves around the master strategy of isolating a single enemy, a devil figure who is materialized in the form of international Jewry. The result is a "heads I win, tails you lose" philosophy. If Jewish people do not seem overtly to reflect Hitler's description of their iniquity, they are simply being cunning in their perpetration of the international Jewish conspiracy. If Aryans behave divisively and impede the instauration of the unified German state, they have been seduced by the villainous Jew. Such sexual symbolism, Burke maintains, pervades *Mein Kampf*. Germany is a de-horned Siegfried; its masses are feminine and desire to be led by a dominating male; this male must overcome the rival Jewish male, a seducer who would poison Aryan blood by intermingling with the folk. An associative cluster emerges; blood-poisoning, syphilis, prostitution, incest, and so on are equated materially with the infection of Jewish blood and spiritually with the infection of Jewish ideas. The symbolism is as dense as that of a literary work, and Burke gives it detailed analysis, showing how imagery and ideation sustain each other.

According to Burke, Hitler's medicine has four main ingredients: inborn dignity, projection device, symbolic rebirth, and commercial use.

Inborn dignity is one of the fruits of racism, for the fiction of a special bloodstream confers on Aryans a genetic superiority. As Burke reflects,

> After the defeat of Germany in the World War, there were especially strong emotional needs that this compensatory doctrine of inborn superiority could gratify. . . . The categorical dignity of superior race was a perfect recipe for the situation. It was "spiritual" in so far as it was "above" crude economic "interests," but it was "materialized" at the psychologically "right" spot in that "the enemy" was someone you could see. (*PLF*, 202, 205)

A projection device brings into effect "the 'curative' process that comes with the ability to hand over one's ills to a scapegoat, thereby getting purification by dissociation" (*PLF*, 202). "One can battle an external enemy instead of battling an enemy within" (*PLF*, 203). Unlike in Christianity, where the victimage of Christ is construed as a universal sacrifice that redeems the sinfulness of all, the Nazi principle of curative victimage is factional, attributing evil not to all people but to some. Given the doctrine of inborn dignity and the projective device of the scapegoat, the Aryan need only convert to Nazism in order to feel as if he has been born again into the purity of his ancestral blood. Symbolically speaking, he votes himself a new identity.

Commercial use comes from the "noneconomic interpretation of economic ills" (*PLF*, 204). The cause of Germany's malaise, which was in reality a product of the Versailles Treaty and the Weimar Republic, Hitler derives from his racial theory. This noneconomic explanation is crucial, for it makes Aryan will to power the only stumbling block, legitimating acts of violence against Jewish finance rather than finance in general and absolving Aryan citizens of any responsibility for the economic mess.

Put all these ingredients together and the result is a crude but devastatingly effective formula for repressive political action. A demoralized and beaten nation now has inborn dignity, an identifiable enemy, a new sense of identity, and a coherent worldview, all of which suggest that the political will to power of Aryan superindividualism (translate as obeisance to leadership but promote as heroism and sacrifice) is the only antidote to Jewish individualism (translate as nothing in particular but describe in terms of everything that is evil—democracy, bolshevism, capitalism, venereal disease, etc.).

Burke's somber conclusion is that

> It may well be that people, in their human frailty, require an enemy as well as a goal. Very well: Hitlerism itself has provided us with such an enemy—and the clear example of its operation is guaranty that we have, in him and all he stands for, no purely fictitious "devil function" made to look like a world menace by rhetorical blandishments, but a reality whose ominousness is clarified by the record of its conduct to date. . . . Hitler appeals by relying upon a bastardization of fundamentally religious patterns of thought. . . . And it is the corruptors of religion who are a major menace to the world today, in giving the profound patterns of religious thought a crude and sinister distortion. (*PLF*, 219)

Given that this essay was written in 1939, Burke's vision is remarkably accurate, and his observations about the corruptors of religion are still timely. Leaving aside the obvious example of Islamic fundamentalism, we see some of the ingredients of Nazi medicine in contemporary born-again Christianity, which shows little hesitancy to impose its dictatorship of the elect on others. Inborn dignity comes from membership in an evangelist sect, a material token of one's spiritual election. The identifiable enemy is secular humanism, a devil figure equated with godlessness, the murder of unborn children, anti-Americanism, the deterioration of family values, the decline of moral standards, the dismantling of nuclear weapons, and so on.[48] Symbolic rebirth comes from being born again. In short, what this system of belief offers is a coherent worldview; believers are materially and spiritually armed for Armageddon.

In "The Rhetoric of Hitler's 'Battle'" Burke is able to render in detail "the grand coalition of [Hitler's] ideational imagery, or imagistic ideation" (*PLF*, 207). Rejecting both the formalism of an intrinsic approach, which regards literature as a self-enclosed universe of discourse, and the determinism of an extrinsic approach, which regards literature as reducible to some other frame of reference, Burke demonstrates that even the formal unfolding of a work—its iterative imagery, recurrent symbolism, appositions (what equals what), oppositions (what versus what), and narrative progressions (what leads to what)—constitute part of its rhetorical force, and that this rhetorical force may lead to real consequences. The intrinsic and extrinsic aspects are mutually dependent.

Burke's insistence on the necessity of a reintegrative point of view is an attempt to bring literary criticism back into the mainstream of social life, and his essay on Hitler gives us a splendid idea of what that sort of criticism involves. As Lentricchia points out, Burke always refuses "to denigrate rhetoric in order to elevate the imaginative."[49] *"Literature makes something happen,"* Lentricchia writes; "if we need to create a slogan for Burke then that would do better than any other . . . it sums up his doctrine of literary rhetoric."[50] The slogan is apt even if at this time the something that literature makes happen only works to sustain the Philosophy of the Bin and thus to exacerbate the social irrelevance of literature and criticism by increasing the gap between high culture and communal life. If serious literature and criticism are directed toward an elite audience, and if popular literature and its variants (advertising, television, etc.) are directed toward society as a whole, then it stands to reason that the academic distinction between the two and the concomitant privileging of serious literature through the canonization of great books are helping to reinforce the status quo. "Tradition," Lentricchia argues, "is always tradition-making . . . a process of historical repression engineered not by the dead but by the living and for those who shall live."[51] As humanist intellectuals, we must "meditate critically upon our historicity as agents of the past and makers of the future."[52]

The cynic might construe Lentricchia's slogan as the compensatory rhetoric of the politically powerless and socially irrelevant literary intelligentsia, but that would be to confuse cause and effect. The overriding point is that one's own allegedly disinterested pursuit of knowledge always ratifies the interests of others who, in the barnyard of human motives, to borrow Burke's metaphor, fear not *les mains sales.* If one avoids politics oneself, one ends up implicitly endorsing someone else's. Using Paul de Man as an example, Lentricchia points out the irony of much of contemporary deconstructionist criticism. Despite its revolutionary rhetoric, such criticism—with its "fatalistic theory of history,"[53] its "absolutization of language,"[54] its "epistemology of failure,"[55] and its celebration of the abyss—is more often a symptom than a corrective of the times. Lentricchia makes this point incisively:

> Deconstruction's useful work is to undercut the epistemological claims
> of representation, but that work in no way touches the real work of

representation—its work of power. To put it another way: deconstruction can show that representations are not and cannot be adequate to the task of representation, but it has nothing to say about the social work that representation can and does do. Deconstruction confuses the act of exposing epistemological fraud with the neutralization of political force.[56]

Burke's dramatism never succumbs to this confusion. "As a form of action in the world the literary is fully enmeshed in the social—it is not an imaginative space apart."[57]

In an article entitled "The Symbolic Inference," Fredric Jameson notes that although the vast corpus of Burke's criticism is given perfunctory recognition, it has not engendered any substantial critical following. The reason for this, I think, is clear—Burke's methodological idiosyncrasies and insufficient "ideological analysis" (Jameson's phrase) notwithstanding.[58] Burke's approach does not guarantee the autonomy of the privileged object of study; it violates canons of compartmentalization, outrages good taste, and is frankly speculative. "Really, universally," says Henry James in the preface to *Roderick Hudson,* "relations stop nowhere, and the exquisite problem of the artist is eternally but to draw, by a geometry of his own, the circle in which they shall happily *appear* to do so."[59] For Burke, the role of the critic is to make sure that we do not forget that relations stop nowhere, for "the synthetic nature of every symbol . . . require[s] a doctrine of 'multiple causation' " (*ATH,* 50).

Burke is obsessed with the variegated functions of symbolic action in general and the whole problem of imputing motives to attitudes and actions. He characteristically regards literature as a casuistry of human motives, for he is profoundly interested in the dialectic and drama of human relations. The literary critic qua critic is free to reject this concern. But he is bound to reduce the rich motivational complexity of the poetic act if he refuses to consider what the poem is doing for the author and reader, to link function with structure, context with text, extrinsic with intrinsic.

Symbolic action is an elusive concept, one that undergoes dazzling sea changes throughout the writings of Kenneth Burke. In order to grasp its mediatory function in the theory of dramatism, its centrality in the intrinsic/extrinsic merger, we need first to examine the implications of the claim that language is symbolic action and that the linguistic model should therefore be given methodological, if not ontological, priority. This problem I shall address in chapters 3 and 4. Before proceeding to do that, however, I should first like to show how Burke's critical terms function when deployed to analyze texts from various genres—first, by making my own application of his ideas to a poem, and second, by examining his own analyses of *Julius Caesar, Antony and Cleopatra, Coriolanus, A Passage to India,* and *A Portrait of the Artist as a Young Man.*

Two

Theory and Practice

ALTHOUGH BURKE HAS written a great deal of practical criticism, he rarely engages in it exclusively. If theoretical issues are not explicitly in the foreground of his discourse, they are always implicitly in the background. How Burke's terms function in the realm of practice is integrally related to what they mean in the realm of theory. My intentions in this chapter are twofold: first, to apply some of his dramatistic categories to a poem by Robert Frost, and second, to explore the unity of theory and practice in some of Burke's literary essays by considering the interrelations among certain key ideas in his critical lexicon: the psychology of form, the rhetoric of identification, the paradox of substance, hierarchic psychosis, categorical guilt, socioanagogic criticism, the tragic rhythm, dramatic catharsis, the principle of the concordance, and so forth. Although my purposes are mainly expository, I shall also discuss the problems of elevating the symbolical at the expense of the grammatical, rhetorical, and ethical, especially insofar as this elevation pertains to the shift from dramatism to logology, the subject matter of chapter 4. One can detect, I think, a similar shift in Burke's practical criticism, for the self-acknowledged progression in his criticism is from self-expression to communication to consummation (tracking down the implications of a nomenclature). The problem with focusing on the latter is that such a focus leads one to regard the work of art as *nothing but* a terminology, the implications of which achieve their consummation in the perfection of the work's intrinsic system, its logologic. Or, to put it another way,

43

the proportional strategy of the dream/prayer/chart triad, which sees the aspects of symbolic action as ingredients in an overall motivational recipe, tends to give way to an essentializing strategy, which sees the symbolic as the essence of the poetic act. Yet the intrinsic fallacy is one that Burke never fully succumbs to, which is why one is forced to use the dubious language of "tendency." And, as Burke reminds us, "a mere tendency to do something is also, by the same token, a tendency *not* to do it" (*GM*, 256).

Symbolic Action in a Poem by Frost

"Mending Wall"

Something there is that doesn't love a wall,
That sends the frozen-ground-swell under it,
And spills the upper boulders in the sun;
And makes gaps even two can pass abreast.
The work of hunters is another thing: 5
    I have come after them and made repair
Where they have left not one stone on a stone,
But they would have the rabbit out of hiding,
To please the yelping dogs. The gaps I mean,
No one has seen them made or heard them made,   10
    But at spring mending-time we find them there.
I let my neighbor know beyond the hill;
And on a day we meet to walk the line
And set the wall between us once again.
We keep the wall between us as we go.   15
    To each the boulders that have fallen to each.
And some are loaves and some so nearly balls
We have to use a spell to make them balance:
'Stay where you are until our backs are turned!'
We wear our fingers rough with handling them.   20
    Oh, just another kind of outdoor game,
One on a side. It comes to little more:
There where it is we do not need the wall:
He is all pine and I am apple orchard.
My apple trees will never get across   25
    And eat the cones under his pines, I tell him.
He only says, 'Good fences make good neighbors.'

Spring is the mischief in me, and I wonder
If I could put a notion in his head:
'*Why* do they make good neighbors? Isn't it   30
   Where there are cows? But here there are no cows.
Before I built a wall I'd ask to know
What I was walling in or walling out,
And to whom I was like to give offense.
Something there is that doesn't love a wall,   35
   That wants it down.' I could say 'Elves' to him,
But it's not elves exactly, and I'd rather
He said it for himself. I see him there
Bringing a stone grasped firmly by the top
In each hand, like an old-stone savage armed.   40
   He moves in darkness as it seems to me,
Not of woods only and the shade of trees.
He will not go behind his father's saying,
And he likes having thought of it so well
He says again, 'Good fences make good neighbors.'   45

The hortatory negative—embedded, par excellence, in the "thou shalt not's" of the Decalogue—finds blunt expression in a familiar prohibition: Private Property, No Trespassing. This pervasive but unpronounced injunction, along with the spirit of the negative that informs it, animates Frost's well-known poem, "Mending Wall." As Burke points out in *The Rhetoric of Religion*, "the negative is not a 'fact' of nature but a function of a symbol system" (*RR*, 20). It is "a peculiarly linguistic marvel," for "there are no negatives in nature, every natural condition being positively what it is" (*RR*, 19). "Nature is emblematic of the spirit imposed upon it by man's linguistic genius" (*LASA*, 362), and to a nature that is positively what it is, language adds the negative and all its proscriptions regarding property, law, behavior, morality, and so forth. Mine and yours, self and not-self, approach and withdrawal, property and propriety, prescription and proscription—these are some of the perplexities that Frost ambiguously entertains in "Mending Wall," a poem whose duplicitous title encapsulates the problem: the neighbors' yearly ritual of mending suggests that the differences between individuals are reconcilable, yet the two men socialize and cooperate only for the purpose of reestablishing and solidifying the wall that separates them. Whereas the speaker is on the surface advocating new prescriptions—his springlike, walls-down feeling would seem to contrast dramatically with the wintry, walls-up feeling of his neighbor—he nonetheless abides by the old proscriptions, as conscientiously remaining on his own side of the imaginary line as the neighbor remains on his. Behaviorally speaking, both men treat the legal fiction of a property line as if it were an empirical fact, thus showing how the linguistic genius of the negative inspirits nature and has positive effects in the realm of nonsymbolic motion. From this point of view, "Mending Wall" can be seen as a sustained meditation on the quandaries of No Trespassing, the burdens of property and propriety. The poem eloquently captures the moment of ambivalence between the optative and the indicative, between the desire for merger on the level of fantasy (dream) and the acceptance of division on the level of reality (chart), the poem being a rhetorical communication that would prove opposites (prayer) and an ethical presentation of the speaker's dilemma (self and social portraiture).

In Burkean terms, what we have is a truncated rebirth ritual. Because the speaker cannot mortify his sense of independent selfhood, he cannot effect a change of identity. Even though he is moving tentatively toward some sort of transformation, he opts ultimately for a strategy of containment and exploits the dialectical resources of tragic ambiguity to achieve this end. While there is a disparity between optative attitude and indicative situation, the poem's symbolic action works toward a qualified acceptance of the reality principle—namely, that limits and separations are necessary to human existence. "If the ingredient of acceptance is uppermost," Burke reflects, "the poet tends to cancel the misfit between himself and the frame by 'tragic ambiguity,' whereby he both expresses his criminality and exorcises it through symbolic punishment" (*ATH,* 209). Tragic ambiguity, then, as Burke understands it, is fundamentally a stance of acceptance, a way of coming to terms with an unavoidable reality. Such a strategy would explain the lack of commitment in the poem, its desire to remain on both sides of the fence at the same time. This is why there is a juxtaposition of both revolutionary and conservative frames, of "Something there is that doesn't love a wall" and "Good fences make good neighbors." Frost expresses the desire for mending the cleavage between self and other but gives it forbidding connotations of homoeroticism and infantile regression. As Norman Holland points out, "It is not difficult . . . to see that the warm, spring-like (but dangerous), walls-down feeling in the conscious content of the poem corresponds to a cosy but risky symbiosis at the fantasy level; or that the neighbour's wintry walls-up sense of privacy and separateness corresponds to the cold, hard reality of individuation."[1]

Holland maintains that after an infant has enjoyed a symbiotic period of oneness with his mother, he is forced to embark upon the long and difficult process of achieving individuation, a process that is coincident with his emergence into the world of language. "His first job in this world," Holland suggests, "is to learn that he is not at one with the world, that there is an inside and an outside, a self and a not-self. In other words he must become individuated; he must learn his own separateness and identity."[2] Frost's poem, Holland goes on to say, "works with some infantile fantasy about breaking down the wall which marks the separated or individuated self so as to return to a state of closeness to some Other."[3] Yet the merger would be with another man and hence homoerotic, which is not to say that the latent content of the poem is homosexual or that the poet desires physical consummation; it is to say, rather, that the poem envisages a loving relation between man and man that challenges accepted social distances and expresses desires for intimacy that are usually repressed. This "nucleus of fantasy" undergirds Frost's poem, for the burdens of individuation are such that one's sense of private property is intimately connected with one's sense of private parts. "The roots of ownership," Burke points out, "reside in *the individual centrality of the nervous system*, in the *divisiveness* of the individual human organism" (*RM*, 130). Infancy knows no "no," and the emergence from inarticulacy into articulacy is an emergence into a morally resonant and highly complicated forensic world of "dos" and "don'ts."

My point here is not to endorse Holland's reading but merely to use it as a frame of reference for our consideration of the poem as dream. As Burke proposes in "Freud—and the Analysis of Poetry" (*PLF*, 258–92), the problem with psychoanalytic interpretation is that it deploys an essentializing rather than a proportional strategy, treating the nucleus of fantasy as an origin or essence at the center of the poem instead of seeing it as but one ingredient in the overall motivational recipe. In regarding language as symbolic action in the fourfold Burkean sense, one looks not for originary causes but for the proportion of grammatical, rhetorical, symbolical, and ethical ingredients. The poem as dream (the symbolic) is simply one of four dimensions; it is not the essence of the poetic act.

Before proceeding further afield, however, we should first look at the poem's intrinsic, internal development from what, through what, to what. Two associative clusters come into view: the first is connected with the archetypal motif of spring as the agent of rebirth and regeneration; the second with the archetypal motif of winter as the agent of death and destruction. In terms of dramatic alignment, we have the speaker versus the neighbor, "Something there is that doesn't love a wall" versus "Good fences make good neighbors," a mischievous and magical sense of outdoor gamesmanship versus a serious sense of the job at hand, play versus work, warmth versus frigidity, the civilized light of liberal open-mindedness versus the primitive darkness of conservative dogmatism, and so on. But even as an initial statement of the poem's oppositional structure, this is inadequate. The speaker may seem to be the voice of civilization, humanism, and liberalism, yet the fantasies he is entertaining on the level of dream, if our initial diagnosis holds up, are more regressive than the alleged primitivism, savagery, and dogmatism of the neighbor. Property and walls are signs of civilization, for although property may be theft from another ideological standpoint, its enforcement demands a complex civilization replete with constabulary and government. Contemplating the smashing of walls is a dangerous courting of anarchism, and the speaker's "loving closeness," therefore, may be more threatening to society than the neighbor's "aggressive distancing."[4] Even the archetypal spring/winter opposition does not altogether work, for the walls-down speaker is imagistically associated with the wall-destroying force of frost/Frost, the frozen-ground-swell of winter. At best, associative clusters and dramatic alignments give us a notion of the variables in the poem's equations. While there is a desire for merger on the level of dream, the stance of tragic ambiguity makes for a rhetoric of ironic acceptance on the level of prayer and for a realistic mode of adjustment on the level of chart. How the poem unfolds is of obvious and paramount importance.

We notice immediately that the syntactic awkwardness of

Something there is that doesn't love a wall,
That sends the frozen-ground-swell under it,

is as disruptive as the force that through the ground-swell spills the boulders. (Compare the aphoristic fluidity and simple parallelism of "Good fences make good neighbors.") Moreover, in accordance with the linguistic genius of the propositional negative—the "it is not" of definition—if there is something there is that doesn't love a wall, there must be, from the point of view of dialectical symmetry, something there is that does love a wall. The first two lines imply the ambivalence that we have already detected in the title itself. The gaps in the wall reflect the gaps in the speaker's consciousness, for his own state of mind is fundamentally divided. For all his desire to obliterate the walls between people, he is the one who lets the neighbor know that it is time to mend the wall. Furthermore, as I mentioned earlier, both of them treat the "thou shalt not" of the property line as if it were a positive reality rather than a hortatory negative—"We keep the wall between us as we go" (l. 15). That the speaker invokes mystery and magic (no one has seen the gaps made or heard them made, and one has to use a spell to make the boulders balance) indicates that motives from the realm of childhood are implicit in this outdoor game. It also stresses the difference between the playful attitude of the speaker and the workmanlike attitude of the neighbor. The dogmatic surety of the neighbor's slogan—"Good fences make good neighbors" (l. 27)—provokes querulousness in the speaker.

> 'Why do they make good neighbors? Isn't it
> Where there are cows? But here there are no cows.
> Before I built a wall I'd ask to know
> What I was walling in or walling out,
> And to whom I was like to give offense.
> Something there is that doesn't love a wall,
> That wants it down.'
>
> (ll. 30–36)

Though the speaker engages in the rebuilding of a fence, he does not want to "give offense," and though he *could* say "Elves" and try to induce his neighbor to examine critically the father's slogan, he does not.

> Bringing a stone grasped firmly by the top
> In each hand, like an old-stone savage armed
>
> (ll. 39–40)

the neighbor aggressively affirms the propriety of his right to property. He says again, "Good fences make good neighbors" (l. 45), and on this note the poem ends. So even though lines 35–36 are a variation of lines 1–2 and thus emphasize the attitude of the speaker, the slogan of the neighbor occupies the position of ultimate emphasis. The opening and closing are contradictory, the propositional negative of lines 1–2 giving way to the aphoristic positive of line 45. Although the poem implies throughout the complexity of the forensic, with all the pre- scriptions and proscriptions of the hortatory negative, it ends on the simplicity of the sloganistic. This fundamental ambivalence expresses itself on the grammatical, rhetorical, symbolical, and ethical levels of the poem's symbolic action.

From the grammatical standpoint, we have two *agents* in a rural New England *scene,* using the *agency* of their hands in the *act* of put- ting boulders together for the *purpose* of mending the wall that sepa- rates their properties. The agents dramatize opposing *attitudes*—the spring-like, walls-down attitude of the speaker, the wintry, walls-up attitude of the neighbor. Both men represent different charts of mean- ing, though it must be remembered, when we come to assess the rela- tive accuracy of their charts, that in striving toward adequate ideas charts of meaning are not "right" or "wrong"—they are relative ap- proximations to the truth.

From the rhetorical standpoint the speaker is trying to encourage his neighbor to go behind the father's saying and to question whether good fences make good neighbors. But since he does not directly con- front his neighbor or overtly try to persuade the man, we may infer that he is as much trying to persuade himself and, by extension, his implied audience. Although rhetoric involves the formation of identity and the establishment and maintenance of affiliation and community, it is predicated upon division and difference, for if identification and consubstantiality were really possible, there would be no need to in- duce them. For Burke, the rhetorical situation is endemic to the human situation.

> The "roots of ownership" . . . reside in the *individual centrality of the nervous system,* in the *divisiveness* of the individual human organism, from birth to death. . . . Bring together a number of individual nervous systems, each with its own unique centrality, and from this indetermi-

nate mixture of cooperation and division there emerge the conditions for the "basic rhetorical situation": an underlying biological incentive towards private property, plus the fact that the high development of production and language owes so much to its public or communal nature. (*RM,* 130)

"Mending Wall" dramatizes this basic rhetorical situation, and the men communicate to the degree that they cooperate. Even if, on the level of dream, the speaker wishes to regress to the symbiosis of the oral stage or progress to some form of homoerotic communion, his desires are sublimated into communication rather than contact. Thus, insofar as he and the neighbor do cooperate and communicate, the infantile wishes are transcended, and insofar as his desire for communion is not converted into overt, practical action, it is substitutive rather than introductory. From the symbolical standpoint the urge may be to embrace symbiosis and renounce individuation, but the rhetorical drive toward communication and cooperation qualifies the symbolic one. Danger is courted but not succumbed to. The motives of communication modify those of self-expression. Whatever estrangement exists between the two neighbors, they overcome it in the cooperative act of mending the wall. The speaker, in spite of his inability to induce a change of attitude in his neighbor, does succeed in inducing his neighbor to participate in the yearly ritual.

All in all, the speaker's chart is realistic and represents a mature adjustment to a complicated situation. The reality principle is reaffirmed by a process that goes through drama rather than avoiding drama. From the ethical standpoint, "Mending Wall" portrays an individuated self who reconciles conflicting motives—the inclination to say "no" to thou shalt not (the pleasure principle) and the obligation to say "yes" to thou shalt not (the reality principle). The reality of division and difference, both on the level of personal identity and private property, is kept in view.

The separation between self and other cannot be entirely overcome. Consequently, the ritual of rebirth is truncated, and the ambiguity is tragic in the sense that it is permanent and unresolvable. The speaker has adopted a stance of tragic ambiguity to cancel the misfit between himself and the objective situation but is seemingly aware of his own equivocality since he knows that the misfit is necessary and that it cannot be really canceled. Even if one were to embrace a rhetoric of social change calling for the abolition of private property, the basic rhetorical situation would still persist—a rhetoric of courtship between biologically isolated individuals whose social roles (even in an order with a noninvidious structure of authority) would be different and thus divisive.

Burke defines rituals of rebirth as "magical incantations whereby the poet effects a change of identity, killing some portion of himself as a technique for membership in a new situation" (*ATH,* 17n). In his rhetorics of motives and religion he discusses at length how killing dignifies, punishes, and transforms—the transformational aspect being both cathartic and dialectical. A grammar of killing includes three modes: the active (killing), the reflexive (self-killing), and the passive (being killed). In any of these modes death is a narrative way of saying mortification; it is a kind of capital punishment. Narratively, then, death is used to suggest guilt. Natural death comes to equal moral mortification. What was originally a natural phenomenon used analogically to suggest the painfulness of a moral phenomenon—the taming of wayward aspects of the self is like killing them or becoming dead to them—becomes so conventionally absorbed and reanalogized that the natural is infused with the moral, the positive with the negative. Death is seen as a kind of punishment or ultimate mortification.

The speaker's urge to mortify his obdurate selfhood lies somewhere between the poles of passivity and reflexivity. He is punishing his desire for more intimate contact with another by knowingly putting himself into a situation wherein the other's point of view will ultimately prevail. This victimage, of course, has a cathartic function for the audience: it expresses vicariously a guilt that is internal to our being and thereby purifies the pollution. It also has a dialectical function: it allows us to transcend the principle of merger that the speaker ambiguously entertains by pushing us toward a higher synthesis. Symbolical motives (the covert self-expression of forbidden and dangerous desires) are triply transformed by rhetorical motives (the need for communication and cooperation, for identification and consubstantiality), grammatical motives (the need for accurate designation and a realistic recognition of the necessity of division and difference), and ethical motives (self and social portraiture, the recognition of the conflict between individual inclination and social duty).

In considering what the poem is doing for the author, we have explored its unconscious or subconscious factors, suggesting that on the level of dream there is a desire for merger that has both infantile and homoerotic connotations. Yet on this level the incipient act is clearly substitutive; it plays a compensatory or therapeutic role, catharsis for the author being the act of self-expression itself. It would be as great an error to regard dream as the essence or origin of the poetic act as it would be to disregard the rich suggestiveness of psychoanalytic interpretation.

In considering the nature of the poem as "addressed," we have explored how the two men, through the inducement of attitudes and actions, have established community and overcome estrangement to the extent that they have joined in a cooperative venture. The speaker, whose point of view dominates the poem, induces similar attitudes in us. To the extent that the poem is a successful communication, we share in his ambivalence; on the one hand, we desire closer contact with others, participating in his magical walls-down attitude and identifying with his playful irreverence toward the dogmas of property and propriety; on the other hand, we admit both the reality of difference and the dangers of regression and contact, knowing, alas, that good fences make good neighbors. We identify with the speaker in that we share his guilt and isolation, yet dissociate ourselves from him in that we are wary of converting our impulses into overt, practical action. The poem immerses us in the ambiguities of attitude, since in its character as incipient action an attitude may be either introductory or substitutive and in the realm of poetic action it is most likely to be both.

In considering the poem as a realistic sizing up of a situation, we may differ in our final judgments. To my mind, it would be excessive to claim that the poem entrenches and naturalizes bourgeois conceptions of private property, mainly because its scene is rural rather than urban and because the separation between the two men is as much biological as social (the two, presumably, enjoying the same class status). It seems to me that the poem productively entertains conflicting impulses in a way that does justice to the complexity of the situation. It does not "*play down* the realistic naming of our situation and *play up* such strategies as make solace cheap" (*PLF*, 299).

As William H. Rueckert points out, one of the general tenets of

Burke's theory of symbolic action is that "all poetry is a rhetoric of rebirth which enables the poet to purge and redeem himself." Rueckert goes on to say that for Burke there are two general kinds of burdens: guilt and identity. "On the one hand, poetry is a ritual of cure which enables the poet to purge his guilt or . . . resolve his tensions and be redeemed; on the other hand, poetry is a ritual of rebirth which enables the poet, by means of symbolic identification, to effect permanent changes of identity."[5] On the level of dream, the poet gives expression to a pattern of identifications and dissociations in order to unburden himself. On the level of prayer, the rhetoric of the poem may induce readers to effect analogous changes in their attitudes or actions. On the level of chart, the poem may offer equipment for living, a realistic strategy for encompassing a real situation. In the realm of symbolic action, dream, prayer, and chart are forever entangled, for "poems can function both as magical forms (structures) for effecting a catharsis and as formulae (statements) for defining situations (problems) and indicating modes of adjustment (solutions)."[6] Poems can also limn an ethical portrait of self and society.

Shifting our vocabulary, we could easily construe "Mending Wall" as an allegory of reading, as a text that with its surplus of signifiers resists totalizing interpretations or even the establishing of hierarchies of meaning, for there is no doubt that the meanings contradict and supplement each other and that the clash between the referential and rhetorical levels of discourse produces undecidability. As readers, we are left in the aporetic double bind of trying to master a text that has neither boundaries nor property lines. In this sense, a Burkean reading is deconstructionist in spirit, although, in accordance with the four levels of symbolic action, we might more properly say that we are left in a quadruple bind. Burke's proportional strategy is as antiessentialist as deconstruction, but his emphasis falls on the multileveled richness of symbolic action rather than on the *mise en abyme* of deferred signification. The difference, as I shall later argue, is as much temperamental as philosophical.

Drama as Rhetoric

From the beginning of his critical career, Burke recognizes the ubiquity of the rhetorical motive in language in general and literature in particular. "If rhetoric is but 'the use of language in such a way as to produce a desired impression upon the hearer or reader,'" he writes in *Counter-Statement,* his first collection of critical essays, "then 'effective literature' could be nothing else but rhetoric" (*CS,* 120). The central premise of the rhetorical approach to literature is enunciated in "Psychology and Form," an essay from this same collection. Although his views become more elaborate over the years, they do not stray very far from this sine qua non.

> Form [is] the psychology of the audience. . . . the creation of an appetite in the mind of the auditor, and the adequate satisfying of that appetite. This satisfaction—so complicated is the human mechanism—at times involves a temporary set of frustrations, but in the end these frustrations prove to be simply a more involved kind of satisfaction, and furthermore serve to make the satisfaction of fulfillment more intense. (*CS,* 31)

Form, "an arousing and fulfillment of desires" (*CS,* 124), has five aspects: "progressive form (subdivided into syllogistic and qualitative progression), repetitive form, conventional form, and minor or incidental forms" (*CS,* 124).

Syllogistic progression follows the logic of linear development and "is the form of a perfectly conducted argument, advancing step by step. . . . Insofar as the audience, from its acquaintance with the premises, feels the rightness of the conclusion, the work is formal" (*CS,* 124). Qualitative progression, on the other hand, is subtler. "Instead of one incident in the plot preparing us for some other possible incident of the plot (as Macbeth's murder of Duncan prepares us for the dying of Macbeth), the presence of one quality prepares us for the introduction of another (the grotesque seriousness of the murder scene preparing us for the grotesque buffoonery of the porter scene)" (*CS,* 124–25). What we have "is a bold juxtaposition of one quality created by another, an association in ideas, which, if not logical, is nevertheless emotionally natural" (*CS,* 39).

Repetitive form is "the consistent maintaining of a principle under new guises. . . . the restatement of a theme by new details" (*CS,* 125). "A succession of images, each of them regiving the same lyric mood; a character repeating his identity, his 'number,' under changing situations; the sustaining of an attitude, as in satire; the rhythmic regularity

of blank verse; the rhyme scheme of *terza rima*—these are all aspects
of repetitive form" (*CS*, 125).

Conventional form "involves to some degree the appeal of form *as
form*" and has an "element of 'categorical expectancy.' . . . Whereas
the anticipations and gratifications of progressive and repetitive form
arise *during the process* of reading, the expectations of conventional
form may be *anterior to* the reading" (*CS*, 126–27). One expects, for
example, a sonnet to exemplify the conventional form of a sonnet.

Minor or incidental forms are aspects of a work "which can be
discussed as formal events in themselves"—"such as metaphor, paradox, disclosure, reversal, contraction, expansion, bathos, apostrophe,
series, chiasmus" (*CS*, 127).

> Their effect partially depends upon their function in the whole, yet they
> manifest sufficient evidences of episodic distinctness to bear considera-
> tion apart from their context. . . . A monologue by Shakespeare can be
> detached from its context and recited with enjoyment because, however
> integrally it contributes to the whole of which it is a part, it is also an
> independent curve of plot enclosed by its own beginning and end. (*CS*,
> 127)

Progressive, repetitive, conventional, and minor forms necessarily
overlap. As Burke points out,

> the lines in *Othello*, beginning "Soft you, a word or two before you go,"
> and ending "Seized by the throat the uncircumcised dog and smote him
> thus (*stabs himself*)" well exemplify the vigorous presence of all five
> aspects of form, as this suicide is the logical outcome of his predicament
> (syllogistic progression); it fits the general mood of gloomy forebodings
> which has fallen upon us (qualitative progression); the speech has
> about it that impetuosity and picturesqueness we have learned to asso-
> ciate with Othello (repetitive form); it is very decidedly a conclusion
> (conventional form), and in its development it is a tiny plot in itself
> (minor form). (*CS*, 128)

Sometimes, however, the forms may conflict, for "an author may
create a character which, by the logic of the fiction, should be destroyed; but he may also have made the character so appealing that the
audience wholly desires the character's salvation" (*CS*, 129).

Although this fivefold conception of form is clearly transgeneric, it is in his drama criticism (the bulk of which pertains to tragedy) that Burke tends to emphasize the rhetorical (along with the ethical) dimension of symbolic action.[7]

"Antony in Behalf of the Play"

Resisting the tendency to consider literature either as a creator's device for self-expression or as an audience's device for amusement and instruction, Burke's avowedly rhetorical approach to *Julius Caesar* stresses the "communicative relationship between writer and audience" (*PLF,* 329) and the psychology of form that the play embodies and enacts by creating, frustrating, reversing, and fulfilling our expectations. In a tour de force Burke imagines Antony addressing the reader or spectator instead of the mob at hand. "Thus we have a tale from Shakespeare, retold, not as a plot but from the standpoint of the rhetorician, who is concerned with the work's processes of appeal" (*PLF,* 330).

In act III, scene ii, Antony enters after Brutus has defended himself before the people and won their sympathy to the conspirators' cause. At this point, Shakespeare's Antony declaims his famous speech—"Friends, Romans, countrymen . . ."—a classic example of what Burke calls minor form. Burke's Antony, however, proceeds to unravel for us the intricacies of the paradox of substance, asking us as implicit coconspirators to consider the burden we now carry. For we have been willing to let Caesar die for slight reasons indeed: his deafness in one ear, his falling sickness, his fever, his aquatic incompetence, his barren wife, his superstition, his imperial appearance on stage in a nightgown—all of which operate on the level of qualitative progression as do the other portents that have been deftly inserted by the playwright.

Shakespeare, Antony tells us, has been careful to establish two principles: a Caesar-principle and a Brutus-principle. Even though we have vicariously conspired in the assassination of an emperor, we nonetheless have sympathy for the victim, for, as Antony points out, a play cannot be profitably built around the horror of a murder if we as an audience do not care whether the murdered man lives or dies. Shakespeare's rhetorical ploy is to make Caesar appealing by proxy. Since Antony is a loyal follower of Caesar, and since we love Antony for a good fellow, his love of Caesar lifts up Caesar in our eyes. Our identification with Antony and the Caesar-principle he represents will prove to be stronger than our identification with the Brutus-principle, whose hegemony is temporary. Speaking in the first person, Antony explains his dual function:

> Not only do I let Caesar shine a bit warmly by his reflection of my glow, but when the actual *persona* of the Caesar-principle is dispatched by daggers, the principle lives on in me, who continues the function of Caesar in the play. . . . Henceforth, I am no mere adjunct to the Caesar-principle. So in expanding to my expanded role, I must break the former mold somewhat. Let *savants* explain the change by saying that carefree Antony was made a soberer man, and a bitter one, by the death of Caesar. But it is an obvious fact that if an important cog in the plot vanishes in the very middle of our drama, something has to take its place. In deputizing for Caesar, I found it impossible to remain completely Antony. Let *savants* explain my altered psychology as they will—*I* know it was a playwright's necessity. (*PLF,* 333–35)

Antony's revelation of the play's rhetorical strategy nicely illustrates the paradox of substance. Through this commentary Burke suggests that it would be a major error in interpretation to view Antony solely as a character unto himself. He must be viewed in terms of the whole play, his attitudes and actions being as much products of discursive necessity as of psychological motivation. Repetitive form is sacrificed to dramaturgic exigency.

At the climax of his speech Antony reverses our expectations and contrives his peripety by metonymic substitution—all under the guise of praising honorable men and burying, not praising, Caesar. He focuses our attention upon Caesar's dagger-pierced and blood-drenched mantle, making a devastatingly effective appeal to pathos. By inciting the audience's desire for vengeance he proves Cassius right: both the persona and the adjunct of the Caesar-principle should have been slain. For "the Brutus-principle, who killed the Caesar-*persona,* is driven to death by the Caesar adjunct" (*PLF,* 341–42). Our own need for catharsis pushes us to make Brutus scapegoat for our crimes. As Antony puts it: "You have been made conspirators in a murder. For this transgression, there must be some expiative beast brought up for sacrifice. Such requirements guided us in the mixing of the Brutus-recipe, for it is Brutus that must die to absolve you of your stabbing of an emperor who was deaf in one ear and whose wife was sterile. . . . In weeping for his death, you will be sweetly absolved" (*PLF*, 334–35). In terms of progressive form, the death of Brutus is both syllogistically and qualitatively appropriate, for it is not only a logical outcome of the plot; it is also a fitting end for a man who "roams about at night, in 'rheumy and unpurged air' sucking up 'the humours of the dank morning,' so that even the quality of swamps is drawn upon to discredit Brutus . . . since he was a conspirator, like a bog" (*PLF*, 335).

Through his masterful deployment of the rhetoric of identification and the paradox of substance, Shakespeare demonstrates eloquently that form is the psychology of the audience. Such rhetoric induces us to conspire in two murders and to be manipulated by our sympathy for Antony. Although Antony frequently enacts his essence, he also behaves according to the dictates of discursive necessity and thereby violates, at least temporarily, the dictates of repetitive form. Whatever frustrations we encounter en route, however, prove in the end to be simply a more involved kind of satisfaction.

Hierarchic Psychosis and the Rhetorical Motive

The need for rhetoric as an agent of symbolic identification arises out of the real differences that plague any given social order. Social malaise and division, Burke argues, are grounded in property structure and in the differentiation of social role imposed upon individuals in a complex heterogeneous society.[8] "In any order," he writes, "there will be mysteries of hierarchy, since such a principle is grounded in the very nature of language and reinforced by the resultant diversity of occupational classes. . . . Language makes for transcendence, and transcendence imposes distance" (*RM*, 279).

Because of such diversity and distance, categorical guilts are implicit in any given social order, and human societies cohere because of symbolic victims that the individual members of the group share in common. Catharsis, a stylistic cleansing of an audience, is effected by the tragic imitation of such victimage. Thus, on the level of the body politic, catharsis is a way of purging and purifying the civic tensions that are endemic to any order, for "tragedy (in its role as a civic ceremony) can *symbolically* transcend modes of civic conflicts that, in the practical realm of social relations, are never *actually* resolved within the conditions of the given social order (and the conflicts 'natural' to it)" (*DD*, 11). Herein resides the social function of tragedy, though catharsis, of course, is not confined to the sociopolitical level; it has bodily, psychological, and familial implications as well, and the great tragedies purge and purify on manifold levels.

Division and difference create the need for identification and consubstantiality, giving rise to what Burke calls a rhetoric of courtship between individuals who occupy different rungs on the social ladder. " 'Hierarchy' is the old, eulogistic word for 'bureaucracy,' with each stage employing a rhetoric of obeisance to the stage above it, and a rhetoric of charitable condescension to the stage beneath it, in sum, a rhetoric of courtship" (*RM*, 118). "By the 'principle of courtship' in rhetoric we mean the use of suasive devices for the transcending of social estrangement" (*RM*, 208). The hierarchic motive is all-pervasive, and "the vocabularies of social and sexual courtship are so readily interchangeable, not because one is a mere 'substitute' for the other, but because sexual courtship is intrinsically fused with the motives of social hierarchy" (*RM*, 217). The attempt to extricate motives of social hierarchy enigmatically concealed in literary representations Burke calls "socioanagogic" interpretation, for "nature is a linguistically inspirited thing," and "what we take as 'nature' is largely a social pageant in disguise" (*LASA*, 378).[9]

"Shakespearean Persuasion: Antony and Cleopatra*"*

In this essay Burke objects to the assumption "that the rhetoric of persuasion has no place in poetics" (*LASA*, 102) and shows how Shakespeare uses amplification as a rhetorical device for paralleling imperialism on the level of world politics with imperialism on the level of sexual politics. "Love is in essence an empire" (*LASA*, 102), and in this play "the motives and motifs of empire . . . aggrandize a love affair, so that it takes place not between two individuals but between no less than Rome and Egypt" (*LASA*, 230).

The basic "tension" that the dramatist exploits for his effects is that "even in the meanest love the lover, however deviously and unconsciously, feels in some way 'ennobled' " (*LASA*, 102). Working on this proclivity in his audience, the dramatist "aims to perfect a plot that will translate the theme of love into terms of imperial 'ostentation'" (*LASA*, 102). "All told, the plot would be a dramatic way of 'acting out' the proposition: 'Implicit in human relations under conditions of emergent empire there are the *forms* of empire as such'" (*LASA*, 104). Because Elizabethan England is an emergent empire, imperial ostentation is a viable strategy for the dramatist to adopt. "In this respect, the tragedy becomes an aesthetic equivalent of the royal *cortege*, using 'world politics' as a means to amplify the story of a love affair. Here the self-flattery implicit in courtship . . . is 'translated' into terms of the grandest 'ostentation'" (*LASA*, 108).

The translation, however, is excessive, and the dramaturgic principle of excess sets up the conditions for victimage and catharsis. Because Antony and Cleopatra are "guilty of gratifying the audience's furtive vanity by being *consummate* lovers," they "must be punished for the very immoderation that allows the audience's timid vanity to wax wanton in principle, through the contemplating of consummations in fiction" (*LASA*, 108). The audience sympathetically involves itself "in the two grandiloquent suicides (each by definition an act of *self*-abuse)," and "the conditions for a purge" are thereby established (*LASA*, 108). With involvement, however, comes separation, for "the humble and moderate can thank God that they personally are not driven by this excessiveness, the imitation of which is designed for their gratification" (*LASA*, 108). Thus does the rhetoric of identification comprehend its dialectical opposite—dissociation, both of which are integral to tragedy. As Burke reflects:

> A tragedy can entertain us by flattery, if it imitates a weakness in us; but by imitating this weakness "consummately," the tragedy can enable us simultaneously to "identify ourselves" with the imitation and to disclaim it. The process involves redemption by vicarious victimage, since we acquiesce to the sacrifice of the persons who were entrusted with the role of imitating our weakness in an amplified form. However sympathetically, we can renounce our representatives, since they represented us only too thoroughly, though this very thoroughness was itself a necessary ingredient in the recipe for a tragic character. (*LASA*, 109)

The imperialist motive, then, expressed in terms of both political and sexual courtship, is at once gratified and punished. Both Antony and Cleopatra die unostentatiously, in humble animality, the pomp and pageantry of empire dissolved by the sheerly biological imperative of death. The deaths of these two titular figures show how much their substance and identity were dependent upon extrinsic factors. Just as Antony's militia and ships (his "Antoniad") are aspects of his substance and identity,

> the description of Cleopatra approaching in her barge contrives to make us feel that the setting is an aspect of her substance, not defining her but reflecting her. This is, of course, the puzzle at the basis of all drama, as it is in life. The major figures can "be themselves" only because the roles of all the characters are related to this end. I call this the "paradox of substance" . . . because one cannot separate the intrinsic properties of a character from the situation that enables him to be what he is. (*LASA*, 107)

The identities of both characters are shaped by their roles in the sociopolitical hierarchy, and their status is contingent upon the magic of this order and the trappings that complement their exalted positions. Social divinity emerges from the mystique of hierarchy.

Although Antony and Cleopatra are consummate lovers, they are punished for their excesses. The implied moral message may very well be, as Burke suggests, "incipiently Puritan" (*LASA*, 108). If a ruler, because of hubristic sexual engrossment, neglects the affairs of state, the wages of sex will surely be death. The self-reflexive nature of suicide accentuates Antony's dereliction of duty (as does the conscientiousness of Octavius), and the message seems to be that world politics should not be superseded by sexual politics. Whether or not one accepts this extrapolation, Burke does succeed in showing how Shakespeare exploits the illusion of imperiousness implicit in courtship and how social motives radically modify sexual motives, both being imbued with hierarchic psychosis.

The Tragic Rhythm

Tragedy, for Burke, is the "representative anecdote" because it is the most thoroughgoing mode of dramatic catharsis and dialectical transcendence. The agonistic or dialectical process is embodied in tragedy, where the agent's action involves a corresponding passion; and from the sufferance of the passion there arises an understanding of the act, an understanding that transcends the act. The act, in being an assertion, has called forth a counter-assertion in the elements that compose its context. And when the agent is able to see in terms of this counter-assertion, he has transcended the state that characterized him at the start. In this final state of tragic vision, intrinsic and extrinsic motivations are merged. That is, although purely circumstantial factors participate in his tragic destiny, these are not felt as exclusively external, or scenic; for they bring about a *representative* kind of accident that belongs with the agent's particular kind of character. (*GM*, 38–39)

The difference between dramatic catharsis and dialectical transcendence is that whereas "catharsis involves fundamentally purgation by the imitation of victimage" (*LASA*, 186), transcendence involves "the building of a *terministic* bridge whereby one realm is *transcended* by being viewed *in terms* of a realm 'beyond' it" (*LASA*, 187). But because both involve formal development—"whereby the position at the end transcends the position at the start, so that the position at the start can eventually be seen in terms of the new motivation encountered en route" (*GM*, 422)—they both give us modes of transformation: victimage and symbolic sacrifice in drama, the treating of contingent things in terms of a beyond in dialectic. Key terms are like characters, "but whereas drama stresses the *persons* who have the thoughts . . . the dialectic of a Platonic dialogue stresses the *thoughts* held by the persons" (*LASA*, 188). Both drama and dialectic "exemplify competitive cooperation" (*LASA*, 188).

In *The Idea of a Theater* Francis Fergusson sloganizes Burke's notion of the tragic rhythm of action (*poiema*), passion or suffering (*pathema*), and understanding (*mathema*) into the alliterative trio of purpose, passion, and perception.[10] The hero engages in purposeful action, making in the process a fatal error in judgment. As a result, he undergoes a purgatorial process of suffering and self-examination. In the end he achieves perception, a deeper knowledge of reality, even though this awareness comes too late to reverse the tragic flow of events. The assumption is that rational beings learn about reality by having their purposes stymied and their excesses or errors exposed, there being in tragedy, of course, a drastic disproportion between crime and punishment.

In *King Lear* the mistaken purpose is Lear's banishing Cordelia, an error in judgment reflective of his hubris—his pride or excess. As a result, he is forced to suffer the ravages of raw nature, his personal disorder finding an external image in the tempest. This suffering imposes a self-revelation, which is the precondition for perception and redemption. His personal redemption consists in the recognition and perception of his error in judgment even though the pressure of a tragic reality takes its toll upon both him and Cordelia. This is a reductive schema, but it does give some idea of what Burke means by the tragic rhythm.

The tragic rhythm may be truncated, and much of modern drama achieves its characteristic effects precisely by doing so. Indeed, it is a commonplace to say that modern theater does not present Aristotelian action but dramatizes a static condition, giving us not imitation of actions, but life as it is, which lacks the comprehensible chain of cause and effect, the purposeful flow of beginning, middle, and end, the cathartic effect of completed events. With playwrights such as Chekhov, the Aristotelian pattern of action becomes problematic, for there is no real pattern of action, just the texture of selected moments of life, purposeful action and eventual gain of new perception being very much overshadowed by consequent endurance of suffering. The focus, then, is on the passion of the characters, their process of undergoing experience. What we have is a blend of comedy and tragedy bringing the mode of passion to the foreground. There is a tragicomic disparity between the existential attitudes of the characters and the objective reality those attitudes would encompass.

In *The Cherry Orchard* the aristocratic attitudes of noblesse oblige that the impoverished owners of the cherry orchard wield are totally out of joint with their own financial circumstances and with the new mercantile reality of Russian society after the emancipation of the serfs and the breakdown of the old feudal order. Nothing happens; the orchard, symbol of the old order, is sold; the characters gain no perception of the inadequacy of their attitudes, values, beliefs, and ideas. Nonetheless, with Chekhov's expert manipulation of dramatic irony, the audience is able to gain perception, even if only a perception of the fact that there is a necessary disparity between existential attitudes and sociohistorical situations. If all we know is that life is tragicomic, at least we know something. Our perspective is more inclusive than that of the characters, and the playwright's irony is stable in this regard.

With Beckett the truncation of the tragic rhythm achieves its apotheosis. In *Waiting for Godot* the irony is unstable and corrosive—it dissolves, deranges, dislocates. The audience's perspective is as benighted as that of the characters. There is no purposeful action, no attainment of a deeper knowledge of reality, just suffering, enduring, waiting—waiting for a vague and undefined person, with a vague and undefined hope. There is no purpose (save that of waiting) and no perception, for the possibility of perception hinges on Godot's coming, and he does not come. A beginning is impossible, for the characters have no memory to speak of and no sense of time or history (the set is virtually barren and the sociohistorical situation is bracketed). An end is impossible because closure depends on Godot; the characters, moreover, are not even capable of the purposive action that suicide requires. They are perpetually in the middle of things, conscious only of their present suffering, the longeurs of their waiting. Nothing to be done.

I adduce these modern examples in order to affirm the centrality of Aristotelian action, the tragic rhythm that Burke describes. Even in its truncated form, where the motive of deliberate violation is uppermost, its presence is felt as absence. This is why Burke insists that the drama and dialectic of tragedy is representative of the fullness of human thought.

"Coriolanus *and the Delights of Faction*"

In *Coriolanus* the tragic rhythm operates somewhat differently. Even though the hero undergoes passion as a result of his mistaken purpose, he attains little, if any, perception. As we have seen, the usual formula for tragedy is this: "The hero acts; in the course of acting, he organizes an opposition; then, in the course of suffering the opposition (or seeing 'in terms of' it) he transcends his earlier position—and the audience, by identification with him, undergoes a similar 'cathartic' transformation" (*LASA*, 95). In the case of *Coriolanus*, however, the hero never really matures, and gains no significant insight into the excesses of his character that have caused his downfall. Even his killer addresses him as "thou boy of tears." "And the ultimate insight is in the audience's own

developments rather than in their sympathetic duplication of a higher
vision on the part of the sacrificed hero" (*LASA,* 95).

The hierarchic motive is all-pervasive in this play, for its central
"moral problem, or social tension . . . is purely and simply a kind of
discord intrinsic to the distinction between upper and lower classes"
(*LASA,* 81). Although the expectations and desires of the audience are
shaped by the psychology of form embodied within the play, "the
topics exploited for persuasive purposes *within* the play . . . have strategic relevance to kinds of 'values' and 'tensions' that prevail *outside*
the play" (*LASA,* 81). Shakespeare achieves distance by setting his
play in ancient Rome rather than contemporary London—"the *malaise* of the conflict between the privileged and the underprivileged"
being "stated in terms of a struggle between the patricians and plebeians of old Rome" (*LASA,* 82)—but his contemporary audience was
no doubt aware that in May and June of 1607 there were insurrections
in the counties of Northampton, Warwick, and Leicester. Rioters de-
molished hedges and ditches designed to enclose common land, and
this violence against the Enclosure Acts lasted several weeks. The
story of Coriolanus, an arrogant nobleman contemptuous of the lower
classes and more inclined to a rhetoric of vituperation than to one of
courtship, was very much a timely topic. To dramatize the tension
Shakespeare created a character who intensifies the tension.

Coriolanus—noble and brave, yet also volatile, vengeful, blunt,
and proud, a man whose virtues are suited for the military prowess
that has already won him acclaim—sues for high political office and
refuses to "court" the plebeians, so alienating them in the process that
he is banished. In exile he aligns himself with a commander he had
formerly defeated in order to lead a force against his own country. His
mother, however, persuades him not to attack and thereby uninten-
tionally creates the conditions whereby the commander is able to arrange for Coriolanus's assassination. His military virtue makes for
tragic dignification, and his political ineptitude (he loves not the common people and "seeks their hate with greater devotion, than they can
render it him"—II, ii) reveals his tragic flaw, his excess. His response
to banishment—"I banish you" (III, iii)—epitomizes his contempt for
his inferiors.

Though his illustrious military accomplishments speak for themselves, a character such as Coriolanus, whose first words in the play
address the citizenry thus:

> What's the matter you dissentious rogues
> That rubbing the poor itch of your opinion,
> Make yourselves scabs?
>
> (I, i)

must be made appealing by proxy. "Coriolanus' courage and out-spokenness make him a sufficiently 'noble' character to dignify a play by the sacrificing of him. And excessive ways of constantly reaffirming his assumption that only the *social* nobility can be *morally* noble indicts him for sacrifice" (*LASA*, 84). Again we encounter the paradox of substance. Coriolanus "cannot 'be himself' unless many others among the dramatis personae contribute to this end." His "very essence . . . is in a large measure defined, or determined, by the other characters who variously assist him or oppose him" (*LASA*, 84).

His mother, Volumnia, "is portrayed as a pugnacious virago of whom the son became a responsive masculine copy" (*LASA*, 85). She has great influence over him and is a discursive necessity of the plot in that she persuades her nonpolitical son to venture into politics and, after Coriolanus has been banished, she persuades him not to attack his homeland. His wife, Virgilia—sensitive, gracious, and silent—reflects well on him, as do the two generals who admire and respect him. Menenius, a nobleman whom both the commoners and the audience respect and who is thus an ideal link between the patrician and plebeian factions, also reflects well on him. Most strategic, perhaps, is Shakespeare's use of Aufidius, the noble and worthy opponent of Coriolanus and the orchestrator of his death, to deliver his eulogy in the final lines of the play. "Though Aufidius must be plotter enough to fulfill his role in Coriolanus' death, he must be of sufficient dignity so that his final tribute to the 'noble memory' of Coriolanus will serve to give the audience a parting reassurance that they have participated in the symbolic sacrifice of a victim worth the killing" (*LASA*, 85). Surrounded by characters who reveal his positive and negative qualities, Coriolanus is thrown into a sociopolitical situation that enables him to be what he is. "The chosen scapegoat can 'be himself' and arrive at the end 'proper to his nature' only if many events and other persons 'conspire' to this end" (*LASA*, 94). *Coriolanus*, Burke maintains, helps us arrive at a formula for tragic catharsis.

> Take some pervasive unresolved tension typical of a given social order (or of life in general). While maintaining the "thought" of it in its over-

all importance, reduce it to terms of personal conflict (conflict between friends, or members of the same family). Feature some prominent figure who, in keeping with his character, though possessing admirable qualities, carries this conflict to excess. Put him in a situation that points up the conflict. Surround him with a cluster of characters whose relations to him and to one another help motivate and accentuate his excesses. So arrange the plot that, after a logically motivated turn, his excesses lead necessarily to his own downfall. Finally, suggest that his misfortune will be followed by a promise of general peace. (*LASA*, 94)

Coriolanus, then, exploits the hierarchic psychosis and the factionalism that estrangement between classes gives rise to. In the practical realm of social relations, such civic tensions and conflicts are rarely resolved; however, in the symbolic realm of tragedy, they may be temporarily transcended through the purgative sacrifice of a worthy victim. "Thereby we are cleansed, thanks to his overstating of our case" (*LASA*, 89). Dramatic catharsis and dialectical transcendence are the agents of this transformation, though the higher vision is vouchsafed only to the audience. For Burke, the notion of the tragic rhythm is suggestive rather than dogmatic.

Although there are always counterexamples to be adduced—the two essays on Goethe's *Faust* (*LASA*, 139–85), for instance, which stress the symbolical and ethical ingredients of symbolic action—Burke's essays on drama tend to stress the rhetorical ingredients in the motivational recipe. He focuses mainly on the communicative relationship between writer and audience, doing justice to both the intrinsic dynamic of the psychology of form and the social tensions and hierarchic psychoses extrinsic to the work in question. His sensitivity to the rhetoric of identification and the paradox of substance is grounded in a pragmatic recognition of the role of dramaturgic exigency, the playwright's choices being as much the products of discursive necessity as of internal consistency.

There is an obvious sense in which drama, a mode of communication overtly directed toward an audience, naturally lends itself to *dramatistic* analysis. And poetry, a mode of self-expression that is overheard rather than heard, is nonetheless an incipient act, a lyric attitude, an "I" talking to its "me." Fiction, however, is another matter, and although Burke's ventures into the analysis of this form are equally impressive and insightful, they are sometimes problematical. To approach fiction in terms of socioanagogic criticism can lead to ideological mystification; to approach it in terms of linguistic consummation can lead to intrinsic reduction.

Fiction as Symbolic Action

"Social and Cosmic Mystery: A Passage to India*"*

Whereas Burke's treatment of *A Portrait of the Artist as a Young Man* is overtly symbolic in that it devotes itself to mapping out the labyrinthine internal consistency of the text, his treatment of *A Passage to India* is as much grammatical, rhetorical, and ethical as it is symbolical. In addition to throwing "light on the ways whereby recurrent terms help establish the internal consistency of the novel" (*LASA*, 232), Burke also delineates the sociohistorical situation, deploys his socioanagogic method to unveil the mysteries of hierarchy, and explores both the quandaries of Forster's liberal humanism and the "mood of ironically sympathetic contemplation" (*LASA*, 225) that attends it.

In this novel Forster offers a "thesaurus of social embarrassments" (*LASA*, 228), India itself being a cornucopia of muddle and mystery.

> The plot and the situation serve to provide us with the *materials* for a comedy of ironically sympathetic contemplation. The muddle of castes and classes in India itself, capped by the essential conflict between the natives and the British officials . . . allows for a maximum of interesting embarrassments in personal relations. Everybody is subtly at odds with everybody else; every situation treated by Forster acutely involves the "mysteries" that result from marked social differentiation—and these are further accentuated by the fact that, since India is in a state of acute transition, along with the *traditional formalities* due to such a clutter of social ratings there is much *improvising of protocol.* . . . Embarrassed improvisings set up the conditions for the incident about which the whole plot hinges . . . the turn that takes place when the honest but sexually muddled English girl, Adela, who has accused the Mohammedan, Aziz, of making advances to her in one of the Marabar Caves, suddenly retracts her charge, to the utter confusion of her British champions and the orgiastic delight of the natives. . . . Embarrassments of

empire invariably have counterparts in *sexual* embarrassments, be they
between members of the same or opposite sexes. (*LASA*, 225–26)

The novel, however, as Burke's title suggests, is not simply a comedy
of ironically sympathetic contemplation; it also has a pronounced
mystical dimension. On the one hand, Forster is a social realist, concentrating on the clash of cultures and the resultant comedy of man-
ners. In this capacity he displays a strong sense of sociohistorical
context and takes an approach that is diagnostic rather than corrective
of the problem, leaving his novel open-ended presumably because history itself is open-ended. On the other hand, Forster is a visionary
symbolist, concentrating on recurrent motifs and symbolic patterns,
on the realm of moral and spiritual value. Though the action of his
novel is firmly riveted in the realm of objective reality, he also furnishes
a cosmic perspective and universal backdrop, the circles beyond the
circles. Thus his zeal for symbolic meanings is kept in balance by the
realism of his social comedy, with all its embarrassments, stupidities,
mysteries, and muddles stemming from cultural and class conflict.
The imperfection of life is never sacrificed to the perfection of form.

A Passage to India asks whether human brotherhood is a real possibility, whether the rational yet skeptical liberal humanism of Fielding
can be united with the imaginative, religious humanism of Godbole
and the sympathetic, emotional understanding of Aziz. "Not yet!"
would seem to be the answer. The rage of the bees and the recalcitrant
terrain of India seem hostile to interracial friendship. Although Fielding sides with Aziz, the two having become friends despite the embarrassments of empire,

> after the native is exonerated, the book closes on the theme of parting,
> since the native refuses to continue their friendship so long as his coun-
> try is subject to imperial rule. The cause of ironic contemplation here is
> particularly favored by an ingenious development of the plot whereby
> the incidents of *personal separation* on which the story closes take place
> during a Hindu ritual proclaiming the principle of *universal unity*.
> (*LASA*, 226)

The triadic structure of the book—"Mosque," "Caves," and "Temple"—reveals the relationship between social and cosmic mystery.

"Despite the novel's comic stress upon the dislocations of society as such, there are traces of a transcendental dialectic. For the presentation as a whole involves a stylistic device whereby *social* motives are viewed in terms of *nature,* and *nature* in turn is infused with glancing references to realms *beyond*" (*LASA,* 227).

The cosmic dimension is visible from the outset. "Except for the Marabar Caves—and they are twenty miles off—the city of Chandrapore presents nothing extraordinary." Thus Forster opens his novel, and gifted with the powers of prophesying after events and knowing the pivotal importance of the caves episode to the plot, we feel the force of this ironic understatement. In a matter-of-fact and distanced tone Forster describes this nondescript city and the "sensibly planned" civil station that neither charms nor repels. "It has nothing hideous in it, and only the view is beautiful; it shares nothing with the city except the overarching sky." At night "the stars hang like lamps from the immense vault. The distance between the vault and them is as nothing to the distance behind them, and that farther distance, though beyond colour, last freed itself from blue." These circles beyond the circles are glancing references to realms beyond the social and the natural that reduce human motives to nothingness. Having adumbrated the mystical strain he is later to develop, Forster changes tone abruptly. "Only in the south, where a group of fists and fingers are thrust up through the soil, is the endless expanse interrupted. These fists and fingers are the Marabar Hills, containing the extraordinary caves." The roughness of tone suggests that nature is at least indifferent, if not malevolent, to human designs. The first chapter is thus a microcosm of the novel and introduces the social, natural, and cosmic dimensions of Forster's dialectic.

The first section, "Mosque," with its Muslim overtones, focuses on the tentative meeting between East and West and takes place in the cool spring (the climate most congenial to Westerners). Here the effort to transcend ethnocentricity and prejudice is paramount, as Aziz and Mrs. Moore establish a secret understanding of the heart and Aziz and Fielding commence their friendship. Embarrassed improvisings result in the fateful trip to the caves.

If "Mosque" suggests the possible transcendence of cultural and class conflict, then "Caves," the second section, with its nihilistic overtones, reveals the worm that is coiled at the heart of being; its malevolent cosmic perspective renders all social and human categories meaningless and shows forth the nothingness beyond good and evil. The trip to the caves takes the Western characters beyond their depth in the midst of the hot, dry summer, a climate antithetical to their dispositions. The Marabar Hills violate the Western sense of proportion and beauty. An echo in the caves distorts Mrs. Moore's sense of the purpose of life, leaving her in a state of spiritual despair and existential emptiness. "Pathos, piety, courage—they exist, but are identical, and so is filth. Everything exists, nothing has value."

> In her absence (for she leaves India and dies on the way home) her presence (her *parousia?*) presides fatally over the course of the trial. And though she dies in a state of mystic drought, the mystery of her spirit pervades the entire plot. . . . And . . . this mystical element must be considered as subplot—and of a sort that is not merely incidental, but radically infuses the comedy with a dimension not generally deemed comical. . . . Here the social mystery is reinforced by connotations of cosmic mystery. (*LASA*, 226–27)

By contrast, Adela's hysteria is both a fear of death and an echo of her sexual repression. In this section human action, cast against a cosmic backdrop, seems insignificant.

The third section, "Temple," with its Hindu overtones, takes place in the wet fall, and although the monsoon brings some measure of relief, it is also potentially destructive. After the chaos of the "Caves" section, this section is an attempt at reconciliation. Godbole's religious ceremony proclaiming universal unity, however, violates Western feelings about propriety and decorum. The individual desires for unity are diffused, and there is no resolution. The novel ends with the parting of Aziz and Fielding, India itself saying "No, not yet" and the sky above saying "No, not there."

> All told, then, what do we have, for the joys of ironically sympathetic contemplation? Much indeed, as regards the comedy of manners, man's picturesque stupidities rooted in hierarchal motives that come to completion in the ills of empire. But how about a world "devoid" of all such "distinctions"? Could we be worthy of it? Could we be equal to its wholly different kinds of responsibility? A doubt of this sort seems to be at least implicit in the structure of *A Passage to India*. It is a dreadful

doubt—but within the conditions of the fiction, it is there for our enjoyment. (*LASA*, 238)

The essay ends on this note, again demonstrating Burke's sensitivity to intrinsic and extrinsic factors, though for the sake of space I have bypassed his discussion of recurrent terms and internal consistency, focusing instead on his sense of the work's triadic structure and the interrelation between social and cosmic mystery. Although I agree that "ironically sympathetic contemplation . . . is essentially a comic mood, and essentially humane (in that the vices depicted in the book are viewed not as villainy, but as folly)" (*LASA*, 225), I do not think that Burke has been quizzical enough about his own definition of the modern liberal novel and about the limitations of socioanagogic interpretation.

In *A Rhetoric of Motives* Burke affirms that socioanagogic interpretation seeks "a 'neutral' approach midway between Marx's rage against 'mystification' and Carlyle's adulation of 'mystery'" (*RM*, 220). In "Social and Cosmic Mystery," however, mystery seems emphasized at the expense of mystification. Certain questions, moreover, pertinent to the realm of ideological analysis, are never posed. To what extent is Forster's liberal humanism and skeptical rationalism itself ethnocentric and paternalistic? Are all Muslims emotional and all Hindus mystical? To what extent does Forster's focus upon interpersonal relationships and cosmic mysteries deflect him from contemplating the political solution to the ills of empire? When is cosmic mystery ideological mystification? What is the relationship between Forster's transcendental dialectic and the historical dialectic it seems to repress? I am not suggesting that there are easy answers to these leading questions. It seems to me, however, that the socioanagogic approach runs the perpetual risk of stressing the anagogic at the expense of the social.

"Fact, Inference, and Proof in the Analysis of Literary Symbolism"

This essay, which uses *A Portrait of the Artist as a Young Man* as a test case, is part of a project called "Theory of the Index" and bases its methodology on the "principle of the concordance" (*FIP*, 145). Burke starts out with the obvious proposition that the individual words of a work are the basic "facts" of that work. The problem for the practical critic is "how to operate with these 'facts,' how to use them as a means of keeping one's inferences under control, yet how to go beyond them, for purposes of inference, when seeking to characterize the motives and 'salient traits' of the work, in its nature as a total symbolic structure" (*FIP*, 145). Burke is quick to point out, however, that the literary work is "at least" words, not "nothing but" words (*FIP*, 146).

The first step is to index the relevant terms into a rough concordance, a procedure that inevitably presupposes a "principle of selection" (*FIP*, 150) and an eye for "key terms" (*FIP*, 151).

> Such concordances are initially noted without inference or interpretation. For whereas purely terministic correlation can serve the ends of "analogical" or "symbolic" exegesis, it is far more tentative and empirical, with a constant demand for fresh inquiry. In fact, one may experimentally note many correlations of this sort without being able to fit them into an overall scheme of interpretation. (*FIP*, 150)

But grounding our concordances in what Burke calls "terminal factuality" is by no means a solution to our problems, for the real question is how the associative clusters, dramatic alignments, and narrative progressions interconnect. We must thus "inspect a work in its *unfoldings*. And we must keep on the move, watching for both static interrelationships and for principles of *transformation* whereby a motive may progress from one combination through another to a third, etc." (*FIP*, 153). We must search for appositions, oppositions, progressions, sequences, synonymizings, desynonymizings, entelechial moments at which a work comes to fruition, and so forth. It is no easy process, for "any connection by synonyms should always be watched for the possibility of lurking antithesis. That is, words on their face synonymous may really *function* as antitheses in a given symbol system" (*FIP*, 158n). Burke makes the point imperatively: "Note all striking terms for acts, attitudes, ideas, images, relationships. . . . Note oppositions. . . . Watch for shifts whereby oppositions become appositions. . . . Note beginnings and endings . . . breaks" (*FIP*, 161).

It comes as no surprise to any reader of Burke that this eminently practical methodology is philosophically anchored in a theory of substance.

That is, in contrast with those "semantic" theories which would banish from their vocabulary any term for "substance," we must believe above all in the reasonableness of "entitling." Confronting a complexity of details, we do not confine ourselves merely to the detailed tracing of interrelationships among them, or among the ones that we consider outstanding. We must also keep prodding ourselves to attempt answering this question: "Suppose you were required to find an overall title for this entire batch of particulars. What would that be?" (*FIP*, 153–54)

Thus it is assumed as a regulative maxim that "all the disparate details included under one head are infused with a common spirit, i.e., are consubstantial" (*FIP*, 153). This organicist assumption, of course, has a built-in deductive aspect. It goes a long way toward ensuring that we shall find what we are looking for—the limits are those of our ingenuity. Our process through a text is one of essentialization by entitlement, as we progressively essentialize the various parts until we arrive at a title of titles that inspirits the whole. One sees here in embryo ideas that are brought to fruition in *The Rhetoric of Religion*, whose logological thesis will be discussed in chapter 4.

Given that *A Portrait of the Artist* is divided into five parts, Burke seeks to determine what their titles should be if we were to try to essentialize their contents. I propose neither to trace Burke's mapping out of the text's internal consistency nor to rehearse in detail his filling out of its stages. Rather, I shall give a skeletal outline of the stages he discovers in *Portrait* through his process of "essentializing by entitlement" (*FIP*, 159).

Because *Portrait* "leads up to the explicit propounding of an Esthetic (a doctrine, catechism, or 'philosophy' of art)" (*FIP*, 155), Burke feels that we should consider the parts from this point of view. The first chapter, he suggests, might be called "Childhood Sensibility" since it deals with "rudimentary sensory perception, primary sensations of smell, touch, sight, sound, taste (basic bodily feelings that, at a later stage in the story, will be methodically 'mortified')" (*FIP*, 155). The aesthetic, then, "begins in simple *aisthesis*. . . . Family relations, religion, and even politics are thus 'esthetically' experienced in this opening part—experienced not as mature 'ideas,' or even as adolescent 'passions,' but as 'sensations,' or 'images'" (*FIP*, 155).

The second chapter, Burke suggests, might be called "The Fall" since its climactic episode is Stephen's succumbing to lust and falling into sexual experience. The sordid reality of his furtive encounters with prostitutes contrasts sharply with his idealized vision of Mercedes, a figure of virginal purity rather than of libidinal desire.

The third chapter, he suggests, might be called "The Sermon," "for that ironic masterpiece of rhetorical amplification is clearly the turning point of the chapter" (*FIP*, 160). The sermon exacerbates Stephen's consciousness of being in mortal sin and leads to his temporary repentance and regeneration.

The fourth chapter, he suggests, might be called either "The New Vocation" or "Epiphany."

> The partially involuntary fall through sexual passion at the end of Chapter II might be distinguished from the deliberate fall of Chapter IV (the choice of a new vocation) somewhat as "passive" is distinguished from "active." It is the latter that Stephen equates with Luciferian pride, epitomized in his many variants of the formula, "I will not serve." . . . By the time the book is finished, the theme of falling has become translated into the theme of ecstatic elevation. (*FIP*, 169)

Stephen's vision of the bird-girl, symbol of his new vocation and manifestation of "mortal beauty" and "profane joy," is the entelechial moment at which the work comes to fruition. However, "when the choice between religion and art is finally made, it is a qualified choice, as art will be conceived in terms of theology secularized" (*FIP*, 160).

The final chapter, Burke suggests, might be called "The New Doctrine," "for what we have here is a catechistic equivalent of the revelation that forms the ecstatic end of Chapter IV" (*FIP*, 160).

"Fact, Inference, and Proof" does not lend itself to effective summary, for the details of Burke's indexings and concordances—his pursuit of such terms as swish, soutane, fly, flight, fall, silence, and so forth—are what give solidity of specification to his consideration of *Portrait* as a total symbolic structure. This intrinsic mode of analysis is remarkably thoroughgoing. Nevertheless, "a way of seeing is also a way of not seeing" (*PC*, 49), and Burke's focus on the symbolic runs the risk of viewing the work as *nothing but* "a circle of terminal relationships" (*FIP*, 152). Whereas there is nothing necessarily anti-dramatistic about this sort of analysis, the context of situation is attenuated to the degree that the intraverbal context is underscored. The

problem of the intrinsic becomes more pronounced in Burke's logological writings, and I shall address it in detail in chapter 4. It is
worth mentioning, however, by way of mitigation, that even within
this very "intrinsic" essay under discussion Burke keeps the dramatistic perspective in view. "The social and linguistic pyramids are 'naturally' interwoven, we take it, as language is a social product. . . . So
our thoughts about hierarchical tension lead us to watch for modes of
catharsis, or of *transcendence,* that may offer a symbolic solution
*within the given symbol-system of the particular work we are analyz-
ing*" (FIP, 165–66).

The symbolic approach to fiction has other shortcomings as well. It
leads one to disregard aspects of narrative that many critics have
found central to an understanding of *Portrait.* I mention these issues
not to chastize Burke for not doing what he had no intention of doing
(the essay is written expressly to demonstrate a method), but to point
out the restrictiveness of the approach. Burke asks no questions about
narrative perspective, point of view, indirect interior monologue, or
authorial distance, and, even more surprising, this master ironist is
strangely insensitive to the possibilities of irony. He takes it for
granted that the doctrine of art is the consummation of the book, "the
explicit propounding of an Esthetic" (FIP, 155).

In general, the symbolic approach invites one to underemphasize the
fact that fiction as a genre gives us its "story" (the "actual" chronological sequence of events) in a particular "discourse" (the sequence in
which these events are related to the reader) from a particular angle of
vision or point of view. Such questions about the rhetoric of fiction are
ones that the "consummatory" approach is likely to leave unposed.
That is, given Joyce's use of indirect interior monologue and his rendering the verbal action primarily from Stephen's point of view, is there an
ironic distance between Stephen's perception of himself and Joyce's
perception of him? Is Stephen an artificer, like his mythological name-
sake Dedalus, trying to escape the labyrinths of Irish society or is he a
rebellious son, like Icarus, doomed to fly too high and to plummet
ingloriously down? Are the epiphanies authentic by definition or does
their sometimes overblown diction indicate other possibilities? Is Stephen's philosophy of art aesthetic gospel or sterile aestheticism? Is his
villanelle anticipatory of mature artistry or of barren formalism? Given
that each of the four chapters ends on epiphany and that the succeeding

chapters begin with a depression of sorts, is the direction of the novel as a whole progressive, a gradual dialectical process toward a crowning synthesis—Stephen's doctrine of art and attainment of freedom—or is it cyclical, a repetitive pattern of rise and fall? Is Stephen's understanding of art and experience adequate, his apprenticeship and education successful? I am not suggesting that these alternatives are mutually exclusive or that Burke should be compelled to answer these questions. But Burke's silent adoption of the "straight" reading is nonetheless significant. For when one approaches a text via the symbolic and assumes its labyrinthine internal consistency, one is apt to downplay questions of genre and narrative technique, what Wayne Booth calls the rhetoric of fiction. One can see this tendency in Burke's later writings. After *A Rhetoric of Motives* Burke's critical essays become more symbolical and less rhetorical. Logology, as I shall argue in chapter 4, is an entelechial fulfillment of essays such as "Fact, Inference, and Proof."

Dramatism, however, is not simply a theory of literature or a method of practical criticism; it is also a philosophy of language. And before examining the shift from dramatism to logology, I shall attempt to put Burke's theory of language into a wider philosophical context.

Three

The Dramatistic Theory
of Language
A Perspective by Incongruity

Nietzsche establishes his perspectives by a constant juxtaposing of incongruous words, attaching to some name a qualifying epithet which had heretofore gone with a different order of names. He writes by the same constant reordering of categories that we find in the Shakespearean metaphor.

(*PC*, 90)

De Gourmont discovered himself for his critics when he used the word "dissociation." He loves to show that a concept which we generally take as a unit can be subdivided. "Man associates his ideas, not in accordance with logic, or verifiable exactitude, but in accordance with his desires and his interests." In his essay, *La Dissociation des Idées,* De Gourmont lets himself loose with this method, and produces a type of writing which is delightfully exact. . . . The method was clearly a companion discovery to symbolism, which sought its effects precisely by utilizing, more programmatically than in any previous movement, the clusters of associations surrounding the important words of a poem or fiction. And writers such as James Joyce and Gertrude Stein are clearly making associative and dissociative processes a pivotal concern of their works. Any technical criticism of our methodological authors of today must concern itself with the further development and schematization of such ideas as De Gourmont was considering.

(*CS*, 22–24)

79

Burke acknowledges Nietzsche's transvaluation of values and Remy De Gourmont's dissociation of ideas as sources for his procedure of perspective by incongruity. The reference to Nietzsche is particularly apt, for Nietzsche, an archconnoisseur of verbal and conceptual dissonance, liked to think of himself as philosophizing with a hammer. Burke, though more modest and humane, has no lack of messianic zeal, no less tendency to attack contemporary orthodoxies with vigor and panache. Although the specific rhetorical strategy of an iconoclast may fall into diverse categories—perspective by incongruity, transvaluation of values, dissociation of ideas, alienation effect, de-automatization of perception, defamiliarization, and so forth—the overriding intention is much the same: to smash the chains of language, which shackle thought and perception by making them conform to habitual patterns, and to reveal how our minds are tyrannized by a prevailing conceptual scheme, a scheme that is reinforced at every juncture by the grammatical structure of a received language.

Any of these methodological procedures for what Burke calls verbal atom cracking has a set of underlying assumptions. It is assumed, as Nietzsche puts it, that "every word is a preconceived judgment"[1] and that "there lies hidden in language a philosophical mythology which breaks out at every moment, however careful one might be."[2] Hence the supreme importance that Burke assigns to the vocabulary of motives that a writer deploys, to what he variously calls ideology, nomenclature, or terministic screen. Since Burke's corpus deals with the broad themes of language, thought, and culture, there is no alternative but to attempt to establish a philosophical framework from which to approach issues notoriously vague and speculative. Only then can one be in any position to evaluate Burke's own terministic screen. I thus propose to juxtapose Nietzsche's nihilism and Burke's perspectivism, a tactic that may itself be another instance of perspective by incongruity—the conclusions the two men derive from similar initial premises are radically different—but a justifiable one insofar as it has heuristic value.

In his second book of critical theory, *Permanence and Change,* Burke confronts the chaos of a world without apparent value, a world wherein conflicting interpretations of value and assignations of motive proliferate to the detriment of any sense of permanence or continuity.

He is painfully aware that "stimuli do not possess an *absolute* meaning. . . . Any given situation derives its character from the entire framework of interpretation by which we judge it. And differences in our ways of sizing up an objective situation are expressed subjectively as differences in our assignment of motive" (*PC,* 35). Since entire frameworks of interpretation are not universally shared in any society where there is differentiation of social role, a modicum of intellectual instability is endemic. In 1935, of course, this necessary intellectual instability was only exacerbated by the economic instability of the Great Depression, for impairment in the modes of social cooperation, Burke maintains, is coeval with impairment in the modes of social communication. This is because he believes that motives are linguistic products, a particular vocabulary of a cultural group. Verbally molded concepts make certain relationships meaningful. "These relationships are not *realities,* they are interpretations of reality—hence different frameworks of interpretation will lead to different conclusions as to what reality is" (*PC,* 35).

In this sort of atmosphere the only constancy is the interpretive attitude itself, and Burke's recourse is to make the communicative medium the object of study. In *Permanence and Change* the focus clearly is on change, particularly on changing interpretations of reality, but the yearning for permanence is omnipresent. By the time he arrives at *The Rhetoric of Religion,* almost thirty years later, permanence has been achieved. Language has been enshrined as the source of all value, and the logological perspective has become the extraperspectival standpoint from which one may evaluate other perspectives. The latter development is an obvious paradox, for by virtue of its own presuppositions Burke's perspectivism must itself by definition be merely another perspective. Nonetheless, in its deviation from and contradiction of initial relativistic premises, Burke's Dialectic of the Upward Way, his heaping of perspective upon perspective in his logological quest for the adequate idea, is similar to Nietzsche's use of the will-to-power not only as an explanatory principle—this is legitimate—but also as a source of ultimate value—this is inconsistent if one truly embraces "the extremest form of nihilism—the insight that every belief, every taking-for-true [Für-wahr-halten], is necessarily false: because there is no *true world* at all."3

Both Burke and Nietzsche realize that *"we cease to think when we refuse to do so under the constraint of language;* we barely reach the doubt that sees this limitation as limitation."[4] Authentic nihilism would condemn its advocates to confront the meaningless chaos of existence in dumb silence. In fact, however, nihilism is often a rhetorical device for assaulting the matrix of values and beliefs that a given society endorses uncritically. Nietzsche himself admits that "to impose upon becoming the character of being—that is the supreme will to power."[5] The point is to be conscious of the interpretations one imposes. To be sure, Nietzsche is more violently destructive in his explosion of linguistic and conceptual proprieties than Burke is, but this is because he was absolutely convinced that "we are not rid of God because we still have faith in grammar."[6] Burke, however, is not prepared to get rid of grammar, so he makes God a component of it. God becomes an ultimate term in a symbol system.

"Against positivism, which halts at phenomena—'There are only *facts*'—I would say: No, facts is precisely what there is not, only interpretations."[7] So reads one of the well-known aphorisms of Nietzsche's posthumous collection, *The Will to Power*. It follows from this assertion that "there are no moral phenomena at all, but only a moral interpretation of phenomena."[8] For Nietzsche, then, "the value of the world lies in our interpretation" and "to demand that our human interpretations and values should be general, and perhaps even constitutive values, belongs among the hereditary idiocies of human pride."[9]

Nietzsche vehemently contends that our beliefs and values do not reflect a self-subsistent order of facts. On the contrary, they are products of our own devising, creations of our own will, which we impose, consciously or unconsciously, upon our experience. Being-in-the-world, to borrow a term from Heidegger, always involves an interpretation by which we actively synthesize the manifold of experience and dominate the world in a certain way. "The 'will to power' is simply Nietzsche's shorthand label for the aggressive character of the relationship of human subjectivity and the world that it subjects to its categories."[10] Arthur Danto expresses Nietzsche's position thus:

> Science he regards not as a repository of truths or a method for discovering them but as a set of convenient fictions, of useful conventions, which has as much and as little basis in reality as any alleged set of

fictions which might be thought to conflict with it. It, no more or no less than religion, morality, and art, was an instance of what he termed Will-to-Power, an impulse and drive to impose upon an essentially chaotic reality a form and a structure, to shape it into a world congenial to human understanding while habitable by human intelligence.[11]

In a sense, then, all beliefs and values are consolations of philosophy. The fictions of science, such as laws of cause and effect, make life possible—they have survival value; the fictions of art make life endurable—they have therapeutic value. Dionysian intoxication obliterates distinctions, yielding one an invigorating sense of primal unity; Apollonian form refines distinctions, yielding one a sense of mastery over chaos. Both have their uses. However philosophically unjustified any of these fictions may be when submitted to exacting nihilistic scrutiny, they are psychologically understandable and in some cases biologically necessary.

Nietzsche affords science none of the magisterial neutrality that it often claims for itself. There is nothing sacrosanct about its so-called observation-language, for "science is not a summary of sense observations but a creative organization of the world, an arrangement which stands to observation in complicated ways."[12] Nietzsche's attitude toward scientific fictions is hauntingly contemporary in that many philosophers of science now reject the correspondence theory of truth, the notion of a match, to use the words of Thomas Kuhn, "between the entities with which the theory populates nature and what is 'really there.'" Kuhn goes on to say that there is "no theory-independent way to reconstruct phrases like 'really there'; the notion of a match between the ontology of a theory and its 'real' counterpart in nature now seems . . . illusive in principle."[13]

Nietzsche's nihilism is a defamiliarizing strategy, a rhetorically flamboyant way of undermining any correspondence theory of truth, any theory, that is, that views truth as a one-to-one correspondence between sentence and fact, or, in the more complicated cases such as those with which Kuhn deals, between theory and nature. For Nietzsche, it is logically impossible that any language, no matter how ideal, could isomorphically represent reality, simply because the very concept of objective reality is a fiction and therefore has no unshakable ontological status. There are no facts. Hence if all our ideas are interpretations that arbitrarily structure chaos, then the significant question is not at all whether they are true—their truth value is irrelevant—but whether we should accept them, whether we should confer value upon them. "The question is to what extent [a belief] is life-promoting, life-preserving, species-preserving, perhaps even species-cultivating."[14] The main criterion is psychological. "Truth is the kind of error without which a certain species of life could not live."[15]

Expressed less dramatically, Nietzsche's philosophy is essentially pragmatist. His notion of will-to-power is not altogether unlike William James's notion of will-to-believe. In fact, many of the pragmatists' formulations are quite compatible with Nietzsche's. Nietzsche, of course, expresses the point of view with characteristic extravagance.

> What then is truth? A mobile army of metaphors, metonymies, anthropomorphisms, a sum, in short, of human relationships which, rhetorically and poetically intensified, ornamented, and transformed, come to be thought of, after long usage by people, as fixed, binding, and canonical. Truths are illusions which we have forgotten are illusions, worn-out metaphors now impotent to stir the senses, coins which have lost their faces and are considered now as metal rather than currency.[16]

What Nietzsche is rejecting, in short, is any conception of the *Ding an sich*, any conception of an autonomous world structure that resides outside the particular perceptions and interpretations of any given human being or group of human beings. There are no pure facts to which particular propositions might correspond, and no sense attaches to any talk of a realm of essences.

Such a position has metaethical consequences. If good and evil are not moral facts existing in the world or in human conscience, then nothing is of ultimate value and no moral principle can ultimately be justified. "Existence and the world seem justified only as an aesthetic phenomenon."[17] We inevitably bring to bear aesthetic criteria when we come to assess the merits of specific values and interpretations. No clear-cut distinction between the aesthetic and the ethical is possible.

Nietzsche shows how Christian morality, through the mechanism of the transvaluation of values, converts individual weakness into collective strength. The weak man finds himself threatened with defeat in battle, so he turns the other cheek and thereby converts his own deficiency into a virtue that is ratified by a religious community. Such a man paradoxically expresses his will-to-power by explicitly denying the value of power. Whether or not one agrees with this description of the genealogy of morals, one has to admit that Nietzsche is entitled to make it on the basis of his own assumptions. But his ethical theory is not simply descriptive; it does not content itself with describing how the transvaluation of values operates. It is emphatically hortatory. We are urged to affirm our wills-to-power, to strive to become overmen rather than last men, and thus to overcome the human-all-too-human. Nietzsche's own transvaluation of values is designed to make us aware of the possible so that we might struggle to realize it. It is, in short, prescriptive. The will-to-power is both an explanatory and evaluative principle, and his nihilistic attitude toward language is part of this overall transvaluating strategy, which, it seems to me, is nothing less than an ethical program for the renovation of mankind. The case of Nietzsche is symptomatic because linguistic nihilism on its own would seem not to be a viable stance; it is usually part of a more comprehensive project. In fact, most nihilistic movements can be seen to presuppose the norms of an extant tradition in the sense that it is only by attacking a structure of norms that a given movement gains its polemical efficacy. The paradox resides in the fact that any radical alterations to traditional procedures are intelligible (and hence communicable) to the degree that they presuppose the very norms, linguistic or otherwise, they are seeking to supplant.

The above is no doubt an inadequate summary of Nietzsche's thought, but its very compression, I think, gives a faint flavor of how to philosophize with a hammer. His own aphoristic style, of course, is more pyrotechnical. My seemingly incongruous propaedeutic is meant to yield us perspective, for Burke struggles with the demoralizing specter of nihilism during his entire career and would probably be the first to admit that perspectivism is but a eulogistic name for relativism. And it is no exaggeration to say, strange as it might seem, that Burke's entire corpus is quite literally directed toward coming to *terms* with a relativistic universe. He seriously believes, however realistic he is about the hopelessness of the task, that language, which is symbolic action, can save us from demoralization precisely because it is a source of value and can thus remoralize a world that science, semantics, and technology have neutralized.

The main point to be derived from the above is this: when one starts with the term "interpretation" as a prime mover in one's conceptual scheme, one is ineluctably led to conflate issues that standard philosophic discourse is at pains to keep apart. For the term "interpretation" is polysemous, and it is relevant to realms putatively as diverse as metaphysics, epistemology, ontology, ethics, aesthetics, and philosophy of language. And it is no accident that one is driven to regard language as the foremost among equals, first because propositions of all sorts are clothed in the material garb of the sentence, and second because language will reveal most clearly the repository of error and prejudice that masquerades under the name of common sense. Common sense, Nietzsche maintains, presupposes a metaphysic. This metaphysic seems innocuous only because cultural tradition has domesticated it, making it seem familiar and self-evident. Language, in other words, contains a structure of interpretations that manifests itself as a structure of facts, and the task of the philosopher is to make us see that what we think of as given and self-authenticating is in reality imposed by human consciousness and culture.

Nietzsche is explicit about the relationship between language, culture, and reality.

> The importance of language for the development of culture lies in this, that through language men erect a world of their own alongside the real world, a position they hold to be so fixed that from it they hope to hoist the other world off its hinges and make themselves master of it. . . . Man really thought that in language he had knowledge of the world. The language-maker was not modest enough to realize that he had only given designations to things. Instead, he believed that he had expressed through words the highest knowledge of things.[18]

Beneath all this is an assumption that language (at least in part) determines worldview, that standard average European languages (SAE), to use Whorf's term, presuppose a philosophy that deals in entities, a philosophy whose prime terms are unity, identity, permanence, substance, cause, thinghood, being, and so forth. In short, Nietzsche, like Whorf, believes that a subject/object grammar makes for a substance/attribute ontology.

When Burke wrote *Permanence and Change* such ideas were very much in the air. In 1931 Edward Sapir, a linguist with whom Burke was familiar, maintained that

> the relation between language and experience is often misunderstood. Language is not merely a more or less systematic inventory of the various items of experience which seem relevant to the individual, as is so often naively assumed, but is also a self-contained, creative symbolic organization, which not only refers to experience largely acquired without its help but actually defines experience for us by reason of its formal completeness and because of our unconscious projections of its implicit expectations into the field of experience.[19]

In a similar vein, Whorf's position entails that "a language constitutes a sort of logic, a general frame of reference, and so molds the thought of its habitual users. . . . Where a culture and a language have developed together, there are significant relationships between the general aspects of the grammar and the characteristics of the culture taken as a whole."[20] This general view, often labeled either the Sapir-Whorf hypothesis or the principle of linguistic relativity, sees a distinctive feature of SAE as residing in its tendency to objectify and spatialize experience, especially with regard to its temporal categories. As one commentator puts it, "speakers of SAE tend to see the world in terms of things, the things themselves built up of a formless stuff given a determinate form. Non-spatial entities are conceived by spatial metaphor."[21] Unlike the language of the Hopi Indians, for example, which Whorf subjects to analysis, SAE implies a substance rather than a process philosophy, a philosophy of being rather than one of becoming.

Subsequent empirical research has neither proved nor disproved the principle of linguistic relativity. If the hypothesis is in fact unable to be verified empirically, it is nonetheless in no worse a position than its competitors. The view that there is an innate linguistic competence that manifests itself in the deep structures of all human languages suffers at this historical moment from the same unverifiability.

Quine sheds some light on the question of the unverifiability of the Sapir-Whorf hypothesis, even though it is not an issue he directly addresses. According to him, it is precisely because there is no extralinguistic perspective to which we have access that translation of any language alien to our own is in principle indeterminate. Moreover, the range of reference that that language intends is in principle inscrutable. He notes that

> we persist in breaking reality down somehow into a multiplicity of identifiable and discriminable objects, to be referred to by singular and general terms. We talk so inveterately of objects that to say that we do so seems almost to say nothing at all; for how else is there to talk?
>
> It is hard to say how else there is to talk, not because our objectifying pattern is an invariable trait of human nature, but because we are bound to adapt any alien pattern to our own in the very process of understanding or translating the alien sentences.[22]

It is inevitable that we read our ontological point of view into an alien language simply because no inquiry is possible without a conceptual scheme, and conceptualization is inseparable from language. "Reference," he writes, "is nonsense except relative to a coordinate system."[23] For Quine, then, ontology is ultimately inscrutable, for questions about ontological items are ultimately circular in the sense that they are always relative to a given coordinate system and conceptual scheme. Quine concludes that "it makes no sense to say what the objects of a theory are, beyond saying how to interpret or reinterpret that theory in another."[24] Yet he wisely recognizes that "for all the difficulty of transcending our object-directed pattern of thought, we can examine it well enough from the inside."[25] That is, according to Quine's notion of ontological relativity, the emphasis falls not so much on the claim that reference is nonsense if considered in ultimate terms as on the necessity of discussing reference in terms of a given conceptual-linguistic scheme. Indeed, it is very questionable whether so-called ontological relativity really has any of the devastating implications that structuralists and deconstructionists claim to derive from it, even though it is true that the notion does deprive language of any *ultimate* referent.

My point here is that if ontological relativity as Quine conceives it is valid, then the principle of linguistic relativity is bound to be empirically unresolvable. There would be no ontologically unloaded way of either verifying or refuting the principle. Indeterminacy of translation and inscrutability of reference would corrupt the neutrality of any investigation. Nonetheless, it is hard to see how ontological relativity could itself be verified or refuted. The same objection, of course, also holds for any of the theories that rely on the existence of innate linguistic structures of consciousness. What kind of evidence could entitle one to say that an alien language *really* has the same deep structures as our own? In discussing these sorts of issues, it would seem, everyone is condemned to some measure of circularity.

Nonetheless, it remains the case that we are born into a conceptual-linguistic scheme that is at once evaluative and descriptive. Spontaneously, as it were, we ingest a worldview by learning a language. But this does not mean that we are ineluctably condemned to that particular prison-house; we may, if we so choose, try to invent another one. Nietzsche and Bergson, after all, wrote in SAE, and the one sought to replace the category of entity with that of power, the other to replace the category of spatial extension with that of durational intension—I am oversimplifying—but both had to labor all the harder and to devise rhetorical strategies all the more radical in order to combat a prevailing conceptual-linguistic scheme. Which again affirms the importance of metaphor—what Burke calls perspective by incongruity—as a tool for wrenching awry an entrenched semantic scheme. For, as he points out, "whole works of scientific research, even entire *schools,* are hardly more than the patient repetition, in all of its ramifications, of a fertile metaphor" (*PC,* 195).

There is, however, a certain ambiguity in the notion of a conceptual-linguistic scheme. This ambiguity arises from the fact that one can use the expression "terministic screen" to refer to either a cultural framework of interpretation or a given scheme within that general framework. In an age of transition and instability, such as the Depression, terministic screens abound. The cultural framework is itself fragmented and heterogeneous, which, of course, increases the importance of attending carefully to divergent vocabularies of motives if one has any desire to gain a perspective upon the rampant incongruities. As Burke reflects,

> By an ideology is meant the nodus of beliefs and judgments which the artist can exploit for his effects. It varies from one person to another, and from one age to another—but insofar as its general acceptance and its stability are more stressed than its particular variations from person to person and from age to age, an ideology is a "culture." . . . But there

are cultures within cultures since a society can be subdivided into groups with divergent standards and interests. . . . An ideology is not a harmonious structure of beliefs or assumptions; some of its beliefs militate against others, and some of its standards militate against our nature. (*CS*, 161–63)

There are at least four possible orientations toward the issue of the relationship between language and reality: positivism, structuralism, deconstruction, and dramatism. In regard to the first three orientations, what follows is admittedly an exercise in summarizing the unsummarizable. "The test of a metaphor's validity," Burke wisely points out, requires "nothing less than *the filling-out, by concrete body, of the characterizations one would test*" (*PLF*, 145). Such a filling-out I shall not attempt. Nonetheless, it seems important to be aware of, at the most fundamental level possible, what these different points of departure assume and entail, in order to get clear about what the dramatistic point of departure assumes and entails.

Positivism

Positivism strives toward what Burke calls the semantic ideal and makes the meaning of a given term contingent upon its reference. In terms of the dramatistic pentad, the focus of positivism is on the extrinsic environmental scene and on how language corresponds to that reality. Ogden and Richards's *Meaning of Meaning* is paradigmatic of this orientation.

Ogden and Richards believe that a science of symbolism would purge cognitive discourse of any referential opacity by eliminating those terms that are empirically unverifiable. Such crude positivism is reminiscent of the Vienna Circle's verification principle that the meaning of a proposition is its method of verification. According to Ogden and Richards, when Saussure made the referent irrelevant to his theory of linguistics he cut himself off from "scientific methods of verification."[26] It is only fair to reiterate, however, that positivism is one-half of their dichotomous theory of language and that the theory is in part designed to protect literature from being subjected to referential criteria, the onslaught of which, they felt, literature could not withstand. Hence their ideal of a semantically purified scientific language makes room for a semantically unpurified poetic language whose autonomy is guaranteed precisely because it is emotive and thus has no cognitive pretensions. Cognitive meaning, they contend, is contingent upon a word's correspondence to a state of affairs, whereas emotive meaning is somehow contingent upon the mysterious psychological adjustments of the human organism. It is obvious that Ogden and Richards feel that by tying their theory of emotive meaning to psychology they are also tying it to "scientific methods of verification," and equally obvious that the advances of psychology, however impressive in other areas, did not fulfill their optimistic hopes.

A more sophisticated example of a correspondence theory is the early Wittgenstein's picture theory of meaning. In the *Tractatus* Wittgenstein contends that language is composed of propositions that picture the world. Propositions give verbal form to thoughts, and thoughts are the logical pictures of facts. The role of philosophy is to reveal the logical form of propositions; philosophy does not itself picture the world. It is easy to imagine how complicated this alleged correspondence between thoughts, propositions, and facts can get, for the term "picture" is not meant to imply a simplistic, isomorphic representation. Such a representation, of course, would be impossible because the three components—the mental, the verbal, and the factual—are categorically different. Moreover, Wittgenstein's theory has, as Russell points out, a quasi-metaphysical dimension in that the correspondence between thought-elements and world-atoms is in some sense ultimate. Hence Russell's phrase "logical atomism."

There are several ways of attacking the semantic ideal. For tactical reasons I shall not use Burke's examples—Chase, Korzybski, et al. First, Burke's treatment of those who would purify the dialect of the tribe through semantical precision is devastating enough on its own. Second, I am interested in examining the semantic ideal at the level of its most fundamental assumptions, a level that Burke elects to ignore in the heat of the forensic arena. Such an examination cannot pretend in any way to refute or disprove the assumptions of semantic idealism—my summary does not provide even an inkling of the acuity and subtlety that advocates of the correspondence theory can muster. But it will bring into relief the advantages or disadvantages, depending on one's point of view, of the assumptions that Burke's theory endorses and challenges.

Semantic idealism seems to base itself on the primacy of ostensive definition, whose *locus classicus* is found in St. Augustine's *Confessions*. Augustine notes, speaking of his elders, that "when they named a certain thing and, at that name, made a gesture towards the object, I observed that object and inferred that it was called by the name they uttered when they wished to show it to me. That they meant this was apparent by their bodily gestures. . . . So little by little I inferred that the words set in their proper places in different sentences, that I heard frequently, were signs of things."[27]

Such a view is implicitly nominalistic in that it equates the development of linguistic competence with the ability to name an ever increasing range of objects. It assumes, in other words, the priority of word over sentence in the order of explanation, which, however commonsensical on the surface, is in fact an illusion. Later I shall discuss Burke's experimental reversal of the slogan "words are the signs of things."

This notion of the primacy of ostensive definition is entangled, as we have seen, with a traditional view of truth—the correspondence theory—and with a traditional view of epistemology, which grounds knowledge in self-authenticating immediate experience. Wilfrid Sellars aptly calls the latter "the Myth of the Given," which in his words is the

> idea that there is, indeed must be, a structure of particular matter of fact such that (a) each fact can not only be non-inferentially known to be the case, but presupposes no other knowledge either of particular matter of fact, or of general truths and (b) such that the non-inferential knowledge of facts belonging to this structure constitutes the ultimate court of appeals for all factual claims—particular and general—about the world. . . . The idea that observation, strictly and properly so-called, is constituted by certain self-authenticating nonverbal episodes, the authority of which is transmitted to verbal and quasi-verbal performances when these performances are made "in conformity with the semantical rules of the language," is, of course, the heart of the Myth of the Given.[28]

A foundationist philosophy, then, accepts the dualism of scheme and content, theory and observation, sentence and fact. There are many ways of expressing this dualism but the essential point remains the same. Immediate experience—brute and raw—is self-authenticating and provides a foundation for knowledge. According to this idea of sensory givenness and incorrigible knowledge, truth involves a correspondence between the unmediated, nonconceptual, and nonlinguistic data of experience and the mediated, conceptual, and linguistic scheme that represents them. In contrast, an antifoundationist philosophy rejects the correspondence theory of truth and the myth of the given on which it is based. In *Philosophy and the Mirror of Nature,* Richard Rorty argues that "the notion of knowledge as accurate representation, made possible by special mental processes, and intelligible through a general theory of representation, needs to be abandoned."[29] Stressing what he calls the theory-ladenness of observation, Rorty adopts the "coherentist" view that objectivity is just intersubjectivity and that no ultimate distinction can be made between linguistic convention and brute experience or between scientific theory and scientific observation. As Quine puts it, "immediate experience simply will not, of itself, cohere as an autonomous domain."[30]

The notion of self-authenticating immediate experience, of some sort of indubitable Cartesian basis, is an understandable misconception. The conceptual confusion emerges from the fact that while we are engaged in perceiving, what we perceive is the world as our conceptual-linguistic scheme structures it. What we do not perceive is that we structure it. We do not see the world as invested with a certain conceptual-linguistic scheme, nor can we distinguish absolutely those aspects of experience that are objectively there from those imposed by human subjectivity.

In the quotation above, Sellars manages neatly to isolate the dichotomous characteristics of the semantic ideal. According to the semantic idealist, there is a realm of fact separable from the conceptual-linguistic scheme that represents it and accessible to immediate experience. The task of the language user is to find the semantically pure verbal expressions that correspond precisely to that which is directly given. These verbal expressions constitute referential language par excellence.

Much the same process goes on in extrinsic literary theories, for these theories must implicitly rely on a foundationist epistemology. The language of a given literary text is thereby parasitic upon its context. Granted, the way in which a text corresponds to its frame of reference is inordinately complex and extremely difficult to disentangle—the excavation of the subtext requires much hermeneutical ingenuity—but that frame is in some sense thought to be the foundation of the text's "real" meaning. The extrinsic critic is as much committed to the autonomy of the referent as the intrinsic critic is to the autonomy of the text. Even critics such as Holland and Jameson, whom I cited earlier as sophisticated practitioners of extrinsic criticism, have to view the referent as independent of the text that transforms it, however attentive they are to what the one calls "the process of transformation from fantasy to intellectual significance" and the other "the dialectical interaction of work and background." From the dramatistic point of view, however, it makes little difference whether one valorizes the frame of reference or the system of signs. For in either case one has subordinated one order to the other and has thereby neglected the essential ambiguity of their transaction, which, for Burke, is the entire point. The extrinsic is loaded in favor of the grammatical; the intrinsic, in favor of the symbolical.

Structuralism

In terms of the dramatistic pentad, the focus of structuralism is on linguistic agency—on the semiological codes that undergird all discourse and on the system of language as a functioning totality. This system Saussure calls *langue*—"the whole set of linguistic habits which allow an individual to understand and to be understood."[31] Anticausal and antiphilological, structuralism deliberately ignores the historical origins of the various elements of language, the external context of linguistic acts, the agents who use language, and the individual speech acts themselves (*parole*). The structuralist orientation is intrinsic in that it regards language as a self-enclosed system, embracing the arbitrariness of the sign, bracketing the referent, and generating a now familiar vocabulary of oppositions, all of which are more or less synonymous: *langue* and *parole,* system and event, synchronic and diachronic, signifier and signified, code and message, metaphor and metonymy, paradigmatic and syntagmatic, selection and combination, substitution and context, similarity and contiguity, and so on. In each case the first term is privileged. A text, then, is seen as a system of relations, for "in the linguistic system there are only differences, without any positive terms."[32]

Although Saussurian linguistics is its paradigm, what is of interest here is how structuralism analogically extends Saussure's terms into the analysis of literature. Barthes is a good example. "Literature is simply a language, a system of signs. Its being (*être*) is not in its message, but in this 'system.' Similarly, it is not for criticism to reconstitute the message of a work, but only its system, exactly as the linguist does not decipher the meaning of a sentence, but establishes the formal structure which allows the meaning to be conveyed."[33] Jonathan Culler spells out the implications for criticism.

> Critical attention comes to focus not on a thematic content that the work aesthetically presents but on the conditions of signification, the different sorts of structures and processes involved in the production of meaning. Even when structuralists engage in interpretation, their attempt to analyze the structure of the work and the forces on which it depends leads to concentration on the relation between the work and its enabling conditions and undermines, as the opponents of structuralism seem to sense, the traditional interpretive project. . . . The categories and methods of linguistics, whether applied directly to the language of literature or used as the model for a poetics, enable critics to focus not on the meaning of a work and its implications or value but on the structures that produce meaning. . . . Languages and structures, rather than authorial self or consciousness, become the major source of explanation.[34]

As a consequence, the subject is dissolved into a series of systems, deprived of his role as a source of meaning, and thereby decentered. "The self is an intersubjective construct over which the person has no control."[35] In addition, the reader is privileged at the expense of the author, for "the text is a kind of formless space whose shape is imposed by structured modes of reading:"[36] The operative concept is intertextuality. "We now know," Barthes writes, "that the text is not a line of words releasing a single 'theological' meaning (the 'message' of an Author-God) but a multi-dimensional space in which a variety of writings, none of them original, blend and clash. The text is a tissue of quotations drawn from innumerable centers of culture." Nevertheless, he goes on to say, "there is one place where this multiplicity is focused and that place is the reader, not, as was hitherto said, the author. The reader is the space on which all the quotations that make up a writing are inscribed. . . . A text's unity lies not in its origin but in its destination."[37] Intertextuality, then, "is the general discursive space that makes a text intelligible,"[38] for "in the act of writing or speaking [we] inevitably postulate . . . an intersubjective body of knowledge . . . a prior body of discourse."[39] "It is the nature of a code to be already in existence."[40] Codes, according to Barthes, equal the already read (*déjà lu*), and the reader is the place where the various codes are located.

This same anti-intentionalist bias is evident in Chomsky's linguistics, the focus of which is on how language is structured rather than on how it is used. It is assumed that there is a fundamental antithesis between use and structure. Chomsky endorses "the view that syntax is the theory of meaningfulness, and semantics the theory of meanings. If syntax, thus viewed, is to be an autonomous empirical discipline, we must be able to discover what is meaningful in L [a language] without discovering what anything means in L."[41] In other words, L has a structure, comprehending a set of generating principles, that allows certain syntactic transformations, and these are to be analyzed as being independent of particular meanings. Hence the idea of generative or transformational grammar, which focuses on the laws of transformation within the realm of deep structure and on a posited homology between these laws and innate structures of mind. As Chomsky puts it, "a distinction must be made between what the speaker of a language knows implicitly (what we may call his *competence*) and what he does (his *performance*)."[42]

If it is true, as structuralism maintains, that "elements of a text do not have intrinsic meaning as autonomous entities but derive their significance from oppositions which are in turn related to other oppositions," then "the relational nature of signs produces a *potentially infinite* process of signification."[43] The deconstructionist project is thus implicit in the structuralist project, for if you undermine the scientific pretensions of structuralism by showing how its focus on the systematic undercuts itself and how its privileging of *langue* over *parole* can be upset and reversed, you are left with the free play of signifiers and an elastic context that can be infinitely extended.

Deconstruction

Unlike structuralism, which privileges structure over event, deconstruction insists on the paradox of structure and event. "Theory," therefore, "must shift back and forth between these perspectives," and this shifting results in "an irresolvable alternation or aporia."[44] In terms of the dramatistic pentad, the focus of deconstruction, paradoxically, is on religious purpose, its linguistic nihilism being a product of both epistemological skepticism and mystic drought. Its quasi-mystical celebration of the abyss would seem to be a product of displaced religious impulse and frustrated metaphysical desire.

Deconstruction is "a careful teasing out of warring forces of signification within the text,"[45] and because there is no outside the text, once one is inside the text one is everywhere and nowhere at the same time. As Culler puts it, "there is a metalinguistic function—language can discuss language—but there is no metalanguage, only more language piled upon language."[46] Consequently, "texts are already riven by the contradictions and indeterminacies that seem inherent in the exercise of language."[47] Given that "texts undo the philosophical system to which they adhere by revealing its rhetorical nature," undecidability is a key concept, and it "is always thematized in the text itself in the form of metalinguistic statements."[48] Because every figure can be read referentially or rhetorically, the reader is unable to arrive at any ultimate decision and is left in the aporetic double bind of trying to master a text that has no boundaries. "One is urged to choose while the possibility of correct choice is eliminated."[49] In sum, "a deconstruction involves the demonstration that a hierarchical opposition, in which one term is said to be dependent upon another conceived as prior, is in fact a rhetorical or metaphysical imposition and that the hierarchy could well be reversed."[50]

The essential rhetoricity of all discourse, then, undoes any metaphysics of presence or logocentrism, any "orientation of philosophy toward an order of meaning—thought, truth, reason, logic, the Word—conceived of as existing in itself, as foundation."[51] Because philosophy is but a mode of discourse, it suffers from the same undecidability that infects discourse in general.

Deconstruction's central point is that "total context is unmasterable, both in principle and in practice. Meaning is context-bound, but context is boundless."[52] A double bind is thus produced, for meaning is contextually determined on the one hand, and context is infinitely extendable and thereby indeterminate on the other. "One cannot simply or effectively choose to make meaning either the original meaning of an author or the creative experience of the reader,"[53] for neither intention nor context ever provides a full determination of meaning.

Meaning, therefore, has a double character; it is both the property of a text and the experience of a reader, and to privilege one over the other is simply to make an ideological choice without foundation. Nevertheless, the deconstructionist choice to focus on the clash of referential and rhetorical levels of discourse rather than on authorial intentions is also an ideological choice. Once you abandon foundations your choices are between nihilism and pragmatism, and the issue becomes as much one of temperament as of philosophy.

Despite its revolutionary rhetoric, much deconstructionist criticism—with its "fatalistic theory of history,"[54] its "absolutization of language,"[55] and its "epistemology of failure"[56]—is more often a symptom than a corrective of the times. In *Criticism and Social Change* Lentricchia makes this point incisively, and it is worth quoting the passage again.

> Deconstruction's useful work is to undercut the epistemological claims of representation, but that work in no way touches the real work of representation—its work of power. To put it another way: deconstruction can show that representations are not and cannot be adequate to the task of representation, but it has nothing to say about the social work that representation can and does do. Deconstruction confuses the act of unmasking with the act of defusing, the act of exposing epistemological fraud with the neutralization of political force.[57]

Like Burke, Lentricchia contends that theory "is a type of rhetoric . . . an invitation to practice, not epistemology. . . . History, then, is a kind of conversation . . . whose discourse is rhetorical and without foundation and whose ends are never assured because rhetorical process, unlike teleological process, is free. It assumes that people do things not because they must but because they are persuaded to do them."[58] "To set aside the classical claim of philosophy for representational adequacy" is not to negate "the materialist view that theory does its representing with a purpose."[59] Even though representation is philosophically unanchored, it has a causal efficacy of its own in its power to induce attitudes and actions. "The epistemological undecidability of discourse is always politically irrelevant—since discourse by definition is always in use, always in force, always ideologically directed."[60] As Roland Barthes puts it, "language is always a matter of force; to speak is to exercise a will for power; in the realm of speech there is no innocence, no safety."[61]

Derrida's animadversions against the "logocentric" worldview and its concomitant "metaphysics of presence" seem based on the misguided claim that because language has no ultimate referent or "transcendental signified" its entire communicative efficacy is undermined. I call his claim misguided because ontological relativism only enjoins that reference is nonsense *except* as it is relative to a coordinate system; one can thus make sense of it in terms of any given conceptual scheme. Hence, that language lacks an ultimate referent does not in itself undermine its communicative efficacy, representational purpose, and social power. Derrida is certainly free to obliterate, as he chooses, substance/attribute ontologies or subject/predicate grammars or ego psychologies, but how this process can generate deconstructed concepts that nonetheless "designate the crevice through which the yet unnameable glimmer beyond the closure can be glimpsed"[62] is not at all clear. How can designation make sense except as it is relative to a conceptual scheme? But argument is futile, for the position is as unanswerable as it is indefensible.

Having lost the plenitude of a world of reference, the linguistic nihilist luxuriates in its absence. By contrast, the Burkean pragmatist and rhetor rejects the all-or-nothing posturing and tempers his antifoundationism with the recognition that language is already in the world and does its work of power regardless of our philosophies. That contexts are infinitely extendable and unmasterable, that indeterminacies are inherent in the exercise of language, that every figure can be read referentially or rhetorically, that knowledge has no ultimate foundation, that hierarchies of meaning are perpetually reversible, that the shifting between structure and event produces paradox, that representation cannot be ontologically anchored in some transcendental signified or objective frame of reference—these are not threatening notions. They do not alter our pragmatic picture of how we do things with words, and in this domain they have no empirical cash value. The grammatical, rhetorical, symbolical, and ethical functions of language remain intact.

It must be acknowledged, however, and it cannot be overstated, that the above characterization of deconstruction only applies to one aspect of the theory and to the domesticated variants of it fashionable in certain academic circles. Not every poststructuralist tells the same dreary and monolithic story about the allegory of uninterpretability. Derrida's critiques of logocentrism, phonocentrism, closure, totalization, and reference as well as his championing of *écriture*, the endless deferral and differing of meaning, have profoundly upped the ante and have spawned both in his own writing and in that of feminists and other oppressed social and racial groups a cogent critique of phallogocentrism, ethnocentrism, and various other discourses of power, authority, and repression. Nihilistic playfulness is only one dimension.

Moreover, there are other poststructuralist writers who are akin to Burke in their shifting of allegiances to symbols of authority and their deployment of perspective by incongruity as a rhetorical tactic for subverting a given hegemonic discourse from within. Engaging in "the violation of linguistic and conceptual categories already established" (*PC*, 108) and in "a deliberate cultivation of logical disorders" (*PC*, 110), these writers recognize "the heuristic or perspective value of a planned incongruity" (*PC*, 121). Foucault's analyses of historical systems of institutional and discursive practices, his recognition that knowledge is governed by power relations, truth relies on institutional support, and disciplines constitute a system of control in the production of discourse, his focus on desire and power, sexuality and politics, madness and reason, speaking the truth and being in the truth (*dans le vrai*)—these ideas immediately come to mind. Barthes, as well, recognizes that power is legion and that it is inscribed in language. "Language," he writes, "is neither reactionary nor progressive; it is quite simply fascist."[63] He persistently exposes myths and stereotypes, systems of values masquerading as systems of fact. Myth transforms history into nature, and the demythologist can only cheat speech, shifting ground and having the courage to abjure his discourse once it has been co-opted by society. Barthes, in short, is a major adept in the art of perspective by incongruity. These and other poststructuralist writers can hardly be accused of being insensitive to the social work that representation can and does do. Lentricchia's point, however, still holds as a general statement about the reactionary domestication implicit in some of the popular versions of contemporary deconstruction. Whatever else can be said, the salutary effect of poststructuralism has been to ensure that Western culture can no longer be unequivocally regarded as the culture of reference.

Dramatism

The dramatistic orientation is based on the premise that language is as much, if not more, a mode of action as it is a means of conveying information. Language, as Jonathan Bennett puts it, is "systematic communicative behaviour."[64] Hence any linguistic theory should give "prominence to the use of language in communication between an utterer and an audience"[65] because meaning should be regarded as "a species within the genus intending-to-communicate."[66] Accordingly, issuing utterances is equated with performing speech acts. John Searle expresses the point thus: "All linguistic communication involves linguistic acts. The unit of linguistic communication is not, as has generally been supposed, the symbol, word, or sentence, or even the token of the symbol, word, or sentence, but rather the production or issuance of the symbol or word or sentence in the performance of the speech act."[67] It follows from this that "a theory of language is part of a theory of action"[68] since language itself is "(highly complex) rule-governed intentional behaviour."[69] Within the confines of dramatism even "referring" is seen to be an action that is performed in the issuing of an utterance.

The basic emphasis of a dramatistic theory is on what an utterer, (U), means by his utterance, (x), rather than what (x) means in a language (L). As Grice puts it, "meaning is a kind of intending"[70] and the hearer or reader's recognition that the speaker or writer means something by x is part of the meaning of x. In contrast to the assumptions of structuralism, dramatism holds that the investigation of structure always presupposes something about meanings, language use, and extralinguistic functions. According to dramatism, language is essentially a transaction between an utterer and an audience. As Dewey puts it, "language is specifically a mode of interaction of at least two beings, a speaker and a hearer."[71] Hence even "soliloquy is the product and reflex of converse with others,"[72] an "I" talking to its "me." The utterer and the interpreter must always be imaginatively switching places. E. D. Hirsch makes the point nicely. "Meaning itself is perspective-bound. . . . In order to understand verbal meaning . . . the interpreter has to submit to a double perspective. He preserves his own standpoint and, at the same time, imaginatively realizes the standpoint of the speaker. This is a characteristic of all verbal intercourse."[73] The upshot of all this is, to use Dewey's words, that meaning is "primarily a property of behaviour," not a "psychic existence"[74] or a system of signs that enjoys semantic autonomy.

Much of the pioneering work done in this regard is attributable to the anthropological research of Bronislaw Malinowski, whose well-known essay on primitive languages appears in an appendix to *The Meaning of Meaning*. In his exploration of modes of primitive communication, Malinowski argues for a theory of meaning that is socially and culturally based, use oriented and context dependent. Throughout Burke's writings Malinowski is frequently cited, and if one were inclined toward proffering a genetic account of Burke's dramatism (which I am not), it would not be unreasonable to see Malinowski as a primary source. Malinowski, of course, confines his remarks in this essay to primitive cultures, and it is thus unclear whether or not he would resent Burke's analogical extensions of his ideas into the complexities of contemporary cultures.

Malinowski contends that "language is essentially rooted in the reality of culture, the tribal life and customs of a people" and that "it cannot be explained without constant reference to these broader contexts of verbal utterance."[75] Like Richards in *The Philosophy of Rhetoric*, he considers meaning to be highly context dependent. As I mentioned earlier in my discussion of internal and external contexts, Malinowski feels that the whole "conception of context has to be broadened."[76] First, there is the "context of the whole utterance"[77]—the interinanimation of words within the speech act itself. This is similar to Max Black's idea of "intra-verbal meaning"[78] and to Hirsch's idea of "a construed notion of the whole meaning narrow enough to determine the meaning of a part."[79] But these intrinsic interrelations, Malinowski maintains, only become fully intelligible when placed within a broader "context of situation," a cultural framework extrinsic to the linguistic act. For "the *situation* in which words are uttered can never be passed over as irrelevant to the linguistic expression."[80] This is similar to Black's idea of "extra-verbal meaning"[81] and to Hirsch's idea of "givens in the milieu which will help us to conceive the right notion of the whole."[82]

It follows from this that "the conception of meaning as *contained* in an utterance is false and futile."[83] What U means by x is more important in the order of explanation than what x means in L. Of course, what x means in L exercises a continual drag (like a sea anchor) on what U means by x. U's control is limited.[84] But Malinowski's point is that it is erroneous "to consider Meaning as a real entity, contained in a word or utterance."[85] According to his "ethnographic view of language," his "principle of symbolic relativity," "the clear realization of the intimate connection between linguistic interpretation and the analysis of the culture to which the language belongs, shows convincingly that neither a Word nor its Meaning has an independent and self-sufficient existence. . . . The meaning of a word must always be gathered, not from a passive contemplation of this word, but from an analysis of its functions, with reference to this given culture."[86] Malinowski's functionalist argument against the notion of meaning containment, against what Richards calls the Proper Meaning Superstition, works toward regarding language as a mode of action. "Language in its primitive forms ought to be regarded and studied against the background of human activities and as a mode of human behaviour in practical matters. . . . In its primitive uses, language functions as a link in concerted human activity, as a piece of human behavior. It is a mode of action and not an instrument of reflection . . . a mode of social action rather than a mere reflection of thought."[87] He freely admits that his is a "pragmatic conception of language" and sees the strength of the perspective of ethnographic empiricism as residing in its classing "human speech with the active modes of human behaviour rather than with the reflective and cognitive ones."[88] "Words," he concludes, are "strongly bound up with the reality of action."[89]

Quine also rejects the conception of meaning containment. He argues that "there is no sharp line between what a sentence means and what it implies through well entrenched contingent generalizations," that "we cannot extricate a pure core of meaning."[90] According to the inextricability thesis, as Michael Dummet calls it, the meaning of a term like cube extends from the simple and banal—an object that will not roll down an incline—to the complex and abstruse—a term that encompasses a network of mathematical equations. What something means and what something implies are not categorically separable, for words are not semantically autonomous; they do not contain a pure core of extricable meaning.

Only context, in both its intraverbal and extraverbal senses, can provide the clues for the valid construing of meanings and implications. While it is true, as Hirsch points out, that "linguistic norms at the very least always impose limitations on verbal meaning," we need to appeal to a "principle of sharability" (what I have elsewhere called intelligibility or communicability) in order to make sense out of any given utterance or series of utterances.[91] We need, in other words, to attempt to construe the intention of the utterer, to discover the "intrinsic genre"[92] that determines the boundaries of his utterance as a whole. I shall later consider Hirsch's cogent "description of the genre-bound character of understanding"[93] in connection with Burke's version of the hermeneutic circle—the tautological cycle of terms. It seems to me that Hirsch's treatment of meaning, implication, intentionality, and genre is incisive. Whether it can lead to a probabilistic theory of validity in interpretation is another issue. I do not believe that it can. Nonetheless, Hirsch's version of the principle of linguistic continuity is entirely consonant with the thrust of this chapter, for, as he maintains, "the immense universe of verbal meaning stretching from casual conversation to epic poetry is uniformly governed by the social principle of linguistic genre and by the individual principle of authorial will."[94] And as Max Black affirms, referring to what he calls the "principle of context-dependence," "the words used, however central and important, must be regarded as only a part of the total speech-act."[95]

It is Malinowski's theory of primitive languages, with its emphasis on the fallacy of meaning containment, and the Sapir-Whorf hypothesis, with its emphasis on the interconnection between language, thought, and reality, that together constitute (in terms of analysis if not of genesis, for, as Burke would say, we need not temporize essence) the cornerstone of Burke's dramatism. These views, as we have seen, are unabashedly relativistic—Malinowski uses the term "symbolic relativity," and linguistic relativity is an epithet used synonymously for the Sapir-Whorf hypothesis. Moreover, a person of Nietzschean temperament would consider these views to be nihilistic in their implications. I shall argue later that Burke's hypersensitivity to the nihilistic chaos that such views about language could engender if pushed to their extremes is precisely what drives him to logology and his theory of the negative.

In *Criticism and Social Change* Lentricchia chooses not to discuss

Burke's shift from dramatism to logology—perhaps he does not need to be reminded how difficult it is to regard one's own philosophy as a rhetorical voice in the foundationless conversation of history—but he astutely diagnoses the reasons for it:

> With no way of making a unified interpretation of Babel, with no totality ("totalization") possible, Burke would seem to have denied a shared basis for the interpretive process, would seem to have plunged interpretation so deeply into the temporal and cultural differences of human particularity as to have engendered an asocial vision of history as a chaos of interpretive attitudes, of innumerable histories, all inaccessibly locked away within their various prison-houses of language.[96]

Logology converts methodological priority—the heuristic method of treating communication as primary to all categories of experience and of adopting the poetic perspective of man as communicant, a dramatistic method first developed in *Permanence and Change*—into ontological priority—the logological view that language is the source and origin of all value because it affords the peculiar possibility of the negative, the possibility of saying "no" to "thou shalt not," a view that finds its ultimate expression in *The Rhetoric of Religion*. If logology seems in part an abandonment of some of the tenets of dramatism (and in the next chapter I shall try to make clear the ways in which I think that it is), the motivation behind Burke's hardening of the categories is obvious enough. For Burke envisages his perspectivism as a way of coming to terms with the chaos of conflicting interpretations endemic to an era of instability, as, to use his own expression, a frame of acceptance. Over the years, it would seem, he comes to feel the necessity of imposing some sort of absolute value on language itself. And for Burke logology is in some sense a surrogate theology. The analogies he makes for heuristic purposes betray a psychological need for a sense of permanence akin to a religious faith in the curative power of the word made flesh.

Malinowski's anthropological speculations are an appropriate point of departure because such themes and their variations pervade much of twentieth-century philosophy of language. In *Philosophical Investigations* Wittgenstein abandons the picture theory of meaning that he articulated in *Tractatus Logico-Philosophicus*, embracing instead the idea of language-games. He contends that "to imagine a language-game means to imagine a form of life"[97] and goes on to say that "the term 'language-*game*' is meant to bring into prominence the fact that the *speaking* of language is part of an activity, or a form of life."[98] Words, he insists, are like tools, and they must be understood in terms of a context of situation, for linguistic and nonlinguistic human behavior intertwine. Language is communal in its nature. Words and the context of situation together define the language-game. The meaning of a word, then, is not the referent to which it points, the object for which it stands; "the meaning of a word is its use in language."[99] "A name functions as a name only in the context of a system of linguistic and non-linguistic activities."[100] This is why words cannot acquire meaning by ostensive definition alone and why reference only makes sense in terms of a shared coordinate system. Unlike Derrida, Wittgenstein starts with the assumption that language is the game that is played. Its lack of ultimate referent or "transcendental signified" notwithstanding, language is communicatively efficacious and communally oriented. It is *not* a symbolic system that can be regarded as intrinsically self-sufficient, as, to use Piaget's terms, a structure that is whole, capable of transformation, and self-regulating.

Wittgenstein's work, of course, is addressed to specific philosophical problems and has logical intricacies that reach beyond my competence. What is of relevance is how he focuses on language as a mode of action, a form of life. But there is a problem regarding legitimacy of application that should be addressed. It is tempting to invoke again the blanket rationalization implicit in the idea of perspective by incongruity, but that will hardly suffice. Furthermore, to compound the confusion, I have consistently used the term "dramatism" as if it really demarcated a common intellectual space that the various philosophers I have cited occupy. Yet the parallels, however real, are admittedly enforced.

It is one thing to say, as I have said—albeit more authoritatively than strict canons of evidence would allow—that the linguistic theories of various philosophers provide informative parallels to Burke's dramatism, but quite another to say that there are substantive connections between them, as I have implied. For one thing, insofar as it is possible, the role of the analytical philosopher is to disambiguate problematical utterances for the sake of logical clarity, whereas the role of the literary theorist is to delimit the range of ambiguous possibility that a given utterance subtends for the sake of literary sharability. Second, the principles that may serve to explicate sentences such as "the cat is on the mat," "I find you guilty," and so on may well prove to falter when marched out to meet a sentence such as

> The tragedy, proclaimed, as they made their way up the crescent of the drive, no less by the gaping potholes in it than by the tall exotic plants, livid and crepuscular through his dark glasses, perishing on every hand of unnecessary thirst, staggering, it almost appeared, against one another, yet struggling like dying voluptuaries in a vision to maintain some final attitude of potency, or of a collective desolate fecundity, the Consul thought distantly, seemed to be reviewed and interpreted by a person walking at his side suffering for him and saying: "Regard: see how strange, how sad, familiar things may be.[101]

Even though the latter sentence is punctuated at this point with a period, the imagined person's quotation in fact goes on for almost the same length as the section of the passage that I have quoted above. The entire passage is effectively one colossal sentence. Moreover, it is a sentence that must be understood in terms of an entire universe of discourse, not to mention in terms of the extraliterary situation that the novelist's literary strategy encompasses. Nonetheless, according to the hypothetical principle of continuity between the various sorts of linguistic action, the differences between such sentences are to be seen as ones of degree rather than kind. This, at any rate, is the governing assumption. One hopes that the advantages of calculatedly misapplying concepts to areas foreign to their progenitors' designs outweigh the dangers of committing fundamental category mistakes. Unfortunately, as Wittgenstein points out, "language is a labyrinth of paths. You approach from one side and know your way about; you approach the same place from another side and no longer know your way about."[102]

Austin's *How to Do Things with Words* is another work that falls under the rubric of dramatism, given my usage of the term. Austin commences by enunciating a reasonably clear-cut distinction between constative and performative utterances, a distinction the initial rhetorical strategy of the book induces us to believe is one that will be further refined and clarified throughout the course of his argument. In fact, quite the opposite occurs. By the end of his book Austin is using such dyslogistic terms as "the true-false fetish" and "the value-fact fetish"[103] and has come to the conclusion that constative and performative are not categorically separable even though they can do useful conceptual work as relative terms.

According to Austin, an utterance is constative if it describes or reports or constates some state of affairs such that one could say its correspondence with the facts is either true or false. That is, constative utterances have what Ogden and Richards call cognitive meaning. Performatives, on the other hand, "A. they do not 'describe' or 'report' or constate anything at all, are not 'true' or 'false'; and B. the uttering of the sentence is, or is part of, the doing of an action, which again would not *normally* be described as saying something."[104] On the simplest level, "the issuing of the utterance is the performing of an action."[105] Marrying, betting, bequeathing, umpiring, passing sentence, christening, knighting, blessing, firing, baptizing, bidding, and so on involve performatives.

> Where, as often, the procedure is designed for use by persons having certain thoughts, feelings, or intentions, or for the inauguration of certain consequential conduct on the part of any participant, then a person participating in so invoking the procedure must in fact have those thoughts, feelings, or intentions, and the participants must intend so to conduct themselves . . . and further must actually so conduct themselves subsequently.[106]

In short, then, the constative utterance is true or false, whereas the performative utterance is felicitous or infelicitous, sincere or insincere, authentic or inauthentic, well invoked or misinvoked, and so on. An examination of a constative utterance focuses on its correspondence with facts. An examination of a performative utterance focuses on what we might loosely call the intentionality of the utterer.

Once Austin has recourse to the notion of speech acts, however, the sharpness of the distinction begins to erode.

> In order to explain what can go wrong with statements we cannot just concentrate on the proposition involved (whatever that is) as has been done traditionally. We must consider the total situation in which the

utterance is issued—the total speech act—if we are to see the parallel between statements and performative utterances, and how each can go wrong. Perhaps indeed there is no great distinction between statements and performative utterances.[107]

Above, then, is another version of the principle of context-dependence.

Austin divides the linguistic act into three components. First, there is the locutionary act—"the act of 'saying something.'"[108] Second, there is the illocutionary act—"the performance of an act *in* saying something as opposed to the performance of an act *of* saying something."[109] Third, there is the perlocutionary act, for "saying something will often, or even normally, produce certain consequential effects upon the feelings, thoughts, or actions of the audience, or of the speaker, or of other persons: and it may be done with the design, intention, or purpose of producing them."[110] In other words, a locutionary act has meaning—that is, sense and reference. It is the act of producing a recognizable grammatical utterance in a given language. An illocutionary act has force. It is informed with a certain tone, attitude, feeling, motive, or intention. A perlocutionary act has consequence. It has an effect upon the addressee. By describing an imminently dangerous situation (locutionary component) in a tone that is designed to warn the addressee (illocutionary component), the addresser may actually frighten him into moving (perlocutionary component). Or, to give another example, "he said $x = y$" is locutionary; "he argued that $x = y$" is illocutionary; "he convinced me that $x = y$" is perlocutionary. Yet even this simpler example is not without complexity. From my point of view as addressee I have to assume that if U said $x = y$ and if U is not deliberately trying to deceive, then the illocutionary force of the utterance is that U believes $x = y$. It would be a very strange situation indeed (to my mind psychologically implausible) if simultaneously U said that $x = y$ was the case and believed that $x = y$ was false. How could U describe a state of affairs in factual terms unless he believed it to be true? Moreover, if U argues that $x = y$, then I have to assume not only that U believes $x = y$ but also that he would be prepared to make a factual utterance constating $x = y$ to be the case. Third, for me to be convinced that $x = y$ I have to assume not only that U is sincere (though, strictly speaking, it is possible for me to be convinced that $x = y$ even while suspecting U's motives) but also that $x = y$ is true. Hence even in a simple example the components overlap. The more complex the speech act, the more the components interfuse. None of this, Austin maintains, is particularly surprising.

> That the giving of straightforward information produces, almost always, consequential effects upon action, is no more surprising than the converse, that the doing of an action (including the uttering of a performative) has regularly the consequence of making ourselves and others aware of facts. To do any act in a perceptible or detectable way is to afford ourselves and generally others also the opportunity to know both (a) that we did it, and further (b) many other facts as to our motives, our character or what not which may be inferred from our having done it.[111]

Originally, then, to recapitulate, Austin contrasts the performative with the constative utterance, saying that "(1) the performative should be doing something as opposed to just saying something; and (2) the performative is happy or unhappy as opposed to true or false."[112] Yet he comes to the conclusion that constating something is doing something and is likely to be happy or unhappy as well as true or false. It would be unhappy, for example, if my describing a dangerous situation to you did not have the force of a warning and the consequence of frightening you into moving. As Austin points out, "once we realize that what we have to study is not the sentence but the issuing of an utterance in a speech situation, there can hardly be any longer a possibility of not seeing that stating is performing an act."[113]

"With the constative utterance," he writes, "we abstract from the illocutionary (let alone the perlocutionary) aspects of the speech act, and we concentrate on the locutionary: moreover, we use an oversimplified notion of correspondence with the facts. . . . With the performative utterance, we attend as much as possible to the illocutionary force of the utterance, and abstract from the dimension of correspondence with facts."[114] His radical conclusion is that "the familiar contrast of 'normative or evaluative' as opposed to the factual is in need, like so many dichotomies, of elimination."[115] We must rid ourselves of both "the true-false fetish" and "the fact-value fetish."[116]

If a philosopher so firmly riveted to the homely realities of ordinary language ultimately argues that everyday speech situations resist clean separation into referential and nonreferential components, then it is clear how simplistic any dichotomous theory of linguistic functions is. So-called "ordinary" language has many of the complexities and ambiguities that are often associated only with so-called "literary" language. Referential/emotive, scientific/literary, semantic/poetic, extrinsic/intrinsic, denotative/connotative, context/text, or other distinctions of the same ilk do not suffice, for they depend upon a strictly nominalist definition of "referent" that, as Quine points out, begs the ontological question. It is impossible to separate thought from its verbal manifestation. Conceptual scheme and linguistic embodiment cross-fertilize, and the symbol-using animal has no perspective from which to survey the scene with magisterial neutrality. Austin, to be sure, would be unsympathetic toward much of the speculative posturing in this chapter, but his commonsensical account of how locutionary, illocutionary, and perlocutionary acts tend to overlap is not inconsonant with many of the ideas discussed earlier. At the very least, Austin is committed to something akin to a principle of continuity between the various sorts of linguistic action.

In the first chapter I examined Burke's division of the poetic act into dream, prayer, and chart—the symbolical, the rhetorical, and the grammatical. His division has interesting affinities with Austin's tripartite scheme, though the grids are by no means coextensive. As I pointed out, dream refers to symbolic action as symptomatic action, as having a compensatory or therapeutic role; prayer refers to symbolic *action* in that it focuses on the communicative function of language and the rhetorical inducing of attitudes and actions; chart refers to *symbolic* action, to language as symbolic *of* something, as a verbal parallel to a pattern of experience, a realistic sizing up of a situation. Chart, then, has obvious affinities with the locutionary or constative dimension. Prayer encompasses aspects of both the illocutionary dimension (the performative) and the perlocutionary dimension in that prayer may have both force and consequence. Dream is problematic. It would have to be subsumed somewhere under illocutionary force, for its reflexive nature focuses its relevance upon the intentionality of the utterer, even though the intentionality may paradoxically be unconscious. There is less of a problem, however, if we regard intentionality in nonpsychologistic terms and thereby translate "unconscious intentions" into "implications of meaning." Implications are part of an intentional verbal act, even if the utterer is not aware of them. The problem here is really one of vocabulary. Note, however, that this construal of the matter does not infringe upon what Hirsch calls the individual principle of authorial will or give credence to the notion of meaning containment. The temporal character of both communicating and understanding makes unsurprising the fact that an utterer sometimes does not know the full implications of what he intended to communicate until some time later, if at all. The same applies *mutatis mutandis* to the addressee.

Each of the various characterizations of language that I have labeled dramatistic try to cover much the same territory, albeit with different emphases. Whether one sees language as symbolic action (in the threefold sense delineated above) or as systematic communicative behavior or as rule-governed intentional behavior, one is trying to capture in definition the same range of features—that language is a mode of action as much as it is a means of conveying information; that it is a self-contained, creative, symbolic organization as well as an inventory of ontological items in a given context of situation; that it depends on both intraverbal and extraverbal contexts; that it operates under the force of an utterer's will because meaning is a species of the genus intending-to-communicate, not something totally contained in an utterance; that it is sharable because it is a communally oriented and communicatively efficacious form of life, having as its substratum some set of reinforceable or destructible human expectations; and that there is a principle of continuity between the various sorts of linguistic action.

For these reasons it seems reasonable to maintain that (1) literature is not linguistically or semantically autonomous, (2) formal and sociological approaches to literature are not mutually exclusive, and (3) literature is not discontinuous with other realms of human action, with the drama and dialectic of human relations in general. As Roger Fowler points out, "the language of literature is not different in essence from language at large . . . and this fact guarantees 'reference out,' connection with the outside world."[117] Literary categories have cultural content; they are defined and delimited by distinct cultural situations. His well-taken point is that "language is essentially, and not only in literature, a fiction-making device—a capability consequent upon its having a semantic dimension."[118] Language, he continues, conditions perception, for the limits of a given language are the limits of its articulated world. Different semantic organizations imply different worldviews. "Man is a fiction-making animal. . . . Language assists the making and stabilization of fictions. . . . What we really do is partition our universe fictionally by an imposed grid of language."[119]

Insofar as Fowler's argument stresses "the mutual interpenetration of language, conceptualization, and cultural organization,"[120] his insights seem solid, but his endorsement of Leach's postulation that "the world is a representation of our language categories, not vice versa,"[121] succumbs to structuralist reductionism. That language lacks an ultimate referent only entails that reference be understood in terms of a given conceptual-linguistic scheme. It does not deny that language subserves a realistic function. The attitude of naive verbal realism, which we most often adopt in our quotidian existence, has survival value; it is communicatively efficacious. Our charts more or less work.

As Burke points out, there is the realm of symbolic action, which comprises both verbal and nonverbal symbol and communications systems, and the realm of nonsymbolic motion, which comprises the spatiotemporal world of cause and effect, the sheer thrownness of things, facticity. Although we posit the world-in-itself as a limiting concept, we have no access to that world save through our conceptual-linguistic schemes. In this resides the peculiar ambiguity of the human situation. Culture and nature intersect; where precisely we cannot say. Yet to say that this means that we are not subject to the recalcitrance of reality, brute and inhuman as its resistance to our schemes sometimes seems, is surely absurd. We ought to recognize that fictionality has degrees and that while the quest for adequate ideas is lifelong, whatever freedom we enjoy is based on the recognition of necessity. We succumb to the false allure of a supreme fiction at the peril of abdicating from the dialectical process of striving toward adequate ideas. Even though such ideas are unrealizable by definition, given the ambiguity of our situation, this lack of ultimate adequacy in no way undermines the validity of the enterprise. To abdicate from that dialectical process is only to indulge in the supreme form of ethical cowardice. And because literature is "an incipient form of action . . . an implied code of conduct" (CS, 18), our critical attitude toward it has a moral dimension.

Value-ridden from the outset, language, for Burke, is intrinsically rhetorical, and "the nature of language as petition, exhortation, persuasion, and dissuasion implies that . . . words will be modes of posture, act, attitude, gesture" (*RR*, 288). Because Burke feels that "language is primarily a species of action, or attitudinizing, rather than an instrument of definition" (*D*, 325), he espouses dramatism as an alternative to scientism in general and to behaviorism, mechanism, and determinism in particular. Dramatism represents "the grammar of action" and is predicated on "the proposition that action cannot be reduced to motion" (*D*, 329).

> The Dramatistic concept of a "scene-act ratio" serves to admonish against an overly positivistic view of descriptive terms, or "empirical data," as regards an account of the conditions that men are thought to confront at a given time in history. For insofar as such a grammatical function does figure in our thoughts about motives and purposes, in the choice and scope of the terms that are used for characterizing a given situation there are implicit corresponding attitudes and programs of action. And thus it is impossible to select terms in which policies of some sort are not more or less clearly inherent. In brief, whatever terms are chosen to define the scene, matters of policy will necessarily be debated *in terms of* them. In the selection of terms for *de*scribing the scene, one automatically *pre*scribes the range of *acts* that will seem "reasonable," "implicit," or "necessary." (*D*, 341)

Since every dialectic transposes and disposes the terms of the dramatistic pentad in a uniquely constitutive fashion and with a uniquely exhortative attitude, every dialectic implies a rhetoric of action. Though a Marxist might see the historical and economic scene as determinative of the acts and attitudes that agents engage in, his "scenic" grammar implies a program of social change that urges the strategic deployment of linguistic and political agency for the purpose of revolution. "The dramatistic view of language, in terms of 'symbolic action,' is exercised about the necessarily *suasive* nature of even the most unemotional scientific nomenclatures" (*LASA*, 45).

Whereas a scientistic approach to the nature of language "begins with questions of *naming*, or *definition*," a dramatistic approach views "the power of language to define and describe . . . as derivative" (*LASA*, 44). According to dramatism, the essential function of language "may be treated as attitudinal or hortatory: attitudinal as with expressions of complaint, fear, gratitude, and such; hortatory as with commands or requests, or, in general, an instrument developed through its use in the social processes of cooperation and competition" (*LASA,* 44). Whereas a scientistic approach "builds the edifice of language with primary stress upon a proposition such as 'it *is,* or it is *not*'" (*LASA,* 44), a dramatistic approach "puts primary stress upon such hortatory expressions as 'thou *shalt,* or thou *shalt not*'" (*LASA,* 44). For Burke, the imperative takes precedence over the indicative, the negative command over the negative proposition. His focus is on the performative rather than on the constative, on illocutionary force and perlocutionary consequence rather than on locutionary meaning. For language is a form of life, and the negative is at the center of our linguistic and moral activity. Although "the negative is a purely linguistic convenience," it is instrumental in "the inculcating of guilt" (*D,* 329) and is an integral part of morality and religion in their dual functions as systems of solace and control. Moreover, to use language at all, one must have a spontaneous grasp of the negative.

> Symbol using demands a feeling for the negative (beginning in the Korzybskian admonition that the word for the thing is *not* the thing). A specifically symbol-using animal will necessarily introduce a symbolic ingredient into every experience. Hence, every experience will be imbued with negativity. Sheer "animality" is not possible to the sensory experiences of a symbol-using animal. (*LASA,* 469)

Terministic screens "direct the *attention*" (*LASA,* 45). "Even if any given terminology is a *reflection* of reality, by its very nature as a terminology it must be a *selection* of reality; and to this extent it must function also as a *deflection* of reality" (*LASA,* 45).

> Not only does the nature of our terms affect the nature of our observations, in the sense that the terms direct the *attention* to one field rather than to another. Also *many of the "observations" are but implications of the particular terminology in terms of which the observations are made.* In brief, much that we take as observations about "reality" may be but the spinning out of the possibilities implicit in our particular choice of terms. (*LASA,* 46)

Behavior "isn't something that you need but observe; even something so 'objectively there' as behavior must be observed through one or another kind of *terministic screen,* that directs the attention in keeping with its nature" (*LASA,* 46).

As Socrates points out in the *Phaedrus,* composition and division are the two basic dialectical resources, there being but "two kinds of terms: terms that put things together, and terms that take things apart" (*LASA,* 49). As Burke reflects:

> We *must* use terministic screens, since we can't say anything without the use of terms; whatever terms we use, they necessarily constitute a corresponding kind of screen; and any such screen necessarily directs the attention to one field rather than another. Within that field there can be different screens, each with its ways of directing the attention and shaping the range of observations implicit in the given terminology. All terminologies must implicitly or explicitly embody choices between the principle of continuity or discontinuity. (*LASA,* 50)

The lurking danger, of course, is relativism, for if empirical observations are reduced to terminological implications, then everything becomes relative to the terminology of the observer. "Must we merely resign ourselves," Burke asks, "to an endless catalogue of terministic screens, each of which can be valued for the light it throws upon the human animal, yet none of which can be considered central? In one sense," he answers, "yes" (*LASA,* 52). For every human being is "thrown" into a unique set of circumstances—biological, physiological, existential, social, political, historical, etc.—and every human being undergoes a unique combination of experiences. In this sense, there are as many worldviews as there are people.

> At the other extreme, each of us shares with other members of our kind (the often-inhuman human species) the fatal fact that, however the situation came to be, all members of our species conceive of reality somewhat roundabout, through the various *media* of symbolism. Any such medium will be, as you prefer, either a way of "dividing" us from the "immediate" (thereby setting up a kind of "alienation" at the very start of our emergence from infancy into a state of articulacy somewhat misleadingly called the "age of reason"); or it can be viewed as a paradoxical way of "uniting" us with things on a "higher level of awareness," or some such. (*LASA,* 52)

Whatever the differences between our terministic screens (the principle of discontinuity), "they are all classifiable together in one critical respect: They all operate by the use of symbol systems; thus all in their various ways manifest the resources and limitations of symbol systems" (*LASA*, 57) (the principle of continuity). The reflexivity of human symbolism entails that we may move from "the criticism of experience to the criticism of criticism. We not only interpret the character of events . . . we may also interpret our interpretations" (*PC*, 6).

In an obvious sense dramatism can only be a terministic screen, a screen that "involves a methodic tracking down of the implications in the idea of symbolic action, and of man as the kind of being that is particularly distinguished by an aptitude for such action" (*LASA*, 54). Burke, however, is very much convinced that there is "more to be learned from a study of tropes than from a study of tropisms" (*PLF*, 114), and he is moved to assert that his perspectivism is not simply another perspective. Hence his investment in logology, as I shall argue in the next chapter. Although he is willing to admit that we may be "but things in motion," he is unwilling to relinquish the point that we necessarily "think of one another (especially of those with whom we are intimate) as *persons*" (*LASA*, 53). According to the logologic of a dramatistic terminology, things move, persons act. Personhood and the idea of freedom it implies may be ontological illusions, but they are linguistic realities and integral components of the logic of action. "If *action* is to be our key term, then *drama;* for drama is the culminative form of action. . . . But if *drama,* then *conflict.* And if *conflict,* then *victimage.* Dramatism is always on the edge of this vexing problem, that comes to a culmination in the song of the scapegoat" (*LASA*, 54).

Guilt, redemption, hierarchy, victimage—these are the great persecutional words of dramatism. Within the realm of social action and human relations, some variant of the tragic rhythm would seem to be inescapable, for categorical guilt, hierarchic psychosis, curative victimage, and dramatic catharsis would seem to be endemic to all social orders. The best we can hope for is that our victims be symbolic rather than literal, and that the competitive cooperation of our discordant voices leads to a dialectical transcendence of our differences and moves us, as the epigraph to *A Grammar of Motives* reads, *ad bellum purificandum.*

As Lentricchia accurately points out, "the subject of subjects in Burke" is rhetoric.[122] And the most important message to derive from the above is that words are agents of power; that they are value-laden, ideologically motivated, and morally and emotionally weighted instruments of purpose, persuasion, and representation; that the semantic ideal of neutral naming is part of a hegemonic discourse that negates the sociohistorical individual by effacing him; and that the most morally bankrupt of all things is to be the neutral namer or disinterested specialist, what Socrates calls in Plato's *Phaedrus* the nonlover. Rhetorical personhood is the real reality. As literary critic or manual laborer, one is already in the forensic arena. One did not ask to be "thrown" into this historical conversation, but here one is. And though no amount of scientific and philosophic analysis can tell one what to do, one always ends up doing something, directing one's allegiance to this or that symbol of authority, working hegemonically or counterhegemonically, as the case may be. "To exist socially," Lentricchia reminds us, "is to be rhetorically aligned."[123] "Not all social power is literary power, but all literary power is social power. . . . The literary act is a social act."[124] One's own ideological persuasions notwithstanding, literature makes something happen.

Four

Words and the Word
Burke's Logological Thesis

THE DRAMATISTIC orientation, which I attempted in the last chapter to put into a philosophical context, is congruent with the Burkean claim that when we discuss words "as modes of action, we must consider both [their] nature as words in themselves and the nature they get from the non-verbal scenes that support their acts" (*PLF*, xvii). That is, we must attend to questions of both internal structure and act-scene relationships, intraverbal and extraverbal contexts. This is because "words are a mediatory realm, that joins us with wordless nature while at the same time standing between us and wordless nature" (*ATH*, 373). From the dramatistic point of view, act equals form, and it makes little difference whether one valorizes the system of signs or the frame of reference. In either case one has subordinated one order to the other and has thereby neglected the essential ambiguity of their transaction.

The character of the transaction between symbolic action and non-symbolic motion is difficult to delineate. Since we have no non-linguistic access to the structure of reality—culture and nature intersect—we also have no neutral standpoint from which to describe the mediatory function of symbolic action. Dialectical instability is necessarily a permanent feature of any attempt at explanation. Moreover, as Burke acknowledges, "the realm of symbolicity" can be "an originating force in its own right,"[1] which further complicates any process of disentanglement. As Hugh Duncan notes in his introduction to *Permanence and Change,* "Symbolic forms affect conduct because of the ways in which they affect communication and thus all action. . . . Motive lies not in some kind of experience 'beyond' symbols, but also *in* symbols. In sum, symbolism is a motive because symbolism is a motivational dimension in its own right" (*PC*, xx–xxi).

Burke insists that "a terminology for the discussion of . . . social behavior must stress symbolism as a motive" (*PC*, 75) simply because man is by definition the symbol-using animal—genus: animality, differentia: symbolicity. "With a symbol-using animal, the logic of symbols must be 'prior' to the effects of any 'productive forces' in the socioeconomic meaning of that expression" (*RM*, 177). (I shall return to the problematical status of the word "prior" shortly.) Whereas symbolism is grounded in biological and socioeconomic conditions, it is not reducible to them; it has, in other words, a creative capacity and causal efficacy of its own. This is because "once associations have been established between words and extra-verbal situations, a new order of motivation arises through resources internal to words as such" (*LASA*, 455).

It is important to keep in mind that the rhetorical manipulation of symbols has a perlocutionary dimension and subserves a realistic function, for rhetoric is but "the use of language as a symbolic means of inducing cooperation in beings that naturally respond to symbols" (*RM*, 43). Rhetoric highlights "the persuasive aspects of language, the function of language as *addressed*" (*RM*, 43–44), and however idealistic the terms deployed may be—honor, patriotism, national will, predestination, and so forth—their function is realistic. People are often ready to cooperate to death with them. "Communication," Burke maintains, "is grounded in material cooperation" (*PC*, xlix), and again we note how indissolubly linked are communication and cooperation in his way of thinking. Whereas chart—symbolic action as symbolic of something—clearly accentuates the realistic factor, prayer, in its capacity to induce attitudes and actions, is also realistic in that it may affect conduct.

Given this connection between communication and cooperation, and given that symbolism comes to be a motivational dimension in its own right because of resources internal to words as such, what does it mean to say that the logic of symbols must be "prior"? Obviously, a great deal is at stake, depending upon the moves one makes with that term. For, as Burke points out throughout his writings, it does not take much terministic maneuvering to convert logical priority into chronological priority through the process of temporizing essence. For the time being let me pose the question thus. Are Hobbes and Rousseau offering us an account of the *genesis* of civil society out of a state of nature or are they offering us an *analysis* of civil society in terms of a concept of a state of nature that is employed as a logical tool? The first kind of explanation deals with origins and sources; it makes historical claims and posits ontological items. The second deals with essences and natures; it establishes a heuristic methodology and uses concepts to regulate inquiry.[2]

Let me try to express the point in terms of poetics in particular. According to Burke, the sort of question we should ask ourselves if we wish to adopt an essentialist method when dealing with, say, literary genres is: Based on our familiarity with works in a certain genre, what would constitute that genre's entelechial fulfillment? (Entelechy, of course, is Aristotle's term for a thing's internal principle of motivation, its incentive to attain the kind of perfection proper to the kind of thing it is.) We should not search for some primal source, some fundamental myth upon which everything else is a variation, but rather we should seek to excogitate the principles of composition that would explain the structure of the perfection of the form. Burke contends that to do such is to do what Aristotle did in the *Poetics*, wherein the latter tried to describe the essence of Greek tragedy. Burke feels that the critic should "aim at a conceptual architectonic which will somehow contrive to translate the poet's intuitions into the terms of their corresponding critical principles."[3] Such principles are logically prior, if not temporally prior, to the text under scrutiny. "Regardless of how any work arose . . . the critic should aim to formulate the principles of composition implicit in it. Then he should test the power and the scope of his formulation by reversing the process. Thus, 'prophesying after the event,' he would proceed by showing how, if his formulations are adequate, the poem should be 'logically deducible' from the principles he has formulated."[4] Burke is committed to the view that a poet "necessarily writes a certain *kind* of poem. Insofar as the poem is effective, it will necessarily produce a certain *kind* of effect. And the poem is necessarily composed of the elements by which it produced the particular kind of effect 'proper' to that particular kind of poem."[5] The same logic would apply *mutatis mutandis* if we were seeking to formulate the principles of composition appropriate to a kind in general, for we would seek to isolate the entelechial drive within the form itself in order to discover its hypothetical perfection. We would not search for an Ur-text that would function as a generic source for texts that came afterward in time. "In this sense the principles of a poetics could be treated as prior to the poems that exemplify them, *though they are formulated afterwards in time,* as with Aristotle's reduction of Greek tragedy to Poetics, or the codifying of the grammar implicit in a language" (*LASA,* 34).

Despite his alertness in spotting the temporizing of essence in the works of others, Burke is sometimes guilty of speciously resorting to the same maneuver. In saying this I do not mean to imply that temporizing of essence is by definition a fallacy. On the contrary, spinning out into narrative a series of logical relationships is endemic to human understanding. In fact, given the temporal character of communicating and understanding, we are condemned to translate our chordal visions into narrative arpeggios (Burke's metaphor).[6] Temporizing of essence is only vicious when it results in a genetic fallacy. My point is that even though logology as a mode of analysis equips us with a vocabulary for discovering and comprehending the temporizing of essence, logology itself temporizes essence in a questionable way. This is because logology converts methodological priority—the heuristic method of treating communication as primary to all categories of experience and of adopting the poetic perspective of man as communicant, a dramatistic method first developed in *Permanence and Change,* into ontological priority—the logological view that language is the source and origin of all value, a view that finds its entelechial fulfillment in *The Rhetoric of Religion.* The problem is that such a language-centered view of reality tends toward the kind of reductionism that dramatism is designed to overcome. Burke's infatuation with his tautological cycle of terms, with labyrinthine internal consistency and organic interrelations, is symptomatic of this tendency. While it is true that focusing on a "closed complex of mutual implications"[7] obviously stresses the *logical* relationships among terms—there is no overt genetic fallacy in this sort of intrinsic analysis—it tends at the same time to ignore act-scene relationships, the reality of action with which words are strongly bound up, the context of situation. I say "tends" advisedly because at no point could it be said that dramatism, with its philosophy of the act, is entirely abandoned; it is only temporarily suspended. The implicit claim regarding the ontological status of language, a claim imbedded in the logological notion that language is literally the generator of value because language affords the peculiar possibility of the negative, is the reason for Burke's efficient overstressing of the intrinsic ingredients in his theoretical recipe.

I have already suggested a reason for the hardening of the categories in Burke's dialectic. Let me rehearse the general claim before proceeding to chart the pattern in detail. I mentioned that it is no exaggeration to say that Burke's entire corpus is directed toward coming to *terms* with a relativistic universe. He is constantly trying to develop a vocabulary that will handle the complexities of living in an era of instability and *"make one at home* in the complexities of relativism, whereas now one tends to be *bewildered* by relativism" (*ATH*, 229). Language, which is symbolic action, can save us from demoralization precisely because it is a source of value and can thus remoralize the world that science, semantics, and technology have neutralized. Considering the poetic ideal to be more inclusive than the semantic one, the dialectical and dramatistic thinker would cure us through the medium of words as much by training us in a distrust of words as in anything else. By allowing us to translate back and forth between semantic schemes that are traditionally kept apart, perspective by incongruity is both a methodological device for giving us a handle on the bewildering diversity of interpretations with which we are bombarded and a rhetorical technique for subverting a given hegemonic discourse from within. In the final analysis, however, perspectivism is but an honorific name for nihilism, and since Burke comes to believe that dramatism is superior in its representation of reality to scientism, he is pressured into imposing some sort of absolute value on language itself. For it is one thing to be sensitively attuned to the dialectical possibilities of linguistic transformation, the resources of catharsis and transcendence, and quite another to let one's own dramatistic theory of symbolic action dissolve in collision with other perspectives. It is difficult to be a perspectivist when it comes to assessing the validity of one's own perspective.

The dramatism/scientism opposition manifests itself in various forms throughout Burke's writings. A selective catalogue, moving in a roughly chronological fashion from *Counter-Statement* to *Dramatism and Development,* will give an idea of its pervasiveness: form/information, ritual/revelation, action/knowledge, symbolism/nature, imagination/bureaucratization, social sciences/physical sciences, act/scene, acts/events, tropes/tropisms, free will/determinism, representative anecdote/informative anecdote, dramatistic pentad/mechanistic reductionism (stimulus-response, cause and effect), synecdochic representation/metonymic reduction, grace/nature, symbolicity/motion, mental action/mechanical motion, form/perception, ontology/epistemology, symbolicity/animality, definition—it is or is not—propositional negative/act—thou shalt or shalt not—hortatory negative, dramatism/behaviorist reductionism, and so on.

It cannot be overstressed, however, that Burke construes the opposition to be dialectical rather than diametrical. Burke's dramatism/scientism opposition is not an alembicated variant of Richards's poetry/science dichotomy. The two terms of Burke's opposition, whatever form they take, are not mutually exclusive, for dramatism is the more inclusive and comprehensive term. "Behaviorism, with its view of man as *in essence* a machine rather than as a symbol-using animal subject to mechanistic frailties, is the figurative approach to things concerned with human motivation."[8] Whereas the machine metaphor has utilitarian and scientific value vis-à-vis the realm of nonsymbolic motion, it results in distortion if applied to the realm of symbolic action. Note, however, that Burke does not at all claim that man is exempt from biological and physical laws. In fact, whatever freedom man enjoys is derivable from his recognition of scientistic necessity. For Burke freedom is not contracausal.

> A Dramatistic terminology of motives, based on a generating distinction between action and motion, would not look for the ultimate roots of freedom in either physicist or biological notions of indeterminacy. . . . Insofar as a state of freedom is possible, Dramatism would seek it in the realm of symbolic action (the dimension that the determinist, Spinoza, called "adequate ideas"). . . . "Freedom" would be grounded in the realm of symbolic action (or "adequate ideas" about the nature of necessity), though by the same token it is also necessarily true that the "inadequate ideas" subject us to the risk of bondage.[9]

Burke seems to be saying that freedom and determinism are compatible within the confines of a dramatistic terminology of motives.

They are compatible because freedom is the recognition of necessity, the dialectical struggle to devise adequate ideas. Embodied in symbolic action is the logic of freedom.

The crux of the supposed clash between freedom and determinism centers on the notion of moral responsibility. The libertarian indeterminist holds that to embrace determinism is to entail the elimination of moral responsibility. Surely this is wrong, for even a convincing refutation of determinism does not necessarily validate moral responsibility; in fact, it runs the risk of ruling out responsibility. Desperately recoiling from any intimation of causation in his analysis of a particular action, the indeterminist ultimately arrives at a conception of free will largely based on chance, whim, or accident. He feels so compelled to show that an individual's actions are a result of unfettered choice that he overasserts the randomness of the will.

The issue is simple. Choice is either random or it is not, and if there is randomness in it, as the indeterminist seems obliged to contend, then it is illogical to hold an individual responsible for his actions. The point is that if one wishes to conceive of free will as devoid of all elements of causation, then any notion of responsibility is absurd. The same reasoning would apply to notions of praise, blame, resentment, gratitude, and other members of that general cluster.

As Burke suggests, moral responsibility tends to presuppose elements of both freedom and determinism. The action must be free, that is, avoidable, and yet not a matter of pure chance. We need to posit, in other words, the logical freedom of the moral agent, which is very different from positing any sort of contracausal or metaphysical freedom—an example of which would be Kant's notion of noumenal freedom, the human power to initiate a sequence of events that is unaffected by the causality of natural phenomena. What I have in mind is something analogous to Kant's weaker claim that "every being which cannot act otherwise than under the idea of freedom is thereby really free in a practical respect."[10] That is, human beings are so constituted as to be unable to think of themselves as causally determined, and to be unable to think of oneself except as free is in effect to be free.[11] Given this, there is no a priori reason to suppose that logical freedom and moral agency are incompatible with determinism. The matter, I would submit, requires some elucidation, and while this will take me into the dubious realm of what Burke "really" means, the excursion will prove relevant when we come to consider *The Rhetoric of Re-*

ligion. After all, what is predestination, whether of people or of words, but the harmony of freedom and determinism?

In *Obligation and the Body Politic* Joseph Tussman refers to two perspectives from which human behavior can be regarded—the descriptive-predictive perspective of the observer and the normative-practical perspective of the actor.

> The relation of these two perspectives to each other raises the traditional problem of freedom and determinism. The same activity, the activity of the decision-maker, is treated in two different sets of terms; on the one hand it is regarded as predictable; on the other hand it is seen as a kind of choosing. And the greater our success in predicting, the more inclined we are to dismiss "choice" as unreal or illusory. . . . There is really no difficulty in regarding an act as both free and predictable. . . . The error consists in substituting "compelled" for "predictable," so that an act which, unobjectionably, is both predictable and free seems instead an act which is both "compelled" and "free."[12]

All compulsion is causation but not all causation is compulsion.

For Tussman the fundamental tenet of political freedom is the reality of human agency, for the agent who has a practical problem and is deliberating about what to do must regard himself as being free to choose and implement alternative courses of action within a finite range of possibilities, the bounds of necessity. This is because, logically speaking, he cannot abandon the perspective of the actor without lapsing into something resembling Sartrian *mauvaise foi.* If he soars into transcendence, he derives false solace from the transformational powers of symbolic action, abandoning the quest for adequate ideas and sustaining himself with supreme fictions. If he retreats into facticity, he derives false solace from the supposedly paralyzing necessity of mechanical motion, failing to grasp the nature of that necessity so that he might be able to identify those elements in his situation which are alterable. As Sartre puts it, the reality of human being is metastability, the constant vacillation between transcendence and facticity, the ambiguous transaction between symbolic action and nonsymbolic motion.

In *Principles and Persons,* an ethical interpretation of existentialism, Frederick Olafson gives trenchant expression to the view that human action should be understood in terms of logical rather than contracausal freedom.

> In denying the reflexive applicability of deterministic modes of thought to human beings, the existentialists are not saying that the human organism and human behavior cannot be studied causally, but rather that there are other modes of conceptualizing the latter and that whatever its value in its own sphere, causal explanation cannot, without becoming explicitly and inadmissibly metaphysical, claim to override or to absorb all other modes of conceptualizing our experience—in particular, the evaluative mode. . . . What the existentialist line of argument establishes, if it is successful, is not that from some external and absolute "God's-eye-point-of-view" man is free, but rather that within the human situation the notions of predictability and freedom are complementary and interdependent.[13]

Olafson goes on to say that if the prediction of an agent's behavior, as well as the theory from which it derives and the sequence of events that theory projects, become known to him, that is, become elements in his situation, then he can react in a number of ways that are not determined by the theory itself. Prediction may be falsified as a result of becoming known.

In other words, our decisions make a difference in determining our courses of action. Agency arises from the fact that we are able to enact certain decisions that we make. As Rousseau notes in *The Social Contract*, "every free action has two causes which concur to produce it, one moral—the will which determines the act, the other physical—the strength which executes it."[14] There is will and strength, the decision and the enactment. Compulsion only occurs when the decision-making process of the agent is not genuinely instrumental in the production of his actions or when his decision to do a particular action arises from some aspect of himself beyond the efficacy of all moral, rhetorical, and deliberational pressures. The alcoholic's decision not to have another drink, for example, exerts no influence on his subsequent behavior. It is fair to talk of agency when action flows from deliberation and decision precisely because they are antecedent causal conditions. For the concatenation of causal factors that determines the eventual action includes the deliberation and the decision. Agency, therefore, comprises having a practical problem, deliberating about what to do, and then acting in accordance with a decision. The agent in a moral situation must act as if he were free and thereby shoulder all the responsibilities he would have if he were free. In such a situation the agent cannot adopt the perspective of the observer because of his unique position in being the agent, for with respect to self-prediction, as we have already seen, the "I" who is to be observed is the "I" who is to do the observing, so that any discovery the "I" may make automatically changes the subject matter.

What we normally think of as human action, then, is not threatened by determinism, for within the human situation the notions of predictability and freedom are complementary and interdependent. Otherwise, any notion of responsibility is vacuous. Nonetheless, it is simply the case that if determinism of the most rigorous variety were true, then every human action would be in principle wholly predictable by someone. But even that would not negate the freedom we must exercise within the confines of our situation.

In short, there are degrees of freedom, and only when one understands one's freedom of choice is one free to choose. Insofar as one's ideas adequate themselves to the nature of necessity one is less subject to bondage. This dispositional interpretation of human freedom means that the movement toward higher levels of freedom involves the progressive development and exercise of a capacity that all of us possess to a greater or lesser degree.

In "Prologue in Heaven" (*RR*, 273–316), an imaginary dialogue between the Lord and Satan, Burke has the Lord declare that the human "ability to be wrong within limits will also argue the ability to be right within limits. And insofar as these creatures are right, they will share in that higher freedom which we equate with necessity, an identity's inevitable necessity of being, in all its parts, the simple self-consistency that it must be, in order to be precisely what it is" (*RR*, 282). Here we see how the notions of human entelechy and adequate ideas are intertwined.

Satan's elaboration of this point reinforces what I have been arguing—namely, that Burke's is a conception of logical as opposed to contracausal or metaphysical freedom. Citing Rousseau, Satan claims that human beings "are in a sense 'forced to be free,' since they will think of themselves as persons, and the idea of personality implies the idea of action, and the ideas of both freedom and necessity are intrinsic to the idea of an act." The intrinsic connection between both free-dom and necessity stems from "the dramatistic nature of [human] terminology" (*RR*, 283), not from any metaphysical reality labeled freedom. "Whereas ontologically or theologically we may say that by being endowed with free will man is able to act morally, the corre-sponding logological statement would be: Implicit in the idea of an act is the idea of free will. . . . That is, even if we hypothetically suppose, with strict behaviorists, cyberneticists and the like, that there is no such thing as 'free will,' that all 'action' is reducible to terms of me-chanical 'motion,' it would still remain true that implicit in the idea of action there is the idea of freedom" (*RR*, 187–88).

According to Burke, human life is a dialectic of the upward way, a heaping of perspective upon perspective in a logological quest for the adequate idea. For "the mind," as Spinoza tells us, "is more passive in proportion as it possesses inadequate ideas, and more active in pro-portion as it possesses adequate ideas" (*GM*, 147). That our ideas are necessarily incapable of total adequacy makes all thinking a version of the quest motif and renders significant the dialectical process itself.[15] The necessary inadequacy arises from our having no extrasymbolic access to the structure of reality. Moreover, a concomitant ambiguity arises from the impossibility of knowing absolutely where the factic-ity of nonsymbolic motion and the transcendence of symbolic action begin and end. Culture and nature intersect; where precisely we can-not say.

Dialectically considered (that is, "dramatistically" considered) men are not only *in nature*. The cultural accretions made possible by the lan-guage motive become a "second nature" with them. Here again we confront the ambiguities of substance, since symbolic communication is not merely an external instrument, but also intrinsic to men as agents. Its motivational properties characterize both "the human situa-tion" and what men are "in themselves."

Whereas there is an implicit irony in other notions of substance, with the dialectic substance the irony is explicit. For it derives its character from the systematic contemplation of the antinomies attendant upon the fact that we necessarily define a thing in terms of something else. "Dialectic substance" would thus be the overall category of dramatism, which treats of human motives in terms of verbal action. (*GM*, 33)

In *A Grammar of Motives* Burke's central claim is that "a linguistic factor at every point in human experience complicates and to some extent transcends the purely biological aspects of motivation" (*GM*, 318). Yet he is scrupulously careful to keep in mind two points he made in earlier books: first, that "to say that you can't talk about anything except by exemplifying the rules of talk is not identical with saying that our world is 'nothing' but the things we say about it" (*PLF*, xvi); second, that "vocabularies are not words alone but the social textures, the local psychoses, the institutional structures, the purposes and practices that lie behind these words" (*PC*, 182). In *The Rhetoric of Religion* and *Language as Symbolic Action,* however, the "nothing but" mentality makes itself felt at various junctures.

From *Counter-Statement* to *A Rhetoric of Motives* the dialectical model of the relationship between ideology, language, and sociohistorical reality predominates. Burke's virtuoso performance in *A Grammar of Motives,* wherein he dialectically manipulates the dramatistic pentad of act, agent, scene, agency, and purpose in order to show forth the combinatory possibilities of various philosophical systems (act = realism, agent = idealism, scene = materialism, agency = pragmatism, purpose = mysticism), indicates his awareness of how conceptual scheme, linguistic embodiment, and human reality cross-fertilize. The necessary ambiguity in the various ratios is traceable to the problematics of substance. If all determination is negation, then all definition is dialectical. (One can see how Burke's preoccupation with negation leads to his later view that the linguistic marvel of the negative is the origin and source of all value.) Yet, as I have already mentioned, within the ambiguous transaction language is treated as the foremost among equals and, for the purposes of analysis, as logically prior to the other factors. Its priority is in accordance with a methodology of treating man as the symbol-using animal. The temptation to temporize essence is there from the start.

Much of what goes on in *Permanence and Change, Attitudes Toward History,* and *The Philosophy of Literary Form* has already been documented, especially in the first chapter. Whether it be the ambiguousness of the relationship between text and context, strategy and situation, intrinsic and extrinsic, or the terms of the dream-prayer-chart triad, I have consistently emphasized the transactional model. My task now is to examine what happens to dramatism when it becomes, as it were, logologized in *The Rhetoric of Religion* and *Language as Symbolic Action*. That there is a discontinuity between dramatism and logology is my own invention to the extent that I offer a more rigid definition of dramatism than Burke himself does. That is, I insist upon dialectical transaction, and, as Burke would say, a reader does well to beware the strategic synonymizings and desynonymizings that an author's linguistic transformations yield. For Burke there is no discontinuity between the two; there is apposition rather than opposition. My position, however, is not without its contradictions, for I am also committed to the view that there is an entelechial drive in Burke's entire symbol system toward the "perfection" of logology. In this sense, I would insist upon a continuity. All this is a long-winded way of saying that logology is reductive only when it is not integrated with dramatism, in the most comprehensive sense of the latter term. To the degree that one downplays the transactional model, one tends to lapse into intrinsic criticism. In spite of this imposed value judgment I believe that logological analysis can do useful conceptual work for the practical critic, a belief the validity of which I hope to demonstrate by subjecting parts of Eliot's *Four Quartets* to such analysis.

"A way of seeing is also a way of not seeing," writes Burke in *Permanence and Change*. He extends the idea in *A Grammar of Motives*.

> Men seek for vocabularies that will be faithful *reflections* of reality. To this end, they must develop vocabularies that are *selections* of reality. And any selection of reality must, in some circumstances, function as a *deflection* of reality. Insofar as the vocabulary meets the needs of reflection, we can say that it has the necessary scope. In its selectivity, it is a reduction. Its scope and reflection become a deflection when the given terminology, or calculus, is not suited to the subject matter which it is designed to calculate. (*GM*, 59)

Burke's emphasis on the formative role of any vocabulary is meant to be a corrective on empiricism, for we must be reminded that "*our instruments are but structures of terms, and hence must be expected to manifest the nature of terms*. That is, we must always be admonished to remember, not that an experiment flatly and simply reveals *reality*, but rather that it *reveals only such reality as is capable of being revealed by this particular kind of terminology*" (*GM*, 313). The point is that "every vocabulary has its limits, imposed by the internal logic of its terms" (*GM*, 466). "We derive kinds of observations in accordance with the nature of the terms featured in the given philosophic idiom" (*GM*, 471).

Terministic screens, to use the parlance of *Language as Symbolic Action*, direct the attention.

> Not only does the nature of our terms affect the nature of our observations, in the sense that the terms direct the attention to one field rather than to another. Also, *many of the "observations" are but implications of the particular terminology in terms of which the observations are made*. In brief, much that we take as observations about "reality" may be but the spinning out of possibilities implicit in our particular choice of terms. (*LASA*, 46)

The passage above is symptomatic of what I have characterized as the later Burke in that it evinces a preoccupation with the implications of terminology. The inductive method, one may well agree, is hardly innocent. Paradigm in part determines significant fact, as Thomas Kuhn would say. But one must avoid the temptation to say that observations are nothing but the implications of the terminology in terms of which the observations are made. For the most part, Burke avoids that temptation. Yet it is worth noting how close his phrasing in the passage above comes to that reductionism. This is not to deprecate in any way Burke's well-taken point that one must acknowledge and take into account "the built-in 'deductive aspect' in any nomenclature" (*DD*, 22).

Consider, for example, Burke's incisive critique of R. S. Crane in an appendix to *A Grammar of Motives* entitled "The Problem of the Intrinsic." According to Burke, Crane's canonization of a neo-Aristotelian inductive method and his accompanying polemic against those critics who move from general principles to particular texts is fallacious precisely because it ignores the built-in deductive aspect in any nomenclature.

> If you consider philosophic or critical terminologies as languages, however (languages from which we derive kinds of observation in accordance with the nature of the terms featured in the given philosophic idiom), you find reasons to question his [Crane's] claims in advance. For the critic does not by any means begin his observations "from

scratch," but has a more or less systematically organized set of terms by which to distinguish and characterize the elements of the poem which he would observe. In this sense, one's observations will not be purely "inductive," even though they derive important modifications from the observing of the given poem. They will also in part (and in particular as to their grammar, or form) be deduced or derived from the nature of the language or terminology which the critic employs. Such languages are developed prior to individual observation (though one may adopt the well known philosophic subterfuge: "Let us begin simply by considering this object in front of us, just as it is"). . . . A given vocabulary coaches us to look for certain kinds of things rather than others—and this coaching of observation is a deductive process, insofar as one approaches the poem with a well-formed analytic terminology prior to the given analysis and derives observations from the nature of his terminology. (GM, 471–72)

This deductive aspect, then, undermines the self-sufficiency of any putatively intrinsic method. There is an ambiguous transaction between empirical observations and terminological implications. The irony is that Burke's sensitivity to critical terminologies as languages itself generates the critical terminology of logology, a terminology that at times succumbs to the intrinsic fallacy precisely by ignoring the transaction between observations and implications.

"The end is implicit in the beginning; all conclusions are foregone conclusions, once we have selected our ancestral principles" (GM, 312). It is easy to see how such a concentration upon the built-in deductive aspect of any terminology suggests a religious metaphor— the predestined implications of terms. Moreover, the more one focuses on the intrinsic interrelationships among terms within a system, the less one attends to the recalcitrance of reality. What starts out as an argument against the self-proclaimed innocence of the inductive method ends up becoming a method in itself. This is not to deny the importance of seeking out predestined implications and of recognizing the internal dynamics of the architectonic motive. Burke's contribution to the analysis of imagistic and conceptual patterns is impressive and sophisticated. He is able to isolate the three features that are essential to this sort of analysis: (1) dramatic alignment—what versus what, opposition, dissociation, desynonymization; (2) associative clusters—what equals what, apposition, association, synonymization, metaphor of chord; (3) narrative progression—what leads to what, metaphor of arpeggio. These three features, of course, are not altogether separable, for to be dialectically attuned to the possibilities of linguistic transformation is to attend to the resources of substitution, condensation, and displacement that any symbol system yields. My point is that such analysis needs to be complemented with the situation/strategy design of *The Philosophy of Literary Form*. Yet even in "Fact, Inference, and Proof in the Analysis of Literary Symbolism," the article in which Burke comes closest to endorsing intrinsic criticism per se by developing a critical procedure based on a theory of the index and a principle of the concordance, the social situation is kept in view.

> All told, one proceeds from such places, where the work comes to a temporary head. One radiates in search of labyrinthine internal consistency, while at the same time watching for progressions. One tries to be aware of one's shifts from "factuality" (the words on the page as they occur and recur, their concordance) and "thematic" generalizing (the inferences which a critic draws from that concordance). One watches for overall social tensions, and for the varying tactics of "purification" with regard to them. And one is thereby talking about symbolism, willy-nilly. (*FIP*, 172)

Before attempting to make sense out of the labyrinthine internal consistency of *The Rhetoric of Religion* it will prove useful to make a distinction between positive terms, dialectical terms, and ultimate terms. According to Burke, there are no negatives in nature; everything is positively what it is. Positive terms, then, denote observable referents. They refer to what Bentham called "real entities"—trees, chairs, buildings, and so on. (See *RM*, 183.) When we adopt an attitude of naive verbal realism, which, pragmatically speaking, we adopt most of the time, such terms provide no problem; in a normal context they are devoid of any referential opacity. This is not to say that Burke is abandoning the claim that reference is relative to a given conceptual scheme; he, in fact, prefers to regard terms as titles for situations rather than names for things and emphatically insists that nature is a linguistically inspired realm, not something given or separable from language. What he is saying is that at the simplest level of ordinary discourse we share an array of positive terms that is more or less indisputable. On the other hand, dialectical terms—Bentham's "fictitious entities"—are more or less disputable, even in a normal context.

> Here are words that belong, not in the order of *motion* and *perception*, but rather in the order of *action* and *idea*. Here are words for *principles* and *essence*. . . . We equate his [Bentham's] "fictitious entities" with "dialectical terms" because they are more concerned with *action* and *attitude* than with *perception* (they fall under the head of *ethics* and *form* rather than *knowledge* and *information*). You define them by asking how they behave; and part of this will be revealed by the discovery of secret modifiers implicit in the expression itself; hence Bentham's project for filling out the expression (phraseoplerosis) and discounting its image (archetypation). (*RM,* 184–85)

In other words, they are terms that cannot be properly understood except in regard to their opposites. To understand "order" we must understand "disorder." The same goes for justice and injustice, freedom and compulsion, beauty and ugliness, etc. The opposition, of course, is not always given in advance. Democracy can be dialectically opposed to any number of other political systems, and there is nothing unusual about two people calling each other antidemocratic. Rhetoric, as Aristotle said, is the art of proving opposites. "By 'positive' terms," then, "would be meant terms that imply no direct 'logical opposites,' as distinct from 'polar' terms that do imply logical opposites" (*RM,* 23n).

Ultimate terms, or god-terms, are a special subset of dialectical terms. They are the summarizing principles in various conceptual hierarchies. In certain symbol systems democracy is an ultimate value, and everything else is to be understood in *terms* of it. The same can be said for goodness, God, spirit, reason, psychic integration, or any other terms that function as ultimate values in given symbol systems. In *The Grammar of Motives,* for example, dramatism is a god-term, for everything else is to be understood in terms of Burke's dramatistic pentad.

In *The Rhetoric of Religion* Burke's central contention is that because theology deals with ultimate terms par excellence, it is uniquely qualified to provide the sorts of analogies that yield insight into the internal logic of symbol systems in particular and of language in general. "It is our 'logological' thesis," he writes, "that, since the theological use of language is thorough, the close study of theology and its forms will provide us with a good insight into the nature of language itself as a motive" (*RR*, vi). "What we say about *words*, in the empirical realm, will bear a notable likeness to what we say about *God*, in theology" (*RR*, 13–14). Logology (words about words) discovers in theology (words about God) the perfectionism implicit in all discourse. The movement in language toward higher and higher levels of abstraction and generalization Burke calls the entelechial motive, entelechy being Aristotle's term for the force that impels an entity to strive toward the kind of perfection appropriate to the kind of thing that it is. Theology strives toward God; language toward god-terms. The logological thesis, however, presupposes the dramatistic thesis that "in the study of human motives, we should begin with complex theories of transcendence (as in theology and metaphysics) rather than with terminologies of simplified laboratory experiment" (*RR*, 5).

Burke notes that there are four realms to which words may refer. First, there are words for the natural realm, "words for things, for material operations, physiological conditions, animality, and the like" (*RR*, 14). Such words are what we might call positive terms, in the sense described above. Second, there are words for the sociopolitical realm, "words for social relations, laws, right, wrong, rule, and the like" (*RR*, 14). Third, there are words about words, "the realm of dictionaries, grammar, etymology, philology, literary criticism, rhetoric, poetics, dialectics" (*RR*, 14)—all that Burke likes to think of as coming to a head in the discipline of logology. Fourth, there are words for the supernatural. These words exist whether or not one wishes to ascribe a truth value to them. Even the most rigorous of logical positivists, who would claim that supernatural statements are meaningless because they are incapable of scientific verification, would have to admit the empirical fact that such words exist in natural languages.

> However, even if one assumed it as beyond question that there really *is* a realm of the supernatural, nevertheless our *words* for the discussion of this realm are necessarily borrowed by analogy from our words for the other three orders: the natural, the socio-political and the verbal (or the

symbolic in general, as with the symbol systems of music, the dance, painting, architecture, the various specialized scientific nomenclatures, etc.).

The supernatural is by definition the realm of the "ineffable." And language by definition is not suited to the expression of the "ineffable." So our words for the fourth realm, the supernatural or "ineffable," are necessarily borrowed from our words for the sorts of things we can talk about literally, our words for the three empirical orders (the world of everyday experience). (*RR*, 15)

The analogical status of the fourth realm is elucidated in Burke's article "The Poetic Motive."

Since "God" by definition transcends all symbol-systems, we must begin, like theology, by noting that language is intrinsically unfitted to discuss the "supernatural" literally. For language is empirically confined to terms referring to physical nature, terms referring to sociopolitical relationships, and terms describing language itself. Hence, all the words for "God" must be used analogically—as were we to speak of God's "powerful arm" (a physical analogy), or of God as "lord" or "father" (a socio-political analogy) or of God as the "Word" (a linguistic analogy). The idea of God as a "person" would be derived by analogy from the sheerly physical insofar as persons have bodies, from the socio-political insofar as persons have status and from the linguistic insofar as the idea of personality implies such kinds of "reason" as flower in man's symbol-using prowess (linguistic, artistic, philosophic, scientific, moralistic, pragmatic). (Cited in *RR*, 15)

Even though words for the supernatural are parasitic upon words for the empirical, which comprise the first three realms, the fourth realm is best equipped to reveal the essence of symbol-systems in general. This is because the systematic rigor and perfectionism of theology, with its preponderance of ultimate terms, brings into relief the entelechial drive within all terministic screens, however inductive employers may claim those screens to be. This assumption, at any rate, is the first of Burke's six analogies.

According to the second analogy, "words are to the non-verbal things they name as Spirit is to Matter. . . . Verbal or symbolic action is analogous to the 'grace' that is said to 'perfect' nature" (*RR*, 16).

Again we see evidence of the dramatism/scientism opposition I earlier referred to, for the difference between symbol and symbolized is in some sense qualitative. As Burke puts it, "A duality of realm is implicit in our definition of man as the symbol-using animal. Man's animality is in the realm of sheer matter, sheer motion. But his 'symbolicity' adds a dimension of action not reducible to the non-symbolic—for by its very nature as symbolic it cannot be identical with the non-symbolic" (*RR*, 16). It is worth remembering, however, that while the difference between these two realms is conceived as being qualitative, the symbol-using animal is in no position to make absolute distinctions (except in theory). For from the point of view of his particular perception, he can only relatively separate out culture and nature. "In all such cases, where symbolic operations can influence bodily processes, the realm of the natural (in the sense of the less-than-verbal) is seen to be pervaded, or *inspirited,* by the realm of the verbal, or symbolic. And in this sense the realm of the symbolic corresponds (in our analogy) to the realm of the 'supernatural'" (*RR*, 17). "Nature," as Burke puts it elsewhere, "is emblematic of the spirit imposed upon it by man's linguistic genius" (*LASA*, 362).

There is no escaping the fact, however, that at times Burke talks more dualistically and less dialectically than my interpretation implies. Two later articles—"Theology and Logology" and "(Nonsymbolic) Motion/(Symbolic) Action"—are symptomatic of this tendency.

In "Theology and Logology" the human capacity for language is described as "familiarity with arbitrary, conventional symbol-systems in general."[16] "Language," Burke writes, "is one vast menagerie of implications—and with each channel of such there are the makings of a corresponding fulfillment proper to its kind, a perfection in germ." Quoting Coleridge, he notes that "language itself does as it were *think* for us."[17] His conception of logology is avowedly dualistic.

> Logology is as dualistic in its way as theology is, since the logological distinction between symbolic action and nonsymbolic motion is as "polar" as theology's distinctions between mind and body, or spirit and matter. Logology holds that "persons" *act,* whereas things but *move,* or are *moved.* And "personality" in the human sense depends upon the ability and opportunity to acquire an arbitrary, conventional symbol-system such as a tribal, familial language.[18]

Whereas "behaviorism is essentially monistic, in assuming that the difference between verbal behavior and nonverbal behavior . . . is but a manner of *degree*. . . . logology is dualistically vowed to the assumption that we here confront a difference in *kind*."[19] In spite of this dualistic language, however, Burke remains sensitive to the importance of context. "There are contexts in the sense that a whole text is the context for any part of the text. There are contexts in the sense of whatever 'background,' historical, geographical, personal, local, or universal, might be conceived of as the scene to which the symbolic act of the author as agent explicitly or implicitly refers, over and above the nature of the text's sheerly internal relationships."[20] The dramatistic awareness of the grammatical, rhetorical, symbolical, and ethical dimensions of symbolic action and of the terministic pentad itself is thus kept in view. Burke does not at all subscribe to poststructuralist textualism. As he observes:

> Although . . . logology is always much more at home with a text than not, it must constantly admonish itself regarding the limitations of a text as the adequate presentation of a symbolic act, and as instructions for the reader to reenact it. In comparison with a well-edited musical score, for instance, the literary text when considered as instructions for performance is seen to be quite deficient. And think how impoverished the text of a drama is, when viewed as instructions for the reader to reenact it in his imagination.[21]

In "(Nonsymbolic) Motion/(Symbolic) Action" the same dualistic attitude predominates. The operative distinction is between selfhood (nonsymbolic motion) and personhood (symbolic action). "In terms of nonsymbolic motion, the Self is a physiological organism, separated from all others of its kind at the moment of parturition. In terms of symbolic action, it becomes a 'person' by learning the language of its tribe with corresponding identities and roles."[22] Self "would be grounded in the realm of nonsymbolic motion and would mature into what one would call a 'person' in the realm of symbolic action."[23] A person, in other words, is an ensemble of social roles and symbolic identifications made possible by the acquisition of a culture-specific language. Whereas the self's sensations are immediately its own, the person is "a member of a community (Culture) characterized by motives in the realm of symbolic action."[24] Although there can be no action without motion and although "the realm of nonsymbolic motion needs no realm of symbolic action,"[25] "symbolic action is *not* reducible to terms of sheer motion. (Symbolicity involves not just a difference of *degree,* but a motivational difference in *kind.*)"[26] From an ontological point of view, then, an absolute duality of realm is implicit in Burke's definition of man as the symbol-using animal. From an existential point of view, the individual human being, despite the obdurate centrality of his own nervous system, has no nonsymbolic access to the structure of reality and must live perforce in the fog of symbols where self and person, action and motion, animality and symbolicity ambiguously intersect.

In the third analogy Burke associates his theory of the negative with negative theology, that procedure whereby one defines God in terms of what he is not—finite, mutable, comprehensible, and so on. "Language referring to the realm of the non-verbal is necessarily talk about things in terms of what they are not" (*LASA,* 5)—a point that follows from the qualitative difference between symbol and symbolized. It is thus the case that "language to be used properly must be 'discounted.' We must remind ourselves that, whatever *correspondence* there is between a *word* and the *thing* it names, the word is *not* the thing. . . . But because these realms coincide so usefully at certain points, we tend to overlook the areas where they radically diverge. We gravitate spontaneously towards a naive verbal realism" (*RR,* 18).

The principle of the negative is closely aligned with the paradox of substance, which derives from our necessarily having to define a thing in terms of something else. As Burke puts it, "the negative is not a 'fact' of nature, but a function of a symbol system" (*RR,* 20). It is "purely a linguistic marvel . . . there are no negatives in nature, every natural condition being positively what it is" (*RR,* 19). The negative, in other words, is a logical device, "not a 'fact' of nature but a function of a symbol system, as intrinsically symbolic as the square root of minus one" (*RR,* 20).

Burke's interest, however, is not in the "*propositional* negative" (*RR,* 20), the "it is not" of definition. Nor is it in the role of the negative as regards matters of expectancy. If I am to meet someone at a bar at a given time and that person has forgotten the appointment, then my expectations have been violated. His absence becomes a positive presence as regards my psychological state. Nor does Burke deal in any detail with the existentialist notion of negativity—the Sartrian claim, for example, that, in its capacity to project possibilities and to envisage worlds different from the contingent reality of the moment, consciousness can constitute a lack in the actual world, rendering the world a nothingness through an imaginative act of nihilation (Sartre's term).[27] Quite properly, Burke insists that "Dramatistically (that is, viewing the matter in terms of 'action'), one should begin with the *hortatory* negative, the negative of command, as with the 'Thou shalt nots' of the Decalogue" (*RR*, 20). The hortatory negative is central because from the logological perspective

> Moral evil arises not from the "positives" of natural existence, but from hortatory resources embedded in the negative, which qua negative is not "positively real," its only "reality" in the "positive" sense being in the sound or look of the word, or in the neural vibrations needed for thinking of it. Since it is "what man adds to nature," and since it defines the discriminatory nature of an act (the yes or no that make the difference between will and will-not), in this sense it is a function of the "will." . . . The ideas of act, will, and the negative mutually imply one another. . . . The principle of the negative is intrinsic to dominion, owing to the role of the negative in the forming of laws. (*RR*, 89–90)

Logology, then, looks upon evil as a species of the negative, that linguistic marvel which is a resource of terministic screens. The very possibilities of obedience and disobedience are grounded in language, for language generates the possibility of the hortatory negative and is thereby the source and origin of all value. Moral disobedience derives not from the breaking of the law but from the very linguistic formulation of it.

> All was permissive in Eden but the eating of the one forbidden fruit, the single negative that set the conditions for the Fall (since, St. Paul pointed out, only the law can make sin, as Bentham was later to point out that only the law can make crime). . . . The word-using animal not only understands a thou-shalt-not; it can carry the principle of the negative a step further, and answer the thou-shalt-not with a disobedient No. Logologically, the distinction between natural innocence and fallen man hinges about this problem of language and the negative. Eliminate language from nature, and there can be no moral disobedience. (*RR*, 186–87)

There is, Burke contends, a cycle of terms implicit in the idea of order such that once "thou shalt not" is posited, everything else follows tautologically. Figure 1 gives an idea of the essence of order and the closed complex of mutual implications that Burke detemporizes and extracts from the first three chapters of Genesis. According to Burke, through its stories of Creation, the Fall, etc., Genesis temporizes essence in that it embodies in narrative form a cycle of terms that tautologically revolve around the idea of order. "'Myth' is characteristically a terminology of quasi-narrative terms for the expression of relationships that are not intrinsically narrative, but 'circular' or 'tautological'" (*RR*, 258). To validate and legitimize the *authority* of a moral order an appeal is made to God as *author* of that order. It may also be the case that in order to validate and legitimize the authority of the order that logological analysis affords, Burke makes an analogous appeal to language as author of that order.

This matter of the negative and the tautological cycle of terms is inordinately complicated, and it will not make complete sense, if it makes sense at all, until we have considered the other analogies. This makes for an interesting note in passing. The very form of Burke's analogies—they are numbered from one to six and dealt with sequentially—illustrates his point about the built-in deductive aspect in any nomenclature, the tautological cycle. For the analogies mutually imply one another, and any order in which they might be presented would be equally as intelligible or confusing as any other, which offers little consolation for the reader but a rhetoric of consolation for the expositor. The chordal vision, though logically prior, must be temporally posterior.

The fourth analogy "involves the linguistic drive towards a Title of Titles, a logic of entitlement that is completed by thus rising to ever and ever higher orders of generalization." It dwells on "the nature of language as a process of entitlement, leading in the secular realm towards an overall title of titles . . . a 'god-term' . . . analogous to the overall entitling role played by the theologian's word for the godhead" (*RR*, 25). A god-term, as I suggested before, is an ultimate term in a hierarchy of terms within a given symbol system, a term whose entitling power essentializes the whole and whose spirit infuses itself throughout the system, "tying the particulars of a work together with the overall spirit signalized by its unitary and unifying title" (*RR*,

FIGURE I. Cycle of Terms Implicit in the Idea of "Order"

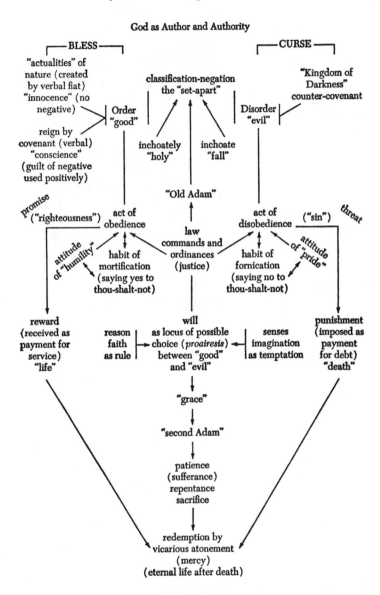

God as Author and Authority

┌─BLESS─┐   ┌─CURSE─┐

"actualities" of
nature (created
by verbal fiat)   classification-negation   "Kingdom of
"innocence" (no   the "set-apart"   Darkness"
negative)   Order   Disorder   counter-covenant
                       "good"   "evil"
reign by
covenant (verbal)   inchoately   inchoate
"conscience"   "holy"   "fall"
(guilt of negative
used positively)
                                 "Old Adam"

promise
("righteousness")   act of   act of   ("sin")   threat
                   obedience   law   disobedience
attitude   commands and   attitude
of "humility"   habit of   ordinances   habit of   of "pride"
                 mortification   (justice)   fornication
                 (saying yes to   (saying no to
                 thou-shalt-not)   thou-shalt-not)

reward   punishment
(received as   reason │ will   senses   (imposed as
payment for   faith │ as locus of possible imagination   payment
service)   as rule│ choice (proairesis) ◄─ as temptation   for debt)
"life"   │ between "good"   "death"
                          and "evil"

                          "grace"

                       "second Adam"

                         patience
                        (sufferance)
                        repentance
                         sacrifice

                      redemption by
                   vicarious atonement
                        (mercy)
                  (eternal life after death)

Source: Burke, *The Rhetoric of Religion.* Reprinted by permission of the University of California Press.

175). Every symbol system, in other words, has an entelechial drive toward attaining the perfection appropriate to the kind of thing it is. To this I shall return shortly.

First, let me disrupt the chronology and briefly characterize the sixth analogy before examining the fifth at length and relating it to what has hitherto been discussed. The sixth analogy likens the relation between name and thing named to the relations of the persons in the Trinity. From the relations of power, wisdom, and love within the Trinity, Burke is able to derive similarities to the power of naming, the knowledge of the thing named, and the communion between the symbolized and the symbol, the latter having something to do with love. I find his subsequent movement from this to Hegelian dialectic and then to Coleridge's dialectical pentad rather confusing. It is not easy to see the point. I am not saying that this section is unintelligible—my mode of presentation is hardly fair—but the sixth analogy does not connect with the issues I find most pertinent, and I shall thus say no more about it.

In the fifth analogy, "the Augustinian distinction between 'time' and 'eternity' is treated in its linguistically analogous form, as the distinction between the unfolding of a sentence through the materiality of its parts and the unitary non-material essence or meaning of the sentence" (*RR*, 3).

> Here the succession of words in a sentence would be analogous to the "temporal." But the *meaning* of the sentence is an *essence,* a kind of fixed significance or definition that is not confined to any of the sentence's parts, but rather pervades or inspirits the sentence as a whole. Such meaning, I would say, is analogous to "eternity." In contrast with the flux of the sentence, where each syllable arises, exists for a moment, and then "dies" to make room for the next stage of the continuing process, the meaning is "non-temporal," though embodied (made incarnate) in a temporal series. The meaning in its unity or simplicity "just *is.*" (*RR,* 27)

The time/eternity metaphor is the master analogy, the hub from which everything else radiates. It connects with the first analogy: the relationship between temporal words and the timeless Word, with the second: matter is to spirit as nonverbal nature is to words corresponds with matter is to spirit as temporal words are to timeless meaning, with the third: the principle of the negative makes for the possibility of terms for order and hence for essences, and with the fourth: if linguistic entitlement leads to a search for the title of titles, then what is a god-term but the unitary essence or meaning writ large so that it might inspirit an entire discourse?

With regard to the latter proposition, the equation reads something like this: Time is to eternity as the particulars in the unfolding of a sentence are to the sentence's unitary meaning, and as the unfolding of the unitary meanings of sentences are to the unitary meaning of the discourse as a whole. The essentializing title of the work (this may or may not be the work's official title) thus corresponds with eternity or, to use a linguistic metaphor, with the synchronic whole, and the narrative unfolding of that work corresponds with time or, to continue the metaphor, with the diachronic sequence of words, the syntagmatic axis of successive meanings. As Burke puts it, "The word is the first full 'perfection' of a term. And we move from it either way as our base, either 'back' to the dissolution of meaning that threatens it by reason of its accidental punwise associates, or 'forward' to its inclusion in a 'higher meaning,' which attains its perfection in the sentence" (*FIP*, 146).

It is obvious that what we are dealing with again is the temporizing of essence, the spinning out into narrative of a series of logical relationships. The tautological cycle of terms, as I suggested in the last chapter, is Burke's version of the hermeneutic circle, that paradoxical interdependence of part and whole, according to which the whole can be understood only through the parts—these are necessarily presented and perceived chronologically—and the parts can be understood only through the whole—this is timeless in that it is logically prior, but it can only be excavated through a temporal process of inference and guesswork along the way; the whole inspirits the parts. "We do confront a problem of *beginnings* here. Insofar as the sentence is an idea, or principle, it proceeds according to a plan that is one kind of 'first,' a sort of 'final cause' that guides the actual choice of words. Yet the wording of the sentence, in its step-by-step temporal sequence, involves another kind of 'first,' since each part of the sentence is 'prior' to the part that follows it" (*RR*, 143). Logologically, then, eternity equals the predestinated implications of terms, their cyclical or tautological aspects, whereas time equals the one-directioned rectilinearity of narrative. In any given discourse, of course, the two aspects interfuse, given the temporal character of communicating and understanding, the paradox of the hermeneutic circle.

Relatively speaking, Burke argues, we can locate two different sorts of style, the narrative or rectilinear style of, say, Genesis (the kind of temporal sequence embodied in the Biblical myth), and the cycle of terms he has found to revolve endlessly about the idea of Order, the timeless terministic cluster, the tautological cycle of terms for order (see Figure 1).[28] Through the temporizing of essence many stories are able to merge a mythic account of origins with a theory of sanctions for a given order of governance. Such a rhetorical device is of much interest, for, according to Burke, we must always be on the lookout for "puns of logical and temporal priority whereby the logical idea of a thing's essence can be translated into a temporal or narrative equivalent by statement in terms of the thing's source or beginning" (*RM*, 13). One can also define essence in terms of the end, as, for example, equating someone's criminal nature with his ending up on the gallows. "We don't usually realize how often we use the quasi-successive of narrative when actually we are but giving a synonym" (*RR*, 225). That is, "terms that are logically synonymous or that tautologically imply one another can be treated narratively as preceding from one to the other, like cause to effect" (*RR*, 208). One can say that death comes from sin, that it is a narrative way of suggesting guilt, a kind of capital punishment. Or one can translate things into a vague, hypothetical past, saying that it was the fruit of that forbidden tree, whose mortal taste brought death into the world and all our woe. In any case, one is talking about the idea of order and its implications, among other things, of course.

(In his brilliant analysis of St. Augustine's *Confessions*, Burke shows how the bipartite structure of the book illustrates the difference between the narrative and essentialist styles. In this instance, the distinction seems to work perfectly. In books one through nine Augustine offers us a narrative of memories, existential instances, whereas from book ten onward he seeks to articulate the principles and philosophy of memory, essential definitions. In Augustine's terms, this is clearly a movement from time to eternity.)

The practical methodology that logological analysis entails is exemplified by an article referred to earlier, "Fact, Inference, and Proof in the Analysis of Literary Symbolism." While there is nothing *necessarily* antidramatistic about this sort of analysis, it does tend toward regarding the work as nothing but a tautological cycle of terms, a cycle that is narratively realized through the temporizing of essence and uses all the resources of dramatic alignments, associative clusters, and narrative progressions to achieve its given end, its entelechial fulfillment. The context of situation is attenuated to the degree that the intraverbal context is underscored. Such a methodology might seem to presuppose the semantic autonomy of the text and to militate against the context theorem of meaning. I shall try to demonstrate that this is not entirely the case by restoring intention through the notion of implication. Yet even in *The Rhetoric of Religion,* the most overtly logological of Burke's works, he remains attuned to "the nature of language as petition, exhortation, persuasion, and dissuasion," the fact "that, first of all . . . words will be modes of posture, act, attitude, gesture" (*RR,* 255). The very theory of the negative, we will remember, depends upon the hortatory dimension of language.

What we have to focus on, Burke claims, is "the relation between narrative unfolding and the cyclical recurrence of key terms" (*RR,* 229). Or, to put it in terms of the chord/arpeggio metaphor first enunciated in *The Philosophy of Literary Form,* we have to watch out for "the narrative kind of equation, whereby *A equals B* because *A leads to B*" (*PLF,* xiv). We have to remember, of course, that his term "terms" refers to both sensory images and ideological concepts.

The notion of essentialization by entitlement is further developed in an essay reproduced in *Language as Symbolic Action* as "What Are the Signs of What? (A Theory of 'Entitlement')." Here Burke reverses the slogan of naive verbal realism—words are the signs of things— into the logological slogan—things are the signs of words. He poses the rhetorical question thus:

> Might words be found to possess a "spirit" peculiar to their nature as words? And might the things of experience then become in effect the materialization of such a spirit, the manifestation of this spirit in visible tangible bodies?
>
> If such verbal spirits, or essences, were enigmatically symbolized in nonverbal things, then their derivation (so far as causes within the natu-

ral world are concerned) could come from both the forms of language and from the group motives that language possesses by reason of its nature as a social product. (*LASA*, 361)

Our concentration, then, should not be so much on the word/thing relationship as on "speech as the 'entitling' of complex nonverbal situations." "The sentence is to be viewed after the analogy of a title, which sums up an essence or trend or slant, rather than describing the conditions that would be required for the thing named really to happen or exist" (*LASA*, 361). The same analogy writ large applies to the discourse as a whole.

> Thus, in mediating between the social realm and the realm of nonverbal nature, words communicate to things the spirit that the society imposes upon the words which have come to be the "names" for them. The things are in effect the visible tangible material embodiments of the spirit that infuses them through the medium of words. And in this sense, things become the signs of the genius that resides in words. The things of nature, as so conceived, become a vast pageantry of social-verbal masques and costumes and guild-like mysteries, not just a world of sheer natural objects, but a parade of spirits. . . . Nature is emblematic of the spirit imposed upon it by man's linguistic genius. (*LASA*, 362)

That Burke emphasizes both the forms of language and the group motives that language possesses by reason of its nature as a social product is evidence that the transactional model, which I associate with dramatism per se, is being resuscitated. If nature is emblematic of the spirit imposed upon it by man's linguistic genius, then in no way can it be absolutely separated from culture. The relationship between the two must be dialectical. The ambiguity of the transaction is the mystery. Burke himself refers to the familiar dramatism/scientism opposition in this essay. He notes that " 'Action' encompasses the realm of entities that respond to words as such. . . . And 'motion' encompasses the realm of entities that do not respond to words as such" (*LASA*, 366). The dramatism side of the opposition emphasizes the poetic and rhetorical uses of language (its functions as expression, persuasion, and inducement to attitude or action). Scientism emphasizes knowledge.

Accordingly, whereas the scientist emphasis spontaneously, almost automatically, begins with problems of the direct relation between the verbal sign and its corresponding nonverbal referent, a Dramatistic approach to the analysis of language starts with problems of terministic catharsis (which is another word for "rebirth," transcendence, transubstantiation, or simply "transformation" in the sense of the technically developmental, as when a major term is found somehow to have moved on, and thus to have in effect changed its nature either by adding new meanings to its old nature, or by yielding place to some other term that henceforth takes over its functions wholly or in part). (*LASA*, 367)

In this sense, I think, the logological and the dramatistic may be integrated.

The problem with logology as it is presented in *The Rhetoric of Religion* is that it tends to downplay the prayer and chart components of symbolic action. The tautological cycle of terms and the methodology of practical criticism that goes with it focus too much attention upon intrinsic terministic interrelationships and neglect too conspicuously the nonverbal scenes that support the verbal acts. Moreover, instead of saying that morality can be fruitfully analyzed in terms of the linguistic marvel of the negative, Burke tends to make language literally the source and origin of all value, thus committing precisely the kind of genetic fallacy that logological analysis is equipped to reveal. For it is one thing to use the hortatory negative as a device for analyzing the moral order, quite another to derive the moral order from it. (Not that I am prepared to say where the moral order really comes from, any more than I would be prepared to say where civil society really comes from. There seems no need to indulge in such speculation. For are we not condemned to understand our prepolitical and premoral selves in terms of our political and moral selves? That complicating linguistic factor would seem to guarantee this.) But the most dangerous aspect of logology is that it might seem to endorse what I have called, somewhat derisively, following Hirsch, the myth of semantic autonomy. I do not think, however, that this is the case.

Burke claims, as I have noted earlier, that the theological notions of providence and predestination are narrative equivalents for the principle of terministic circularity. This, I would suggest, is intentionalist language. Terms are predestinated by an author—this corresponds to what Hirsch calls the individual principle of authorial will—but they must unfold in temporal sequence. Because of the paradox of the hermeneutic circle, we must make some sort of guess regarding a work's "intrinsic genre"—"that sense of the whole by means of which an interpreter can correctly understand any part in its determinacy."[29] Intrinsic genre, then, corresponds to the unitary essence of the discourse.

> Speech-act theory, in the form developed by Grice and Strawson, reasserts the linguistic priority of intention and hence of mind. It asserts the indeterminacy, and hence the partial dependence, of meaning with respect to form and convention. It follows that a guess about intention is in principle a permanent feature of interpretation which no methodological system could ever remove. The guess itself cannot be fully determined by stylistic features, nor can the stylistic features definitively confirm the guess concerning the intended meaning.[30]

Every nomenclature, in other words, has its own built-in deductive aspect.

Terminological implications explain away the whole problem of unconscious intentions. This is because implications are part of an intentional verbal act even if the author is unaware of them. This fact neither infringes upon intentionality nor gives credence to the notion of meaning containment. For the temporal character of both communicating and understanding makes unsurprising the fact that an author sometimes does not know the full implications of what he intended to communicate, that is, of what his terms predestinated, until some time later, if at all. The same applies *mutatis mutandis* to the reader. In this way it may be said that implications seem to derive from the genius of the symbol system itself.

Five

The Rhetoric of Religion
and "Burnt Norton"

THE INFLUENCE OF St. Augustine and F. H. Bradley on the substance of T. S. Eliot's thought has often been recognized, but the extent to which their influence affects the structure of his thought has not received all the attention it might have.

The structure of *The Confessions of St. Augustine* can be broken down into two parts. In books one through nine Augustine presents a narrative of memories, whereas from book ten onward he seeks to define the principles of time and memory. The two parts illustrate the difference between what Burke calls the rectilinear and cyclical styles. The former is chronological in that it deals with a sequence of events; the latter is tautological in that it deals with a philosophic network of logical implications, the cycle of interrelated terms that any discourse gives rise to. In Augustine's view, the movement from chronology to logic, from a narrative of autobiographical confessions to a system of theological professions, is clearly a movement from time (words) to eternity (the Word). I shall suggest that a comparable though less straightforward structure is evident in "Burnt Norton."

The structure of Bradley's *Appearance and Reality* can also be broken down into two parts. The movement of Bradley's dialectic is from a stance of epistemological skepticism to one of philosophical idealism, from the chaos of appearance to the coherence of reality. The first part of his book mercilessly exposes the limitations of discursive reasoning and the paradoxes and contradictions it inevitably produces. According to Bradley, human reason is a defective instrument and therefore incapable of attaining any adequate grasp of ultimate truth. The problem is that his deconstruction of appearance is so devastating that many readers find his reconstruction of reality unconvincing in comparison. I shall suggest that Eliot runs a similar risk, for both men openly admit that their discourse is inadequate to the task they assign it but nonetheless fare forward, attempting to use analogy as a device for transcending the limitations of thought and language.

The connection between Eliot and Burke is less direct. Their mutual concern with Augustine, however, is a common factor; the cornerstone of Burke's *Rhetoric of Religion* is a long and complex essay on verbal action in *The Confessions*. More important, Burke's critical vocabulary in itself—especially as it pertains to his discussion of the perfectionism built into religious language, to his ideas about the rhetoric of the ineffable, and to his view of the oxymoron as the master trope of mysticism—sheds light on Eliot's rhetorical strategy in "Burnt Norton." Religious language, of course, is quintessentially purposive and always gravitates toward teleological rather than mechanistic explanation. Even though words for the supernatural are derived from words for the empirical, "once a terminology has been developed for special theological purposes the order can become reversed" (*RR*, 7). The supernatural can infuse itself throughout the "lower" realms as if it were their source or ground, creating a new hierarchy according to which all purpose flows from God, the term of terms. Language, Burke wryly observes, is rotten with perfection.

According to the dramatistic pentad of *A Grammar of Motives,* the featuring of the term "purpose" culminates in mysticism. This is because a predisposition toward teleological explanation achieves its own perfection in the contemplation of final cause and ultimate purpose. The mystical strategy, Burke suggests, comes to the fore in situations of instability and transition, for "precisely at such times of general hesitancy, the mystic can compensate for his own doubts about human purpose by submerging himself in some vision of a *universal,* or *absolute,* or *transcendent* purpose with which he would identify himself" (*GM*, 288). Certainly, the prewar period during which the first of Eliot's quartets was written and the period of war during which the rest of them were written qualify as times of general hesitancy in this regard. It does not seem unreasonable to propose tentatively that Eliot was moved by the currents of his historical moment to make an "in spite of" spiritual affirmation. In such a context of situation a transcendental strategy is called for, especially if one wishes to endorse an implicitly religious frame of acceptance by way of compensation for the secular chaos of war. Thus, let us say for now, in the spirit of prophesying after the event, that we should expect to find a plethora of teleological terms in *Four Quartets*. Also, in accordance with the transcendental strategy invoked, we should expect to find sophisticated dialectical exploitation of terms for the temporal and terms for the timeless, and all manner of merger and division therein.

On the level of rhetoric the master trope of mysticism is the oxymoron. As Burke puts it, "the incongruity of the grotesque-mystical comes to a focus in the oxymoron: one hears silence, peoples loneliness, and sees in the dark." Mysticism specializes in "twilight states" (*ATH*, 59–60).[1] "And since the mystic communicates ultimately in terms of the oxymoron (the figure that combines contradictory elements within a single expression), we would see in the packing of an image or idea with divergent motives a more or less remote instance of "literary mysticism" (*RM*, 324). We should therefore be on the lookout for "fixed clusters or amalgams that amount in the end to oxymorons, as you find that the poet had fused, by interacting associations, symbols logically at odds: life, death, eternity, mother, sexual desire, castration, health, disease, art, forests or the sea, all linked indiscriminately together, so that he can talk of one by talking of the others, and when he centers upon one, the others flicker about the edges of his imagery" (*ATH*, 64). The analytical process demands less vigilance in the case of Eliot since he is ultimately operating in terms of a Christian vocabulary of motives, and "in the mystery of Christ as sacrificial king, the principle of the oxymoron is obvious, in Christ's double role as victimized and victorious" (*RM*, 328). A martyr's action is identical to his passion.

Also to be attended to is the interaction of dialectical transcendence and dramatic catharsis, which are both agents of transformation—the one on an ideational or conceptual level (the treating of contingent things in terms of a beyond), the other on a bodily or emotional level (purgation by the imitation of victimage). The first mode of transformation calls to mind the logological analogies discussed in the last chapter as well as the general matter of the temporizing of essence, of the rectilinear and cyclical styles. In a mystic frame of reference the second mode would involve the self-victimage of mortification, which, as I pointed out in the second chapter, falls on the suicidal slope of motivation. It connects as well with notions of the negative way. The logological reverberations are unmistakable.

On a purely technical or linguistic level, however, the deployment of the mystic oxymoron (which, it should be understood, I am treating more as a general rhetorical strategy embracing also paradox and contradiction than as a particular trope) raises the problem of expressibility. Only a poet as philosophically astute as Eliot would have the courage to raise within the context of the poem itself the very problem that threatens to undermine the cogency of his presentation. The problem is obvious because "in a sense, of course, literary mysticism is a contradiction in terms. For as [William] James points out, the mystic's experience is 'ineffable.' But poetry being expressive, mystic poetry would have to 'express the ineffable'" (*RM,* 324). Eliot is hypersensitive to the fact that he is trying to express "something that is probably quite ineffable," to use his phrase from "The Dry Salvages."[2] It is simply the case that given the relational and temporal character of thought and language, the limitations of which F. H. Bradley's tactical projection of epistemological skepticism exposes, knowledge of the Absolute is conceptually impossible. How then can a conceptual impossibility be rendered into a poetic possibility? Perhaps, we might predict, through a proliferation of cross-fertilizing analogies derived from the four pyramids of language—the natural, the sociopolitical, the logological, and the supernatural. As we saw in the last chapter, the supernatural is by definition conceived by analogy, though once the analogy is made it can infuse itself throughout the lower orders as if it were their source or ground. One needs empirical terms for gracious experiences.

The problem of expressibility is at the core of the *Four Quartets;* it arises from the very nature of Eliot's subject matter—the relationship between the temporal and the timeless. As Wilhelm Windelband points out, "concepts become poorer in intension in proportion as their extension increases, so that the content *zero* must correspond to the extension *infinity*" (*GM,* 87). In other words, concepts of the greatest generality have the least empirical content. When reference is infinite, meaning is infinitesimal. At an ultimate level purpose and no purpose become identical. Consider, for example, Heidegger treating

Nothingness as the ground of Being. Nothingness seems substantive only because its content is zero, its extension infinity. But in a different context the same could be said for Being. From the logological point of view there is no need to view such concepts as falling under either the rubric of ideological mystification or that of divine mystery. It suffices to view them as rhetorical and dialectical resources and to examine how they work, uncovering the structure of motives they realize and imply. The immediate question is this: where locutionary meaning is at the very least imprecise, can illocutionary force and perlocutionary consequence yet abide? Can religious truth, which by definition cannot be caught in the web of language, nonetheless be analogically apprehended through it?

By way of introduction there is only one more point I wish to make. This concerns the relationship between mystical transcendence and infantile regression, between the eschatological and the scatological. Early in *The Grammar of Motives* Burke contends that

> when we are examining, from the standpoint of the Symbolic, meta-
> physical tracts that would deal with "fundamentals" and get to the
> "bottom" of things, this last set of meanings can admonish us to be on
> the look-out for what Freud might call "cloacal" motives, furtively in-
> terwoven with speculations that may on the surface seem wholly ab-
> stract. An "acceptance" of the universe on this plane may also be a
> roundabout way of "making peace with faeces." (*GM*, 23)

Later on he notes that such fundamentalism often involves a demonic trinity. "The substantial nature of imagery may often produce an unin-tended burlesque of substance, in drawing upon the ambiguities of the cloacal, where are united, in a 'demonic trinity,' the three principles of the erotic, urinary, and excremental" (*GM*, 301–2). The point is made explicitly in reference to Eliot's *Murder in the Cathedral*. "The imag-ery of pollution by which the mystic frequently expresses the sense of drought (as with Eliot's 'Merdes' in the Cathedral, an *ecclesia super cloacam*) suggests that mystic thoroughness ultimately involves the recognition of fundamental tabus at the very moment of their tran-scendence" (*GM*, 302).

My concern in this chapter will be less with the scatological than the infantile simply because the *Quartets* are not particularly amenable to the demonic treatment. The first movement of "East Coker," replete with its flesh, fur, feces, dung, and death, might seem an exception, but it could hardly be said that the cloacal motives are furtively interwoven with abstract speculations; the feces is clearly in view. Of more interest in this regard is a short passage from the opening of "The Dry Salvages." River is the antecedent of "his."

> His rhythm was present in the nursery bedroom,
> In the rank ailanthus of the April dooryard,
> In the smell of grapes on the autumn table,
> And the evening circle in the winter gaslight.
>
> (ll. 11–14)

It does not take much ingenuity to see the rhythm of micturition present in the nursery bedroom—we might even associate the flow of liquid with the tears that often accompany bed-wetting—but it takes a great deal of ingenuity to see the river as seminal in the second line quoted. Nonetheless, it seems to me that the river, with its flowing liquid, is to be seen as the river of linear time (the biological movement of an individual's life, the flow of blood within his veins), of urinary evacuation, and of seminal creation. The ailanthus has both celestial and phallic connotations, corresponding to the higher romantic and lower animalistic aspects of sexuality. It is the tree of heaven on which the silkworm feeds and thrives. Its smell is rank, like that of sexuality itself, as Eliot would have it. (I shall later discuss Eliot's tendency to see final cause in youthful sexuality, examining his treatment of Dante's experience in the *Vita Nuova*.) Accepting my hypothesis, which I leave to the reader to put together explicitly, might we not perceive a connection between the ailanthus and the *ail* of the garlic and sapphires in the mud that clot the bedded axletree? The axletree, of course, is at the still point of the turning world, a principle of heavenly order *bedded* in the material world, an image of the God-man, the Word become flesh. Fecundity itself is part of the clotting factor. Whether one accepts this extravagant collocation is not of consequence. What is of consequence is how any poem affords a coagulation of motives that is not entirely rationally explicable. The celestial and the bodily are condemned to be interwoven in some measure, given the four pyramids of language and their interconnections. In any case, let me now turn to the first of the quartets. For the most part I shall confine my remarks to "Burnt Norton," but the others will be considered insofar as they illuminate specific issues.

The commencement of "Burnt Norton" reverses the movement in Augustine's *Confessions* by dealing at first with the principles of time and memory and then turning to a brief narrative of memories or, to be more accurate, of remembered possibilities, the realm of what might have been. The principles, however, are darkly given.

> Time present and time past
> Are both perhaps present in time future,
> And time future contained in time past.
> If all time is eternally present
> All time is unredeemable.
> What might have been is an abstraction
> Remaining a perpetual possibility
> Only in a world of speculation.
> What might have been and what has been
> Point to one end, which is always present.
>   (ll. 1–10)

The motive underlying this passage is likely subversive, for the passage is difficult to disentangle conceptually, and one suspects that even at this point in his career Eliot still shared Bradley's conviction that "a relational way of thought—any one that moves by the machinery of terms and relations—must give appearance and not reality."[3] Any attempt to conceptualize time proves par excellence reality's recalcitrance to relational ways of thought and language.

According to Bradley, the problem is that "if you take time as a relation without duration, then the whole time has no duration, and is not time at all. But, if you give duration to the whole time, then at once the units themselves are found to possess it; and they thus cease to be units" (*AR*, 33–34). Any moment in time has to be both continuous (otherwise it would have no duration) and discrete (otherwise it would not be a distinguishable point), and these two necessities are contradictory. The moment is specious, and the past is a mental construction of such specious moments, while the future is a mental construction of specious moments that are perpetually about to arrive but never do.

Augustine gives utterance to the same paradox. "If any point in time is conceived that can no longer be divided into even the most minute parts of a moment, that alone is which may be called the present. It flies with such speed from the future into the past that it cannot be extended by even a trifling amount. For if it is extended, it is divided into past and future."[4] Augustine psychologizes the notion of time, contending that "the present of things past is in *memory*; the present of things present is in *intuition* [a more modern translation might use the term 'consciousness']; the present of things future is in *expectation*."[5] "It is in you, O my mind, that I measure my times. . . . It is in you, I say, that I measure tracts of time. The impression that passing things make upon you remains, even after those things have passed. The present state is what I measure, not the things which pass away so that it be made."[6]

Given this preamble, what can we make out of Eliot's opening? The present and the past are both present in the future in that when the future is experienced it is experienced as the present, and what was once the present can then be remembered as the past, just as the past can now be remembered. The "perhaps" simply reflects the fact that we do not remember everything that is impressed on our minds. "And time future is contained in time past" would reflect, in Burke's words (though he is not talking about Eliot), "a more complicated kind of reversibility [that] is to be found in connection with 'final causes.' They are directed 'towards the future'; and thus they can be felt to 'implicitly contain' the future. In this sense the future is felt to 'precede' the stages that lead to its fulfillment. Actually, 'final causes' are not future at all, but continually present (a kind of *nunc stans*) until attained or abandoned" (*RR*, 246). The line from Eliot cited above, then, embodies an entelechial motive in consonance with the teleological terminology we had "prophesied." Entelechy, an aim contained within an entity, is the Aristotelian title "for the fact that the seed 'implicitly contains' a future conforming to its nature, if the external conditions necessary to such unfolding and fulfillment occur in the right order" (*RR*, 246). As Eliot puts it in "Little Gidding,"

> And what you thought you came for
> Is only a shell, a husk of meaning
> From which the purpose breaks only when it is fulfilled

If at all. Either you had no purpose
Or the purpose is beyond the end you figured
And is altered in fulfillment.

(ll. 31–36)

This teleological frame of mind makes for the possibility expressed in "The Dry Salvages" that

We had the experience but missed the meaning,
And approach to the meaning restores the experience
In a different form . . .

(ll. 93–95)

In this sense, memory of the past sometimes contains the purpose of the future. Entelechy literally means that time future is contained in time past. But, as Aristotle points out, potential (*dynamis*) can only achieve its perfect actualization at an appropriate moment (*kairos*) through movement (*kinesis*) in time.

It is of course possible that Eliot's first statement could be a deterministic thesis about the past being an efficient cause of the future. This interpretation seems unlikely to me, but nothing in the language denies it. The statement could also mean that from a God's-eye point of view the future is something already known. God's ability to see the future gives us a dim analogue of what it would be like to occupy an Eternal Present. God foresees the narrative of history by eternally apprehending its essence. In any case, predestination is but a eulogistic name for determinism, as immortality is for death.

If all time is eternally present
All time is unredeemable.

(ll. 4–5)

If in the present, one cannot have expectations or hopes for the future, all time is unredeemable. An Eternal Present is propitious for God (His essence equals His existence) but unpropitious for man (his existence precedes his essence, to borrow Sartre's phrase). Until death, the essence of a man has no irrevocable finality. In hell there are no seasons, no possibilities for change. (The same is true for heaven, of course, but that truth has more beneficent implications.) One is eternally what one was, *un être en soi* rather than *un être pour soi*. Only if hope or expectation can be fulfilled in a present later than the one now occupied is redemption possible, for only then can timeless grace intersect with temporal existence.

It is fine to analogize the eternal by conceiving it as an eternal present—a moving image of eternity, in Plato's phrase, the discount being manifest in the word "moving"—for the present necessarily gives us our image of the *nunc stans,* but if the eternal present is taken literally as an existential possibility, no redemption can take place. Presuming that one is as yet unleavened by gracious experience, what might have been is invidiously speculative. Still, what might have been is a perpetual possibility of the present moment, since, as Bradley points out, consciousness is the present datum of psychical fact, plus its actual past (replete with the potentialities that were not realized) and its conditional future (containing a hope that may or may not be fulfilled).

The line asserting that what might have been and what has been point to one end, which is always present, reminds us that the present of things past (whether those things were actual or potential) is in memory, and an act of memory takes place in the present. Thus, what might have been and what has been *point* to one *end,* which is always a *present* purpose.

The end is a temporal terminus, a cessation, insofar as the present is a distinguishable point. But it is also a purpose, goal, or aim insofar as memory has a point in directing or pointing itself at what might have been or what has been. The temporal and teleological meanings of end "merge in the sense that the fulfillment of an aim and the completion of a development are characterizable as the 'death' of that aim or development" (*LASA,* 388). It is worth noting that Eliot uses the word "point" in an intentionalist manner in his doctoral dissertation on F. H. Bradley. "An object is as such a point of attention, and thus anything and everything to which we may be said to direct attention is an object. . . . There is no absolute point of view from which real and ideal can be finally separated and labelled."[7] What might have been (a realm of ideal objects) and what has been (a realm of real objects) are equally capable of being present points of attention. The purpose or end of a mnemonic act is always a present intention, and this point of attention is its terminus, logically speaking, and the purpose is present (that is, at hand or in view) since consciousness is presently pointing toward or intending a remembered event or remembered possibility. Elizabeth Drew's summation of the passage we have been considering is enlightening.

> As a summing up of time as progression, it says that what has been (the past) and what might have been (the potentialities of the past) point to the present as their conclusion: that is what they have produced. As a summing up of the second idea of the eternal present as a "point," it says that what that points to is both that the present moment is the only actuality, and that what to do in the present is an *aim* or purpose which is always present with us.[8]

Looking at the opening passage as a whole, we have before us a tautological cycle of terms for time. All the preceding speculations are but predestinated implications of the tautology that the present is the present. Tautologically, as it were, past and future can only be thought of as present. One thinks of something—whether in terms of memory, immediate perception, or expectation—*now*. That is simply what "present" means. Everything that presently happens in the mind happens in the present. But this is a deep tautology. Given the temporal nature of communicating and understanding, it manifests itself as paradox, just as any tautological cycle of terms shows forth the paradox of the hermeneutical circle. Everything becomes more complex, of course, when the essence one is trying to temporize is that of time itself. One could speculate endlessly (both forever and probably to no purpose as well) about the implications of the tautology. As long as language and thought condemn us to use the machinery of terms and relations, the paradoxes and contradictions will keep proliferating.

The passage, however, functions rhetorically to perplex our minds with nice speculations of philosophy and to make us more responsive to the imminently forthcoming visionary sequence. It bespeaks the need for some sort of gracious experience to redeem us from the tautological vortex of whirling implications.

> Footfalls echo in the memory
> Down the passage which we did not take

> Towards the door we never opened
> Into the rose-garden. My words echo
> Thus, in your mind.
> But to what purpose
> Disturbing the dust on a bowl of rose-leaves
> I do not know.
>
> (ll. 11–16)

The word "footfalls" echoes a passage in Augustine's *Confessions*.

> However, when true accounts of the past are given, it is not the things themselves, which have passed away, that are drawn forth from memory, but words conceived from their images. These images they implanted in my mind like *footsteps* as they passed through the senses.
> My boyhood, indeed, which no longer is, belongs to past time, which no longer is. However, when I recall it and talk about it, I perceive its image at the present time, because it is still in my memory.[9]

Commenting on Augustine, Burke notes that "by the Memory he can see colors in darkness, or listen to a song in silence (an observation, by the way, which might serve to suggest how the normal experience of memory can provide the makings of that quasi-mystical figure, the oxymoron)" (*RR*, 127). Eliot's memory of what might have been, as we shall see, leads him into the region of mystic oxymorons.

In the second sentence of the Eliot passage just cited the analogy is obvious. Eliot's words echo in our minds and his images implant themselves into consciousness like footsteps, just as memories of what might have been echo in his mind and are transmitted and transmuted into poetry. The hermeneutic process of the reader is analogous to the mnemonic experience and writing process of the author. Footfalls can also echo in the latter's memory down the passage that he did not write. The purpose of the authorial exercise is dubious ("I do not know"), and perhaps the hesitancy is paralleled in the reader as he disturbs the dust on the leaves of his Eliot text. The collaboration required of us is made manifest by the use of the pronoun "we." After the "I" of "I do not know" the only personal pronouns in the garden passage are first person plural.

Having been asked whether or not we should follow the deception of the thrush into our first world, we are faced with two fundamental questions. What is "our first world" (l. 21)? And if we follow the thrush into it, why are we following a "deception" (l. 22)? Though commentators have offered many answers, let us take the logological tack, not in the spirit of exclusiveness, but with a sense of limitation, since we shall only find what our vocabulary allows us to look for. Among other things, then, the problems of relational thought and linguistic expressibility lurk in the garden passage.

The technical problem is this: The prelinguistic, the preconceptual, and the preexperiential can only be expressed in terms of the linguistic, the conceptual, and the experiential. Thus any speculation about childhood experience is by definition speculation about what might have been, since the what-has-been of the child took place at a time when he had no adequate vocabulary in which to express it. Some measure of deception in the reconstruction of such experience is thereby inevitable, for adult exploration into childhood memory is plagued with this irremediable difficulty. But what a compelling metaphor. For do we not confront a similar difficulty when we try to explore the supralinguistic, the supraconceptual, and the supraexperiential? Is not the supraverbal silence of the Word exquisitely analogous to the preverbal inarticulacy of the infant? So when we search for the very essence of words, the Word itself, it is unsurprising to find that, as Burke suggests, "imagery related to the realm of the infantile necessarily provides a radical terminology for the poetic expression of first principle, because the search for essence can so readily be conceived in terms of the mind's beginnings" (*LASA*, 322). The connection between the infantile and the mystical resides in the fact that "the yearning to see beyond the intellect terminates mystically in the yearning to regain a true state of 'infancy,' such immediacy of communication as would be possible only if man had never spoken at all" (*LASA*, 263). The paradox is pointed out by Lancelot Andrewes in a passage that Eliot cites. "I add yet farther: what flesh? The flesh of an infant. What, *Verbum infans,* the Word of an infant. The Word, and not to be able to speak a word. How evil agreeth this!"[10]

"Logologically," as Burke observes, speaking of Augustine but in terms apposite to Eliot,

> we are endlessly enticed to speculate on the paradoxical knot of motives that must be involved when an inveterate wordman thus conceives of eternity under the sign of an ultimate, unchanging Word, itself con-

ceived in terms of wordlessness, (wordless though having attained the very Essence of words). . . . Though silence as so conceived requires the sophistication of a consummate word-man, it nonetheless ties in psychologically with motives vestigially "infantile." It would be a point at which great sophistication and great simplicity could meet. (*RR,* 121)

F. H. Bradley is illuminating in regard to the connection between infrarelational unity (the infantile) and suprarelational unity (the Absolute). Bradley tries to show that given the relational form of thought and language, knowledge of the Absolute is impossible, but that nonetheless the concept of the Absolute is essential to the coherence of experience and can be grasped analogically through a nonrelational sentient experience. The One sought in metaphysics, then, as Frederick Copleston points out, cannot be reached by any logical process but must be given in a basic feeling experience.[11] That is to say, on a nondiscursive level of consciousness there is an experience "in which there is no distinction between [one's] awareness and that of which it is aware. There is an immediate feeling, a knowing and being in one, with which knowledge begins."[12] In fact, "when distinctions and relations emerge in consciousness, there is always the background of a 'felt totality.'"[13] As Eliot puts it, "experience is non-relational. Relations can hold only between terms, and these terms can exist only against the background of an experience which is not itself a term."[14] This is the well-known doctrine of immediate experience. Because immediate experience is not relational it is also not temporal. "Immediate experience . . . is a timeless unity which is not as such present either any*where* or to any*one.* It is only in the world of objects that we have time and space and selves. By the failure of any experience to be merely immediate, by its lack of harmony and cohesion, we find ourselves as conscious souls in a world of objects. We are led to the conception of an all-inclusive experience outside of which nothing shall fall."[15]

Metaphysics in the Bradleyan scheme, as Copleston observes, is the attempt to think the One that is given in a primitive feeling-experience, an attempt foredoomed to failure since thought and its linguistic embodiment are necessarily relational.[16] Nonetheless, a limited knowledge is possible. This is approached by conceiving the Absolute "on an analogy with the basic sentient experience which underlies the emergence of distinctions between subject and object and between different objects. . . . There is an immediate experience of 'a many felt in one,' and . . . this experience gives us an inkling of the nature of the Absolute."[17] Feeling, then, "supplies us with a positive idea of a non-relational unity" (AR, 470), and from "an experience of unity below relations we can rise to the idea of a superior unity above them" (AR, 461–62). The infrarelational experience of unity in the child, which is below the level of thought and language, becomes a model for imagining a suprarelational unity that transcends the level of thought and language.

In effect, Bradley is saying that initially, in a child, there is an immediate and basic feeling-experience in which "the distinction between subject and object . . . has not yet emerged." As the child develops a capacity for thought

> this basic unity, a felt totality, breaks up and externality is introduced. The world of the manifold appears as external to the subject. But we can conceive as a possibility an experience in which the immediacy of feeling, of primitive sentient experience, is recovered, as it were, at a higher level, a level at which the externality of related terms such as subject and object ceases utterly. The Absolute is such an experience in the highest degree.[18]

Richard Wollheim makes the point well.

> Immediate Experience is important because it provides us with a model of the kind of whole that we encounter again at the very peak of human knowledge—or, perhaps, better, would encounter again if that peak were not unattainable; the non-relational immediate felt unity, which is Immediate Experience, prefigures the supra-rational unity of the Absolute, in which thought and its object are united to form Truth, and the difference between the two stages is that, whereas at the former, divisions and relations have not yet emerged, at the latter, they have been transcended; they merge again in the highest experience.[19]

Bradley is painfully aware, however, that if we assert that reality, in contradistinction to appearance, is a self-coherent totality, this is only because we have decided that reality must be this way. As Copleston puts it, "References to a primitive sentient experience of a 'felt totality' will not help us much. The idea of such an experience may indeed serve as an analogue for conceiving the Absolute, if we have already decided that there must be an Absolute. But it can hardly be said to prove that it is necessary to postulate the Absolute."[20] Perhaps reality is fundamentally incoherent, subject to Heraclitean universal flux. Bradley freely concedes that "philosophy demands, and in the end rests on, what may fairly be termed faith. It has, we may say, to presuppose its conclusion in order to prove it."[21]

Given that memory provides the makings of the oxymoron and that the preverbal inarticulacy of childhood is analogous to the supraverbal silence of the Word and supplies us with a positive idea of a nonrelational unity, it is no accident that the leaves of the *Quartets* are full of children, not to mention oxymorons. Once Eliot begins to speak of unheard music, unseen eyebeams, and pools filled with water out of sunlight, we are in the region of the mystic oxymoron where contrary significances abound. The garden of what might have been is real to the extent that it incarnates an immediate feeling-experience of infrarelational unity, an analogue of the visionary or mystic moment, which may or may not have the perlocutionary consequence of instilling a comparable felt totality in the reader. But it is deceptive to the extent that analogues are part of the machinery of terms and relations; strictly speaking, they are *not* what they analogize. The antitype of the sensuous rose may indeed be the mystic rose, but the latter is only a reality if we decide that it must be. We must presuppose the conclusion in order to arrive at it.

The rose garden is earthly love in all its resplendent beauty but it is also a type of divine love. The ecstatic moment in childhood merges sensuous and religious ecstasy. "The rose," Raymond Preston maintains, "carries the sexual and religious associations of the *Roman de la Rose* and the mystic rose of the *Paradiso*."[22] Eliot points out, speaking of the fundamental experience of the *Vita Nuova*, which is an experience of the flesh in some measure, that the attitude of Dante to that experience

> can only be understood by accustoming ourselves to find meaning in *final causes* rather than in origins. It is not, I believe, meant as a description of what he *consciously* felt on his meeting with Beatrice, but rather as a description of what that meant on mature reflection upon it. The

final cause is the attraction towards God. . . . The love of man and woman (or for that matter of man and man) is only explained and made reasonable by the higher love, or else is simply the coupling of animals.[23]

The final cause is logically prior, though chronologically posterior, to the efficient cause. It is the essence of the experience.

This predisposition toward teleological explanation, which Eliot explicitly reveals in the quotation above, exposes the transvaluating drive that is central to the overall dialectic of his poetry. As Burke suggests, "The rock of the parched desert in "The Waste Land" can become the rock of religious fortitude. The early laments about un-fulfilled possibilities as regards one man's indecisions can give way to universal ponderings on human tentativeness. Talk of a rose garden can now stand ambiguously for: (1) purely secular delights; (2) vague adumbrations of exalted delights; (3) the final mystic unfolding and enfoldment" (RM, 322). In a similar vein, dyslogistic acedia can be dialectically transformed into eulogistic negation, "the dark dove with the flickering tongue" ("Little Gidding," l. 83), a plane of war, into the Holy Ghost, and secular meaninglessness into divine mystery.

The natural and supernatural pyramids of language interfuse to produce this moment of the rose. But the rose is also the sociopolitical rose, the "spectre" of "old factions" and "old policies" that "Little Gidding" tells us cannot be revived or restored (ll. 184–86). The ex-foliated rose of this visionary sequence, emblem of sensuous splendor, heart of light, is later to be infolded into the crowned knot of fire, where the fire and the rose are one.

In the context of this visionary sequence the image of lotos is singularly appropriate.

> And the pool was filled with water out of sunlight,
> And the lotos rose, quietly, quietly,
> The surface glittered out of heart of light,
> And they were behind us, reflected in the pool.
>
> (ll. 35–38)

The figure of the lotos involves the packing of an image or idea with divergent motives, an image in which the poet has fused, by interacting associations, symbols logically at odds. The image is ambiguous because of a punning association between lotos and the logos of the epigraph—"although the logos is common to all, each one acts as if he had a private wisdom of his own." The lotos has positive associations in Eastern mysticism (it is a symbol of godhead and mystic wisdom) and is also an obvious sexual symbol. Moreover, we recall that the fruit of the lotos tree induces the kind of forgetfulness of being and indolent sensuous contentment that the Christian Logos seeks to redeem. Ulysses relates that his

> men went on and presently met the Lotus-Eaters, nor did these Lotus-Eaters have any thoughts of destroying our companions, but they only gave them lotus to taste of. But any of them who ate the honey-sweet fruit of lotus was unwilling to take any message back, or to go away, but they wanted to stay there with the lotus-eating people, feeding on lotus, and forget the way home.[24]

Tennyson describes the place where the Lotos-Eaters reside as

> A land where all things always seem'd the same!
> And round about the keel with faces pale,
> Dark faces pale against that rosy flame,
> The mild-eyed melancholy Lotos-eaters came.[25]

The perpetual sameness of dark faces pale against that rosy flame is a perversion or parody of the timeless moment wherein the fire and the rose are one. In Lotos-land timelessness equals forgetfulness of time. The eaters find it sweet "To muse and brood and live again in memory, / With those old faces of our infancy," a pleasure that points out the dangers of memory and infantile regression.[26]

The association with lotos-eating becomes more plausible when we look at the narrative progression. The second movement of "Burnt Norton" focuses on the axletree, which is at the still point of the turning world, a principle of heavenly order bedded in the material world, the Logos become flesh. This logos tree (tree is of course associated with the cross and also with good and evil) may now be cast in opposition to the lotos tree.

Despite the positive quality of affirmation in the garden passage, the ambivalence of the poet's attitude toward analogical procedures and mystifying oxymorons is present in the last five lines. Abruptly, Eliot jerks us back into time present.

> Go, go, go, said the bird: human kind
> Cannot bear very much reality.
> Time past and time future
> What might have been and what has been
> Point to one end, which is always present.
>   (ll. 42–46)

The garden of what might have been is simultaneously illuminating and deceptive. It gives us an inkling of the timeless and yet, tautologically speaking, only the present has reality. The present is the one end of which we can be sure. Too much concentration on what might have been and what has been can induce forgetfulness of being and thereby annul any hope of future redemption. That the lotos combines mystic wisdom, sexual potency, and sensuous indolence in one renders it a perfect image for the context. Eliot's poetical method, like Bradley's philosophical method, has a pronounced element of epistemological skepticism. Humankind cannot bear very much reality because humankind cannot know, conceptualize, or express very much reality, given the relational nature of thought and language.

The lyrical section of the second movement exploits what Burke calls the noblest synecdoche, the identity of macrocosm and microcosm.

> The dance along the artery
> The circulation of the lymph
> Are figured in the drift of stars
>   (ll. 52–54)

Processes in blood and lymph are mirrored in celestial patterns, just as the pursuits of desire, symbolized by the boarhound, are reconciled with their objects, symbolized by the boar, in constellated metamorphosis. Lower desires (garlic), higher desires (sapphires), long-forgotten wars (the sociopolitical rose), ascending seminal sap, are reconciled among the stars. The realities of the various pyramids of language are all conjoined. This harmonious cosmic dance finds its principle of orchestration in the bedded axle tree, which is at the still point of the turning world. Because the axletree is bedded in the earth (like Christ was bedded in the manger, Elizabeth Drew suggests) and because it is representative of a transcendent principle of order, it may be seen as an image of the God-man, the Word become flesh. The latter, we may say, is the noblest oxymoron.

The quasi-discursive passage that follows the lyric is of great interest from the logological point of view. It abounds in oxymorons and deploys negative constructions in a fascinating way. If the garden passage furnished an analogue for the nonrelational, timeless unity of the mystic moment by using words for the natural, this passage attempts to do the same by using words for the logological and by capitalizing on the genius of the negative, that purely linguistic marvel. Here the negative in question is the propositional negative. What the poet cannot say is as important as what he can say.

> At the still point of the turning world. Neither flesh nor fleshless;
> Neither from nor towards; at the still point, there the dance is,
> But neither arrest nor movement. And do not call it fixity,
> Where past and future are gathered. Neither movement from nor
>   towards,
> Neither ascent nor decline. Except for the point, the still point,
> There would be no dance, and there is only the dance.
> I can only say, *there* we have been: but I cannot say where.
> And I cannot say, how long, for that is to place it in time.
>
> (ll. 62–69)

The expressions neither flesh nor fleshless, neither from nor towards, neither arrest nor movement nor fixity, neither ascent nor decline, no dance, only the dance, are quite literally non-sense. Although they negate alternatives they do not denote any. Locutionarily speaking, they are vacuous, having no real substance; they are an eclipse of meaning, just as evil is an eclipse of good. Their illocutionary force, however, has the effect of revealing the impotency of discursive language as a vehicle for grasping the intersection of the timeless with time and of communicating a tone of sublime confusion as we stand before that which cannot be said but can only be shown to be ineffable. Neither arrest nor movement nor fixity conceptually eliminates all the possibilities that language might give utterance to. Whether the passage has the perlocutionary consequence of perplexing the reader with puzzlements of metaphysics or contradictions of language, or of elevating him into that feeling of significance that derives from contemplating the divine mystery of things mystical, or of exasperating him into calling the passage mere mystification, muddle rather than mystery, is an open issue. (As Eliot himself said in his essay on Pascal, speaking of the mystic moment, "You may call it communion with the Divine, or you may call it a temporary crystallization of the mind.")[27] The negative can thus be used to exclude options without delimiting anything positive. This capacity, I would say, comes within the orbit of the oxymoron. There are explicit oxymorons (the still point of the turning world, a white light still and moving) to be found, but the whole passage is, in my extended sense of the term, essentially oxymoronic. Eliot's rhetorical strategy is no doubt to elevate the reader into a feeling of significance, and whether or not one agrees that he has succeeded in that regard, one has to agree that he has succeeded in exposing the limitations of relational language. He approaches the nonrelational through the negative way; he negates the relational.

Compare the passage from "Little Gidding."

> The only hope, or else despair
> Lies in the choice of pyre or pyre—
> To be redeemed from fire by fire.
> (ll. 206–8)

While this passage does not explicitly deploy negative constructions, it is certainly on the surface paradoxical. Unlike the other passage, however, once we subject it to scrutiny we see that it delimits real options. Hope is very different from despair, and the "or's" set up a meaningful opposition. On the one hand we have the fire of sensuous passion, sterile lust, self-love, destruction, world war, torture, Inferno, and so forth; on the other hand we have the fire of purification, illumination, divine love, ecstatic blessedness, the Holy Ghost, the Pentecost, Purgatorio, Paradiso, and so forth. In this context fire is a complex symbol with multiple meanings, but there should never be any doubt about which side of the opposition a given meaning falls on. The first fire culminates in despair, the second, in hope. We have to be redeemed from the first by the second.

A new order of motivation enters in near the end of the second movement.

> Yet the enchainment of past and future
> Woven in the weakness of the changing body,
> Protects mankind from heaven and damnation
> Which flesh cannot endure.
>
> (ll. 79–82)

The enchainment of past and future, the iron bondage of memory and expectation, prevents us from dwelling on our spiritual predicament. But this engrossment with past and future is double-edged: it protects us from both heaven and damnation—from heaven because it renders us inattentive to the perpetual possibility of the gracious moment, from damnation because sin is a perverse twisting of the will demanding an immediate intention.

> Time past and time future
> Allow but a little consciousness.
> To be conscious is not to be in time
>
> (ll. 83–85)

Consciousness of the timeless moment is what is supremely real and what redeems us from the whirling vortex of our normal consciousness of time. Yet supreme consciousness is ephemeral; our normal obsession with past and future allows us few, if any, such moments. The paradox is that we can only remember timeless moments in time. "Only through time time is conquered" (l. 90).

What we have so far is this: the opening section of the first movement enunciates a tautology. Consciousness—whether directed to past, present, or future—intends its object in the present. Tautological as this point may be, it appears paradoxical because of the relational character of thought and language. By the time we arrive at the peroration of the second movement a new possibility of consciousness has been introduced. This is a consciousness transcending the machinery of terms and relations, which redeems us from the time-consuming preoccupation with past and future. In order to furnish an inkling of what that consciousness is like, Eliot has to assail the locutionary power of discursive language and to destroy through overelaboration the law of contradiction.

In the third movement Eliot delineates the normal, time-ridden consciousness, the obsession with time before and time after, the purposelessness of passengers in transit. The darkness of the subway is merely the eclipse of real consciousness; it is neither the plenitude of the fulfilling moment nor the constructive vacancy of the mystic's negative way. In the subway there is

> Only a flicker
> Over the strained time-ridden faces
> Distracted from distraction by distraction
> Filled with fancies and empty of meaning
> Tumid apathy with no concentration
> Men and bits of paper, whirled by the cold wind
> That blows before and after time,
> Wind in and out of unwholesome lungs
> Time before and time after.
>   (ll. 100–108)

The only hope, or else despair, lies in transvaluating the sterile death-in-life of this underground waste land into the consuming life-in-death of the negative way. One must

> Descend lower, descend only
> Into the world of perpetual solitude,
> World not world, but that which is not world,
> Internal darkness, deprivation
> And destitution of all property,
> Desiccation of the world of sense,
> Evacuation of the world of fancy,
> Inoperancy of the world of spirit;
> This is the one way, and the other
> Is the same, not in movement
> But abstention from movement; while the world moves
> In appetency, on its metalled ways
> Of time past and time future.
>   (ll. 115–27)

Ideally speaking, a thorough treatment of this passage would involve considering in detail two works of St. John of the Cross—*The Ascent of Mount Carmel* and *The Dark Night of the Soul*. But there is no point in repeating what other critics, such as Helen Gardner, have covered admirably.[28] Staffan Bergsten's summary is good enough for our purposes: "*The Ascent* deals with the active striving of the soul, describes the road of self-discipline and self-negation. *The Dark Night* represents the passive state of the soul, the necessary spiritual vacuum preliminary to the reception of God's grace."[29] The end of the third movement of "East Coker"—the passage beginning with

> In order to arrive there,
> To arrive where you are, to get from where you are not,
> You must go by a way wherein there is no ecstasy
> (ll. 136–38)

is a free translation of a section from *The Ascent of Mount Carmel*—the passage beginning with

> In order to arrive at having pleasure in everything,
> Desire to have pleasure in nothing.[30]

What is important logologically is the way in which these passages deploy negative constructions that amount in the end to oxymorons.

Also important are the possibilities for transvaluation. Once Eliot posits a timeless still point, all sorts of dialectical manipulation become possible. "Since reduction to terms of highest generalization allows for permanent or 'timeless' principles, and since 'eternity' as so couched equals pure being (which in its transcending of conditions is indistinguishable from nothing) there are now even possibilities of a good meaning for drought, as presented in terms of mortification and the *via negativa*" (*RM*, 322). Again we see the connection between dialectical transcendence and dramatic catharsis. The mystic undergoes purgation by victimizing himself, and this negation of the world of contingencies only makes sense when that world is placed in antithesis to the unconditioned realm of the timeless. Moreover, since the way of plenitude and the way of vacancy intend the same object (union with God), the way up is the way down. The telos is identical in each case, for

> The light is still
> At the still point of the turning world
> (ll. 136–37)

"still" bearing two meanings—motionless and perpetual.

From the logological point of view, the opening of the fifth movement is of paramount importance.

> Words move, music moves
> Only in time; but that which is only living
> Can only die. Words, after speech, reach
> Into the silence. Only by the form, the pattern,
> Can words or music reach
> The stillness, as a Chinese jar still
> Moves perpetually in its stillness.
> Not the stillness of the violin, while the note lasts,
> Not that only, but the co-existence,
> Or say that the end precedes the beginning,
> And the end and the beginning were always there
> Before the beginning and after the end.
> And all is always now.
> (ll. 138–50)

This passage calls back to mind Burke's fifth analogy wherein "the Augustinian distinction between 'time' and 'eternity' is treated in its linguistically analogous form, as the distinction between the unfolding of a sentence through the materiality of its parts and the unitary non-material essence of meaning of the sentence" (RR, 3).

> Here the succession of words in a sentence would be analogous to the "temporal." But the *meaning* of the sentence is an *essence,* a kind of fixed significance or definition that is not confined to any of the sentence's parts, but rather pervades or inspirits the sentence as a whole. Such meaning, I would say, is analogous to "eternity." In contrast with the flux of the sentence, where each syllable arises, exists for a moment, and then "dies" to make room for the next stage of the continuing process, the meaning is "non-temporal," though embodied (made incarnate) in a temporal series. The meaning in its unity or simplicity "just *is.*" (RR, 27)

According to this analogy, time is to eternity as the particulars in the unfolding of a sentence are to the sentence's unitary meaning, and as the unfolding of the unitary meanings of sentences is to the unitary meaning of the work as a whole. The essentializing title of the work thus corresponds with eternity or, to use a linguistic metaphor, with the synchronic whole, and the narrative unfolding of the work corresponds with time or, to continue the metaphor, with the diachronic sequence of words, the syntagmatic axis of successive meanings. It is obvious that what we are dealing with again is the temporizing of essence, the spinning out into narrative of a series of logical relationships. The tautological cycle of terms, as I have stated, is Burke's version of the hermeneutic circle, that paradoxical interdependence of part and whole, according to which the whole can be understood only through the parts—these are necessarily presented and perceived chronologically—and the parts can be understood only through the whole—this is timeless in that it is logically prior in the order of explanation, but it can only be excavated through a temporal process of inference and guesswork along the way; the whole inspirits the parts. "We do confront a problem of *beginnings* here. Insofar as the sentence is an idea, or principle, it proceeds according to a plan that is one kind of 'first,' a sort of 'final cause' that guides the actual choice of words. Yet the wording of the sentence, in its step-by-step temporal sequence, involves another kind of 'first,' since each part of the sentence is 'prior' to the part that follows it" (*RR*, 143). Logologically, then, eternity equals the predestinated implications of terminology, their cyclical or tautological aspects, whereas time equals the one-directioned rectilinearity of narrative. In any given work, of course, the two aspects interfuse, given the temporal character of communicating and understanding, the paradox of the hermeneutic circle.

Words and music in their materiality as physical sounds move only in time. The temporally prior sound "dies" to make room for its successor. "That which is only living can only die." "Words, after speech, reach into the silence" because the meaning of a speech act transcends the sheer nature of the individual words as temporal motions. It is an essence, not reducible to any part of the sentence, or even to the whole of it. The meaning, then, as Burke points out, is nontemporal, though embodied (made incarnate) in a temporal series. From the point of view of the interpreter, the activity of understanding is a psychological process of remembering, perceiving, and expecting. It is only in the temporally posterior postverbal silence that he can grasp the logically prior unitary meaning of the whole. Augustine describes the interrelationship between memory, perception, and expectation, using the recitation of a psalm as an example.

> I am about to recite a psalm that I know. Before I begin, my expectation extends over the entire psalm. Once I have begun, my memory extends over as much of it as I shall separate off and assign to the past. The life of this action of mine is distended into memory by reason of the part I have spoken and into forethought by reason of the part I am about to speak. But the attention is actually present and that which was to be is borne along by it so as to become past. The more this is done and done again, so much more is memory lengthened by a shortening of expectation, until the whole expectation is exhausted. When this is done the whole action is completed and passes into memory. What takes place in the whole psalm takes place also in each of its parts and in each of its syllables. The same thing holds for a longer action, of which perhaps the psalm is a small part. The same thing holds for a man's entire life, the parts of which are all the man's actions. The same thing holds throughout the whole age of the sons of men, the parts of which are the lives of all men.[31]

Silence ensues when expectation has become memory. The temporal process has been terminated, and only its end or essence persists.

Augustine's example involves an act of communicating something he already knows. Yet the psychological process he describes applies equally to acts of understanding as well. With regard to the latter, it would not even matter whether the hermeneutic experience were an act of reading or rereading. "Only by the form, the pattern, can words or music reach the stillness, as a Chinese jar still moves perpetually in its stillness." Only by the intrinsic genre, that sense of the whole which inspirits the parts, can those parts reach the stillness, which I take to be the meaning or essence. The meaning of the whole is still, in that it is both perpetual and silent. What we have, of course, is another version of the hermeneutic circle. Form or pattern is logically prior but it must be understood chronologically through a process of memory, perception, and expectation. This is a complicated process because expectation can be either fulfilled or violated, and one's sense of the whole is something that is open to continual revision and reformulation, even if one is already familiar with the work. Form is the psychology of the audience. What eventually becomes a structure is transmitted as a movement.

The above gives us the possibility of another meaning for "Words move, music moves, only in time." If we take "move" to mean "emotionally affect," then it can be said that words and music only move us fully after we have taken time to undergo the psychological process of listening. A Beethoven quartet, for example, is almost unintelligible upon a first listening, though in time what initially appears to be anomalous becomes expected. The same is true of novels like *Ulysses* or poems like the *Four Quartets*. Punningly, as Burke points out, merging the temporal and teleological senses of "order," "the sounds are formed *in order that* the song may come to be" (*RR*, 151). Process and structure coalesce. The more one undergoes the process, the more capable one is to understand and be moved by the structure, but one cannot undergo the process unless one can anticipate and project a semblance of the structure. The rectilinear and the cyclical are enclosed within a tautological cycle of terms, a hermeneutic circle. Implications may be predestinated but in some measure they manifest themselves as surprise to the interpreter.

"A Chinese jar still moves perpetually in its stillness" in the sense that its structure as a motionless spatial form perpetually affects us aesthetically. Eliot's Chinese jar reminds me of Keats's Grecian urn. (Compare also the "unheard music" of the first movement of "Burnt Norton" to "heard melodies are sweet but those unheard are sweeter" in the second stanza of Keats's ode. It is also worth looking at Burke's treatment of the ode in an appendix to *A Grammar of Motives*.) But the silent form teases the Keatsian persona out of thought as does eternity, whereas for Eliot the silent form is a figure, however impoverished, given the relational character of thought and language, of eternity. That is, the artifice of eternity is to a large degree substitutive or compensatory for a religious conception of eternity that Keats, and for that matter Yeats as well, cannot believe in, whereas in Eliot it is introductory and analogical, an incipient version of metaphysical reality. In Keats and Yeats we see an incipient version of the "supreme fiction" mentality that achieves its entelechy, for better or for worse, in Wallace Stevens. In Keats and Yeats, to be sure, the strenuous dialogue of self and soul throughout their poetry, the constant vacillation, makes their provisional assent to the supreme fiction of an artifice of eternity humanly poignant and authentically ambiguous.

The stillness, Eliot tells us, is *not* the stillness of the violin, while the note lasts. At least, it is not that only. (Again we note the strategic deployment of the negative.) If the stillness refers back to the stillness of a Chinese jar, then Eliot might be saying that the perpetual and motionless essence of a spatial form is dissimilar to that of a temporal form. The durational extension of a note, like that of a moment in time, may be a distinguishable point, but it only has meaning in relation to a chronological sequence. Paradoxically, as we have seen, that sequence only has meaning in relation to the essence that inspirits the whole. That essence logically precedes the work's existence, but has to reveal its structure through a temporal process. In a spatial form existence and essence are simultaneously present, though it is true that the observer must undergo a hermeneutic process in order to be able to apprehend the simultaneity. The innocent eye sees nothing.

In a flurry of repetitive forays into the notion of coexistence—in three lines Eliot repeats the words "end" and "beginning" three times each—Eliot merges temporal and logical priority as well as the temporal and teleological meanings of end. Logically speaking, the end precedes the beginning, but the end and the beginning were always there in that they are implicit in the tautological cycle of terms that the narrative progression makes explicit. The implications of terms are predestinated just as human existence and history are predestinated, as the later quartets reveal. After the fact, both the beginning and end of a work of art are inevitable and coexistent, whereas to an omniscient mind the same is true of human existence and history before the fact. Eliot's constant temporizing and detemporizing of essence get us back to the tautological starting point of the first movement—"All is always now."

Humankind cannot bear very much reality because the Absolute defies the machinery of terms and relations.

> Words strain,
> Crack and sometimes break, under the burden,
> Under the tension, slip, slide, perish,
> Decay with imprecision, will not stay in place,
> Will not stay still.
> (ll. 150–54)

They will not stay still because they are units in chronological movement. They will not stay constant because that chronological movement is a unit in a larger historical movement; contexts and usages change; words hurry to their death, but are continually restored and born anew.

> For last year's words belong to last year's language
> And next year's words await another voice.
> ("Little Gidding," ll. 120–21)

Eliot sees his enterprise as "trying to learn to use words," an enterprise in which every attempt

> Is a wholly new start, and a different kind of failure
> Because one has only learnt to get the better of words
> For the thing one no longer has to say, or the way in which
> One is no longer disposed to say it. And so each venture
> Is a new beginning, a raid on the inarticulate
> With shabby equipment always deteriorating
> In the general mess of imprecision of feeling,
> Undisciplined squads of emotion.
> ("East Coker," ll. 175–82)

It is interesting to observe how the logological strategy is expressed in terms of the historical situation in which it is devised; it is appropriately couched in militaristic terms—raid, shabby equipment, general mess, undisciplined squads—and thus also serves as a cultural comment on the general mess occasioned by the Second World War, where undisciplined squads of emotion ran rampant. For Eliot there is

> At best, only a limited value
> In the knowledge derived from experience.
> The knowledge imposes a pattern, and falsifies,
> For the pattern is new in every moment
> And every moment is a new and shocking
> Valuation of all we have been.
> ("East Coker," ll. 83–88)

Positivistic empiricism, which derives all knowledge from experience, operates only in terms of efficient causes and thus regards experience deterministically rather than teleologically. To use Eliot's critical vocabulary as a metaphor, we might say that such empiricism does not see how the seeds of tradition may find their entelechial fulfillment in an individual talent. The individual case may transvaluate the past.

> What happens when a new work of art is created is something that happens simultaneously to all the works of art which preceded it. The existing monuments form an ideal order among themselves, which is modified by the introstion of the new (the really new) work of art among them. The existing order is complete before the new work arrives; for order to persist after the supervention of novelty, the *whole* existing order must be, if ever so slightly, altered; and so the relations, proportions, values of each work of art toward the whole are readjusted; and this is conformity between the old and new. . . . It [is not] preposterous that the past should be altered by the present as much as the present is directed by past.[32]

In contradistinction to the whirling vortex of temporal words and their implications stands the silent Word at the still point of the turning world. As Eliot puts it in "Ash Wednesday," echoing the Andrewes passage I cited earlier,

> If the lost word is lost, if the spent word is spent
> If the unheard, unspoken
> Word is unspoken, unheard;
> Still is the unspoken word, the Word unheard,
> The Word without a word, the Word within
> The world and for the world;
> And the light shone in darkness and
> Against the Word the unstilled world still whirled
> About the centre of the silent Word.

As Burke reflects, "the 'eternal Word' by which the world was created must have been in silence, for there was as yet no matter and time whereby the syllables could arise and fall in succession" (*RR*, 144). The creative fiat, Augustine maintains, must be coeternal with God himself. Augustine distinguishes speech in which "the syllables were sounded and they passed away, the second after the first, the third after the second, and the rest in order, until the last one came after all the others, and silence after the last"—words, after speech, reach into the silence—from God's "eternal Word in its silence."[33]

> So you call us to understand the Word, God with you, O God, which is spoken eternally, and in which all things are spoken eternally. Nor is it the case that what was spoken is ended and that another thing is said, so that all things may at length be said: all things are spoken once and forever. Elsewise, there would already be time and change, and neither true eternity nor true immortality. . . . Therefore, no part of your Word gives place to another or takes the place of another, since it is truly eternal and immortal. Therefore, you say once and forever all that you say by the Word, who is co-eternal with you.[34]

The main point is that in the fifth movement of "Burnt Norton" Eliot uses the logological as a metaphor for the theological, which, it may be said, is exactly the opposite of what Burke does. The syllables of a sentence are born and they die, but the meaning abides in silence beyond the temporal movement; like meaning or essence, the eternal Word must be conceived in terms of silence. Meaning is made incarnate by the temporal movements of words, as the Word is made flesh in the temporal movements of human history. Only by the form, the pattern, can words or music reach the stillness.

> The detail of the pattern is movement,
> As in the figure of the ten stairs.
> Desire itself is movement
> Not in itself desirable;
> Love is itself unmoving,
> Only the cause and end of movement . . .
> (ll. 160–65)

According to Eliot, love is both the prime mover and the final cause. The latter notion is a way of stating the former in narrative terms, of temporizing essence. Logologically speaking, the two notions are synonymous.

In the final analysis, however,

> to apprehend
> The point of intersection of the timeless
> With time, is an occupation for the saint
> ("The Dry Salvages," ll. 200–202)

and certainly not an occupation for students of literature. Bequeathed to us is

> the intolerable wrestle
> With words and meanings.
> ("East Coker," ll. 71–72)

> We shall not cease from exploration
> And the end of all our exploring
> Will be to arrive where we started
> And know the place for the first time.
> ("Little Gidding," ll. 241–44)

A logological translation might read: we shall not cease from trying to explore the movement of temporal words and from trying to track down their implications, and the purpose and terminus of all our exploring will be to arrive at the ultimate term, the final cause, and know the timeless meaning for the first time.

The reason why logology is to my mind a fruitful methodology when applied to the *Four Quartets* is that Eliot's religious frame of acceptance views historical reality *sub specie aeternitatis* and thus brings to bear upon that reality an essentially ahistorical or synchronic mode of apprehension while paradoxically, at the same time, striving to find the ultimate purpose or meaning of history. Hence the fact that logology tends to downplay the scenic term of the dramatistic pentad makes for a felicitous complementarity.

Postscript

WITH ITS PERSISTENT attentiveness to grammatical accuracy, rhetorical persuasion, symbolical consistency, and ethical portraiture, Burke's dramatism offers us a sophisticated picture of how we do things with words and of the labyrinthine ways in which symbolic action designates, communicates, expresses, and evaluates. His approach, it seems to me, is an exemplary alternative to the linguistic nihilism that pervades much of contemporary criticism. For although Burke is well aware of the fact that critical vocabularies and interpretive strategies are in large measure self-fulfilling prophecies, he is equally aware of the dialectical nature of the transaction between the system of signs and the frame of reference, between verbal implications and empirical observations. To assume that sign systems affect perception but that the external world does not is anathema to Burke; the intrinsic and the extrinsic are mutually dependent. In one sense Burke's dramatistic method, unlike, say, deconstruction, does not undermine the traditional interpretive project of determining what a text means; in another sense, however, it so expands the conception of what a text means (and how it means and why it means) as to be doing something very different from, say, structuralism or New Criticism. Burke approaches the problem of interpretation in a sufficiently complex way so as to link function with structure, context with text, and reader with author. Thus he is able to transcend the formalism of intrinsic approaches, the reductionism of extrinsic approaches, and the indeterminism of poststructuralist approaches. His fourfold conception of symbolic action, as I have argued, is integral to this transcendence.

The grammatical realm, as we have seen, comprises logic, dialectic, knowledge, information, external reference, and objective reality. Symbolic action has a reality-regarding element and has realistic content insofar as it encompasses the situation it represents. The encompassment, however, is necessarily imperfect since we have no nonsymbolic or nonlinguistic access to the structure of reality. In striving toward adequate ideas our charts are relative approximations to the truth. On the grammatical level, the Burkean reader resists the oversimplifications of naive verbal realism and seeks to determine what components of the dramatistic pentad the work emphasizes and deemphasizes and whether the work provides a viable chart for thought and action, a realistic reflection of the way things are.

In the realm of rhetoric we regard symbolic action as audience-directed discourse, focusing upon its nature as communication, persuasion, exhortation, address, prayer, petition, and inducement to attitude and action. Through the use of identification, rhetoric seeks to overcome social estrangement, to foster cooperation, and to establish community. Hierarchic psychosis is endemic to every society, and every work reflects the embarrassments, tensions, and alienations of a given sociopolitical hierarchy. On the rhetorical level, the Burkean reader deploys the socioanagogic method to unveil the mysteries of hierarchy and seeks to determine whether the work induces attitudes and actions that help us to overcome social estrangement and alienation.

In the realm of the symbolic, symbolic action is symptomatic action and plays a compensatory or therapeutic role. It has an author-regarding element and is expressive, either directly or indirectly, of psychological engrossments and avoidances, of patterns of identification and dissociation, of the burdens of guilt and identity, and of the rhetoric of rebirth that the work enacts. The symbolic also attends to the internal consistency of the text and to the architectonic or developmental motive, the narrative unfolding of associative clusters and dramatic alignments, the entelechial drive within any symbol system to attain the kind of perfection appropriate to the kind of thing that it is, the psychology of form that the work embodies. On the symbolic level, the Burkean reader explores the quandaries of self, form, and entelechy.

The realm of ethics and of social and self-portraiture comprises the moral proscriptions of a given social order (its "thou shalt not's") and the kind of identity a personality builds up through the ensemble of social roles a person incorporates. A work always reflects individual and social values, for it is a portrait of both self and society. On the ethical level, the Burkean reader seeks to determine what values the work embodies, what image of self and society it projects.

The four realms, of course, interpenetrate, for the nature of language is such that it is at once grammatical, rhetorical, symbolical, and ethical. Burke's understanding of the interrelationships among these realms, as I have tried to show throughout this discussion, provides a comprehensive theory of literature and language, and one that has a high degree of practical utility.

What ultimately distinguish Burke, however, are his attitudes toward language, life, literature, and method. One can easily get carried away and overstress the systematic nature of dramatism, but what gets lost in the process is the fact that dramatism is fundamentally an ethical and existential attitude, a charitable yet realistic frame of ironic and comic acceptance. The Burkean rhetor passionately participates in the foundationless conversation of history because he believes that people are persuadable, that they can be goaded into moving toward a better life, that words are agents of purpose and power, that freedom and value are embodied in the logic of symbolic action, and that out of the fog of symbols there is a path leading toward the realm of adequate ideas. As William H. Rueckert points out, for Burke "the self in quest" strives to move "out of the waste land towards a better life through symbolic action."[1]

> The orientation is a kind of secular Christianity where Hell, Purgatory, and Heaven have been replaced by their psychological equivalents, and where the redemptive Christ has been replaced by the miracle of symbolic action. . . . The goal is "By and through language," to move "beyond language." The attitude of patience is one of these beyonds; another is the hope that nourishes this patience, the hope that by going through language one can get "glimpses into the ultimate reality that stretches somehow beyond the fogs of language and its sloganizing."[2]

As a vocabulary of motives, dramatism is equipment for living, and Burke's dramatistic definition of man contains four clauses. First, "man is the symbol-using animal" (*LASA*, 3). For in spite of our everyday adoption of an attitude of naive verbal realism, "much of what we mean by 'reality' has been built up for us through nothing but our symbol systems" (*LASA*, 5). But the ability to use symbols, Burke maintains, is also the ability to abuse and misuse symbols, which is why he advocates an attitude of "linguistic skepticism." Nevertheless, he synonymizes this attitude with "linguistic appreciation, on the grounds that an attitude of methodical quizzicality toward language may best equip us to perceive the full scope of its resourcefulness" (*GM*, 441). Because "language referring to the realm of the nonverbal is necessarily talk about things in terms of what they are not" (*LASA*, 5), such quizzicality inhibits us from succumbing to the illusions of naive verbal realism and helps us to avoid being enmeshed in a maze of symbols. "Whatever may be the ultimate ground of all possibility," Burke writes,

> the proper study of mankind is man's tendency to misjudge reality as inspirited by the troublous genius of symbolism. But if we were trained, for generation after generation, from our first emergence out of infancy, and in ways ranging from the simplest to the most complex, depending upon our stage of development, to collaborate in spying upon ourselves with pious yet sportive fearfulness, and thus helping to free one another of the false ambitions that symbolism so readily encourages, we might yet contrive to keep from wholly ruining this handsome planet and its plenitude.[3]

Second, man is "the inventor of the negative" (*LASA*, 9) and is "moralized by the negative" (*LASA*, 16). As I mentioned earlier, particularly in my discussion of *The Rhetoric of Religion*, to a nature that is positively what it is, human language adds the negative and all its proscriptions regarding property, law, behavior, morality, and so forth.

Third, man is "separated from his natural condition by instruments of his own making" (*LASA*, 13). Alienating himself more and more from his own animality, man creates a counternature and becomes the instrument of his instruments. "Hypertechnologism" leads toward hell on earth, and Burke's well-founded fear is that human entelechy may very well be expressed in the perfection of technology itself, which, paradoxically, would be the ultimate form of antihumanism. Burke's humanistic counterstatement takes its stand against such technologism. As he puts it, "an anti-Technologistic Humanism would be 'animalistic' in the sense that, far from boasting of some privileged human status, it would never disregard our humble, and maybe even humiliating, place in the totality of the natural order" (*DD,* 54).

Fourth, man is "goaded by the spirit of hierarchy," "moved by a sense of order" (*LASA,* 15), and "rotten with perfection" (*LASA,* 16). As I mentioned earlier in my discussion of hierarchic psychosis and the entelechial motive, the magic and mystery of social role and status along with the terministic drive toward perfection in any system are intrinsic to language and symbol using. The impulse toward perfection, however, is a mixed blessing, and Burke's phrase "rotten with perfection" nicely captures the ambivalence. We are all too familiar with the obscenity of final solutions to view perfectionism from a neutral standpoint.

Throughout his writings Burke consistently argues against the semantic ideal of neutral naming, favoring instead a dramatic vocabulary, with weighting and counterweighting. The neutral vocabularies of science and technology systematically try to eliminate value, emotion, and attitude. This desire, Burke suggests, may be one vast castration symbol, for "speech in its essence is not neutral. . . . Spontaneous speech is not a naming at all, but a system of attitudes, or implicit exhortations" (*PC,* 176–77).

In "The Phaedrus and the Nature of Rhetoric," Richard Weaver makes a similar point, seeing Plato's "dramatistic presentation" in this dialogue as an argument against preferring "a neuter form of speech to the kind which is ever getting us aroused over things and provoking an expense of spirit."[4] Weaver associates the advocate of semantically purified neuter speech with Socrates' conception of the nonlover. Although such a person can attain some measure of objective understanding and can rationally manipulate things and people, he can move neither himself nor others toward a better life. "True rhetoric," Weaver maintains, "is concerned with the potency of things. The literalist . . . is troubled by its failure to conform to a present reality. What he fails to appreciate is that potentiality is a mode of existence."[5] Rhetorical language, whether directed toward good or evil ends, excites the affections and moves in the realm of potency. Although base rhetoric is exploitative, even demagogic—and there is nothing to guarantee that rhetorical competence will not lead to evil consequences—it is at least vibrant and human, unlike neutral language, which is sterile and inhuman. As Weaver points out,

> We cannot deny that there are degrees of objectivity in the reference of speech. But this is not the same as an assurance that a vocabulary of reduced meanings will solve the problems of mankind. Many of those problems will have to be handled, as Socrates well knew, by the student of souls, who must primarily make use of the language of tendency. The soul is impulse, not simply cognition. . . . So rhetoric at its truest seeks to perfect men by showing them better versions of themselves, links in that chain extending up toward the ideal, which only the intellect can apprehend and only the soul can have affection for.[6]

There may, in fact, be no way out of the fog of symbols, no realm of adequate ideas to match our dialectical aspirations, and no escape from the ubiquitous evil of hypertechnologism. But throughout his long career as a man of letters Burke has persistently been the kind of noble rhetorician whose life and work attest to the value that resides in the struggle and the quest.

Notes

INTRODUCTION

1. Burke, *Permanence and Change*, p. 263.
2. Burke, *A Grammar of Motives*, p. xxii.
3. Burke, *The Philosophy of Literary Form*, p. 1.
4. Rueckert, *Kenneth Burke and the Drama of Human Relations*, pp. xiii–xiv.
5. Lentricchia, "Reading History with Kenneth Burke," pp. 131–32, 134.
6. Burke, *The Rhetoric of Religion*, p. vi.
7. Burke, *Attitudes Toward History*, p. 57.

CHAPTER ONE

1. See Burke, "Kinds of Criticism," pp. 272–82. Here Burke distinguishes between extrinsic criticism—the genetic version of which looks to extraliterary causes, the implicational version of which looks to extraliterary effects—and intrinsic criticism—poetics, genre criticism, reviewing, and textual analysis. "Insofar as the Criticism of Criticism can provide terms that can be extended integrally (not by sheer addition) into all areas of criticism, it brings both Extrinsic and Intrinsic under a single focus" (p. 280). Such integration, I shall argue, is the aim of dramatism.
2. Abrams, *The Mirror and the Lamp*, p. 26.
3. Abrams, p. 272.
4. Ogden and Richards, *The Meaning of Meaning*, p. 150.
5. Richards, *Poetries and Sciences*, p. 60.
6. Richards, *Principles of Literary Criticism*, p. 268.
7. Empson, *The Structure of Complex Words*, p. 7.
8. Wimsatt and Beardsley, "The Affective Fallacy," p. 24.
9. Ransom, *The World's Body*, p. 153.

10. Ransom, p. 113.
11. Ransom, p. 158.
12. Ransom, *The New Criticism*, p. xi.
13. Brooks, *The Well-Wrought Urn*, p. 3.
14. Burke, *Counter-Statement*, p. 39.
15. Winters, *The Anatomy of Nonsense*, p. 13.
16. Pratt, *Toward a Speech Act Theory of Literary Discourse*, p. xii.
17. Jameson, *The Prison-House of Language*, p. 49.
18. Prague School, cited by Pratt, p. xvii.
19. Holland, "The 'Unconscious' of Literature: The Psychoanalytic Approach," p. 142.
20. Holland, p. 143, my italics.
21. Holland, p. 144.
22. Jameson, *Marxism and Form*, pp. 330–31.
23. Brecht, *Brecht on Theatre*, section 38, p. 190. "The 'historical conditions' must of course not be imagined (nor will they be so constructed) as mysterious Powers (in the background); on the contrary, they are created and maintained by men (and will in due course be altered by them)." Also see Barthes, *Mythologies*. In his introduction Barthes notes that "the starting point of these reflections was usually a feeling of impatience at the sight of the 'naturalness' with which newspapers, art and common sense constantly dress up a reality which, even though it is the one we live in, is undoubtedly determined by history. In short, in the account given of our contemporary circumstances, I resented seeing Nature and History confused at every turn, and I wanted to track down, in the decorative display of *what-goes-without-saying*, the ideological abuse which, in my view, is hidden there" (p. 11). Barthes goes on to show how myth "transforms history into nature . . . it is not read as a motive, but as a reason" (p. 129). "Any semiological system is a system of values; now the myth-consumer takes the signification for a system of facts: myth is read as a factual system, whereas it is but a semiological system" (p. 131). Myth naturalizes; it presents values as facts.
24. See Brecht, section 37, p. 190. "And if we play works dealing with our own time as though they too were historical, then perhaps the circumstances under which he [the spectator] himself acts will strike him as equally odd; and this is where the critical attitude begins."
25. Brecht, section 45, p. 192.
26. See Brecht, section 43, p. 192. "The new alienations are only designed to free socially-conditioned phenomena from that stamp of familiarity which protects them against our grasp today."

27. Burke, "Dramatism," p. 332.

28. Burke contrasts "a truly liquid attitude towards speech" with "the deceptive comforts of ideological rigidity" (*ATH*, p. 231).

29. Richards, *The Philosophy of Rhetoric*, p. 11.

30. See Richards, *Interpretation in Teaching*, pp. 48–49. "Thinking is radically metaphoric. Linkage by analogy is its constitutive law or principle, its causal nexus, since meaning only arises through the causal *contexts* by which a sign stands for (takes the place of) an instance of a sort. To think of anything is to take it *as* a sort (as a such and such) and that 'as' brings in (openly or in disguise) the analogy, the parallel, the metaphoric grapple or ground or grasp or draw by which alone the mind takes hold. It takes no hold if there is nothing for it to haul from, for its thinking is the haul, the attraction of likes."

31. See Jameson, *The Prison-House of Language*, p. 60. Citing Shklovsky, the Russian Formalist, Jameson notes that "the basic way of seeing any object anew is 'to place the object in a new semantic row, in a row of concepts which belong to another category.' "

32. Empson, *Seven Types of Ambiguity*, p. 19.

33. Kuhn, *The Structure of Scientific Revolutions*, p. 127.

34. The term "intertextuality" is Julia Kristeva's. As Jonathan Culler points out in *The Pursuit of Signs*, Kristeva defines it as "the sum of knowledge that makes it possible for texts to have meaning: once we think of the meaning of a text as dependent upon other texts that it absorbs and transforms, she writes, 'in place of the notion of intersubjectivity is installed that of intertextuality' " (p. 104). "A text can be read only in relation to other texts, and it is made possible by the codes which animate the discursive space of a culture" (p. 38). Every text is a response to and interpretation of other texts, all of which are a response to and interpretation of an objective situation.

35. Burke, *Language as Symbolic Action*, p. 359.

36. Jameson, *The Prison-House of Language*, p. 37.

37. See Burke, "Fact, Inference, and Proof," p. 146. "But the word is the first full 'perfection' of a term. And we move from it either way as our base, either 'back' to the dissolution of meaning that threatens it by reasons of its accidental punwise associates, or 'forward' to its dissolution through inclusion in a 'higher meaning,' which attains *its* perfection in the sentence."

38. Burke, *A Rhetoric of Motives*.

39. Lentricchia, *After the New Criticism*, p. 44.

40. Lentricchia, *After the New Criticism*, p. 55.

41. Lentricchia, *Criticism and Social Change*, p. 89.
42. See Burke, "The Language of Poetry, 'Dramatistically' Considered," pp. 88–102.
43. Crusius, "A Case for Kenneth Burke's Dialectic and Rhetoric," p. 24.
44. Crusius, p. 31.
45. See Booth, *The Rhetoric of Fiction, passim*.
46. Burke, "The Language of Poetry, 'Dramatistically' Considered," p. 98.
47. Lentricchia, *Criticism and Social Change*, p. 103.
48. *Time* magazine (July 28, 1986) reports that a group of Fundamentalist Christian parents formally opened their legal attack against the public schools of Hawkins County, Tennessee. Their claim is that the county's textbooks endorse secular humanism, a doctrine that elevates man at the expense of God. Vicki Frost, leader of the group, complained that these secular humanist textbooks promote pacifism, child rebellion, situational ethics, and feminism (p. 60). Again we see the elasticity of devil-terms such as secular humanism.
49. Lentricchia, *Criticism and Social Change*, p. 55.
50. Lentricchia, *Criticism and Social Change*, p. 105.
51. Lentricchia, *Criticism and Social Change*, p. 125.
52. Lentricchia, *Criticism and Social Change*, p. 142.
53. Lentricchia, *Criticism and Social Change*, p. 48.
54. Lentricchia, *Criticism and Social Change*, p. 43.
55. Lentricchia, *Criticism and Social Change*, p. 42.
56. Lentricchia, *Criticism and Social Change*, pp. 50–51.
57. Lentricchia, *Criticism and Social Change*, p. 25.
58. Jameson, "The Symbolic Inference; or, Kenneth Burke and Ideological Analysis," p. 509.
59. James, *The Art of the Novel*, p. 5.

CHAPTER TWO

1. Holland, "The 'Unconscious' of Literature: The Psychoanalytic Approach," p. 142. Holland's interpretation is more full-fledged than my summary indicates. He bases his diagnosis of the nucleus of fantasy on the presence of oral imagery in the poem—the references to speech and eating—and sees the references to cows as conjuring up associations of milk and motherhood and as thereby injecting a note of femininity into a poem that deals in the main with male bonding.
2. Holland, p. 137.
3. Holland, p. 139.
4. Holland, p. 150.

5. Rueckert, *Kenneth Burke and the Drama of Human Relations*, p. 97.

6. Rueckert, p. 26.

7. I say "tends" advisedly because (1) in the realm of symbolic action the four dimensions necessarily interpenetrate and (2) there are always counterexamples to be adduced—the two essays on Goethe's *Faust* (*LASA*, 139–85), for instance, which stress the symbolical and ethical.

8. See *PC*, p. 283. "Man's specific nature as the symbol-using animal transcends his generic nature as sheer animal, thereby giving rise to property, rights, and obligations of purely man-made sorts; (2) the necessary nature of property in a complex social order makes for the 'embarrassments' of social mystery in men's relations to one another, thereby giving rise to attitudes that pervade areas of thought not strictly germane to it; (3) the terms 'Bureaucracy,' 'Hierarchy,' and 'Order' all touch upon this realm of social mystery, because of their relation to authority, and to canons of Propriety."

9. For an example of socioanagogic interpretation, see Burke's discussion of *Venus and Adonis* (*RM*, pp. 212–21).

10. Fergusson, *The Idea of a Theater*, p. 31.

CHAPTER THREE

1. Nietzsche, *The Wanderer and His Shadow*, 55. Cited by Danto, *Nietzsche as Philosopher*, p. 83.

2. Nietzsche, *The Wanderer*, p. 11.

3. Nietzsche, *Unpublished Notes*. Cited by Danto, p. 33.

4. Nietzsche, *The Will to Power*, 522, p. 283.

5. Nietzsche, *The Will to Power*, 617, p. 330.

6. Nietzsche, *Twilight of the Idols*, in *The Portable Nietzsche*, p. 483.

7. Nietzsche, *The Will to Power*, 481, p. 267.

8. Nietzsche, *Beyond Good and Evil*, 108, in *Basic Writings of Nietzsche*, p. 275.

9. Nietzsche, *The Will to Power*, 616, p. 330.

10. Olafson, *Principles and Persons*, p. 48.

11. Danto, p. 30.

12. Danto, p. 92.

13. Kuhn, *The Structure of Scientific Revolutions*, p. 206.

14. Nietzsche, *Beyond Good and Evil*, 4, p. 201.

15. Nietzsche, *The Will to Power*, 493, p. 272. Cf. Burke, *PC*, p. 101. "If people believe a belief and live, the fact of their survival tends to prove the adequacy of the belief."

16. Nietzsche, cited by Danto, pp. 38–39.

17. Nietzsche, *The Birth of Tragedy*, 24, in *Basic Writings of Nietzsche*, p. 141.
18. Nietzsche, *Human, All-too-Human*, 11. Cited by Danto, p. 84.
19. Sapir, "Conceptual Categories of Primitive Languages," p. 578.
20. Henle, "Language, Thought, and Culture," pp. 1–2.
21. Henle, p. 15.
22. Quine, *Ontological Relativity*, p. 1.
23. Quine, p. 48.
24. Quine, p. 50.
25. Quine, p. 6.
26. Ogden and Richards, *The Meaning of Meaning*, p. 6.
27. Augustine, *Confessions*, I, 8, p. 51. One also recalls Thomas Spratt's endorsement of the Royal Society's desire "to return back to primitive purity and shortness, when men deliver'd so many *things* almost in an equal number of words," and the burdened philosophers in Swift's *Gulliver's Travels*.
28. Sellars, "The Myth of the Given," pp. 177–78, 185.
29. Rorty, *Philosophy and the Mirror of Nature*, p. 6.
30. Quine, *Word and Object*, p. 2.
31. Saussure, "On the Nature of Language," p. 52. See Saussure's *Course in General Linguistics*, p. 9.
32. Culler, *On Deconstruction*, p. 28.
33. Barthes, cited by Lane, p. 37.
34. Culler, *On Deconstruction*, pp. 20–21.
35. Lentricchia, *After the New Criticism*, p. 108.
36. Lentricchia, *After the New Criticism*, p. 108.
37. Barthes, cited by Culler, *On Deconstruction*, pp. 32–33.
38. Culler, *The Pursuit of Signs*, p. 106.
39. Culler, *The Pursuit of Signs*, p. 101.
40. Culler, *The Pursuit of Signs*, p. 103.
41. Bennett, *Linguistic Behaviour*, p. 246.
42. Chomsky, "Topics in the Theory of Generative Grammar," p. 73.
43. Culler, *The Pursuit of Signs*, p. 29.
44. Culler, *On Deconstruction*, p. 106.
45. Barbara Johnson, cited by Culler, *The Pursuit of Signs*, p. ix.
46. Culler, *The Pursuit of Signs*, p. xi.
47. Culler, *The Pursuit of Signs*, p. 42.
48. Culler, *The Pursuit of Signs*, p. 15.
49. Culler, *On Deconstruction*, p. 234.
50. Culler, *The Pursuit of Signs*, p. 183.
51. Culler, *On Deconstruction*, p. 92.

52. Culler, *On Deconstruction*, p. 123.
53. Culler, *On Deconstruction*, p. 132.
54. Lentricchia, *Criticism and Social Change*, p. 48.
55. Lentricchia, *Criticism and Social Change*, p. 43.
56. Lentricchia, *Criticism and Social Change*, p. 42.
57. Lentricchia, *Criticism and Social Change*, pp. 50–51.
58. Lentricchia, *Criticism and Social Change*, p. 13.
59. Lentricchia, *Criticism and Social Change*, p. 13.
60. Lentricchia, *Criticism and Social Change*, p. 81.
61. Barthes, *A Barthes Reader*, p. 381.
62. Jacques Derrida, cited by Abrams, "How to Do Things with Texts," p. 574.
63. Barthes, *A Barthes Reader*, p. 461. See note 43, chapter I.
64. Bennett, p. ix. If one were to fill out the symmetry of the pentad, the "agent" term would be featured in romantic or phenomenological theories of language.
65. Bennett, p. 6.
66. Bennett, p. 171.
67. Searle, *Speech Acts*, p. 16.
68. Searle, p. 17.
69. Searle, p. 12.
70. H. Paul Grice, cited by Bennett, p. 11.
71. Dewey, *Experience and Nature*, p. 185.
72. Dewey, p. 170.
73. Hirsch, *Validity in Interpretation*, p. 135n.
74. Dewey, p. 179.
75. Malinowski, "The Problem of Meaning in Primitive Languages," p. 305.
76. Malinowski, p. 306.
77. Malinowski, p. 306.
78. Black, *The Labyrinth of Language*, p. 38.
79. Hirsch, p. 87.
80. Malinowski, p. 306.
81. Black, p. 38.
82. Hirsch, p. 87.
83. Malinowski, p. 307.
84. As Black points out, more often it is a question of "rule-governed innovation" rather than "rule-changing innovation" (p. 50).
85. Malinowski, p. 308.
86. Malinowski, p. 308–9.
87. Malinowski, p. 312.

88. Malinowski, p. 317.
89. Malinowski, p. 322.
90. Bennett, p. 254.
91. Hirsch, p. 52. He goes on to say that "verbal meaning is whatever some-one has willed to convey by a particular sequence of linguistic signs and which can be conveyed (shared) by means of those linguistic signs."
92. Hirsch, pp. 78ff.
93. Hirsch, p. 76.
94. Hirsch, p. 127.
95. Black, p. 97.
96. Lentricchia, *Criticism and Social Change*, pp. 57–58.
97. Wittgenstein, *Philosophical Investigations*, p. 8.
98. Wittgenstein, p. 11.
99. Wittgenstein, p. 20.
100. Kenny, *Wittgenstein*, p. 160.
101. Lowry, *Under the Volcano*, p. 65.
102. Wittgenstein, p. 82.
103. Austin, *How to Do Things with Words*, p. 150.
104. Austin, p. 5.
105. Austin, p. 6.
106. Austin, p. 15.
107. Austin, p. 52.
108. Austin, p. 94.
109. Austin, p. 99.
110. Austin, p. 101.
111. Austin, p. 110n.
112. Austin, p. 132.
113. Austin, p. 138.
114. Austin, p. 144.
115. Austin, p. 148.
116. Austin, p. 150.
117. Fowler, "The Structure of Criticism and the Languages of Poetry," pp. 183–84.
118. Fowler, p. 188.
119. Fowler, p. 189.
120. Fowler, p. 194.
121. Edmund Leach, cited by Fowler, p. 189.
122. Lentricchia, *Criticism and Social Change*, p. 145.
123. Lentricchia, *Criticism and Social Change*, p. 149.
124. Lentricchia, *Criticism and Social Change*, p. 19.

CHAPTER FOUR

1. Burke, "Methodological Repression and/or Strategies of Containment,"
   p. 414.
2. See Burke, *The Rhetoric of Religion,* p. 242. Rather than posing the question rhetorically, as I have done, Burke asserts that Hobbes's account of
   the social contract is analytic, not genetic. "Men did not make such a
   contract as Hobbes describes. But they did make such a contract 'in principle.' Or, they are related to one another *as though* they had made such a
   contract." The model, in other words, is heuristic rather than ontological.
3. Burke, "The Principle of Composition," p. 194.
4. Burke, "The Principle of Composition," p. 195.
5. Burke, "The Principle of Composition," p. 196.
6. What is "contain[ed] implicitly, in 'chordial collapse,' [is] a destiny that
   the narrative will unfold explicitly, in 'arpeggio' " (*PLF,* p. 82).
7. Frank, *Kenneth Burke,* p. 142. This is his definition of "logologic."
8. Burke, "Dancing with Tears in My Eyes," p. 28.
9. Burke, *Dramatism and Development,* pp. 30–32.
10. Kant, *Foundations of the Metaphysics of Morals,* p. 66.
11. See Olafson, *Principles and Persons,* p. 146.
12. Tussman, *Obligation and the Body Politic,* pp. 13–14.
13. Olafson, p. 148.
14. Rousseau, *The Social Contract,* p. 101.
15. For a fuller account of Burke's views about "the mystery of the self in
    quest toward a better life," see Rueckert's *Kenneth Burke and the Drama
    of Human Relations,* p. 43.
16. Burke, "Theology and Logology," p. 152.
17. Burke, "Theology and Logology," p. 155.
18. Burke, "Theology and Logology," p. 156.
19. Burke, "Theology and Logology," p. 175.
20. Burke, "Theology and Logology," p. 177.
21. Burke, "Theology and Logology," p. 174.
22. Burke, "(Nonsymbolic) Motion/(Symbolic) Action," p. 814.
23. Burke, "(Nonsymbolic) Motion/(Symbolic) Action," p. 810.
24. Burke, "(Nonsymbolic) Motion/(Symbolic) Action," p. 813.
25. Burke, "(Nonsymbolic) Motion/(Symbolic) Action," p. 811.
26. Burke, "(Nonsymbolic) Motion/(Symbolic) Action," p. 814.
27. As Jameson points out, for Sartre "the very origin of action . . . was
    found in the structure of human being as *lack,* as ontological privation,

attempting to satisfy itself, and thereby to arrive at some definitive state of being" (*MF*, p. 232).

28. As Copi points out, "a cosmo*gony* is not a cosmo*logy*. The one is a narrative sequence in time, the other a pattern of timeless concepts." See "The Growth of Concepts," p. 45.

29. Hirsch, *Validity in Interpretation*, p. 86.

30. Hirsch, "Stylistics and Synonymity," p. 577.

CHAPTER FIVE

1. The grotesque is secular conversion downward, a cult of incongruity without the laughter that humor affords, whereas mysticism is religious conversion upward. See "Poetic Categories" in *ATH*.

2. Eliot, "The Dry Salvages," *Collected Poems*, p. 208, l. 100. All references are to this edition, and line numbers are given in the text.

3. Bradley, *Appearance and Reality*, p. 28.

4. Augustine, XI, 15, p. 289.

5. Augustine, XI, 20, p. 293.

6. Augustine, XI, 27, p. 300. Cf. Kant, *Critique of Pure Reason*, pp. 76–79. "Time is not something which exists of itself, or which inheres in things as an objective determination, and it does not, therefore, remain when abstraction is made of all subjective conditions of its intuition (A 33). . . . Time is nothing but the form of inner sense, that is, of the intuition of ourselves and of our inner state. It cannot be a determination of outer appearances; it has to do neither with shape nor position, but with the relation of representations in our inner state. And just because this inner intuition yields no shape, we endeavour to make up for this want by analogies (B 50). . . . Time is therefore a purely subjective condition of our human intuition (which is always sensible, that is, so far as we are affected by objects), and in itself, apart from the subject, is nothing (A 35). . . . It does not inhere in the objects, but merely in the subject which intuits them (A 38)." A similar psychologizing move is evident in Bergson's notion of the *durée réelle*, as it is in most of the existentialists, phenomenologists, and their idealist predecessors.

7. Eliot, *Knowledge and Experience*, pp. 18, 99.

8. Drew, *T. S. Eliot: The Design of His Poetry*, pp. 186–87.

9. Augustine, XI, 18, p. 291; my italics.

10. Eliot, "Lancelot Andrewes," *Selected Essays*, p. 307.

11. See Copleston, *A History of Philosophy*, p. 229.

12. Bradley, *Essays on Truth and Reality*, p. 159.

13. Copleston, p. 229.
14. Eliot, *Knowledge and Experience*, p. 27.
15. Eliot, *Knowledge and Experience*, p. 31.
16. See Copleston, p. 229.
17. Copleston, pp. 229–30.
18. Copleston, p. 236.
19. Wollheim, "Eliot and Bradley: An Account," p. 173.
20. Copleston, p. 244.
21. Bradley, *Essays on Truth and Reality*, p. 15. The idea of a fall from a prior unity and of a subsequent attempt to recover that unity at a higher level is hardly new. The vocabulary of innocence and experience in its religious and secular variants pervades the Western tradition, as everyone knows. The advantage of regarding the idea from the Bradleyan perspective is that it reveals the technical problem confronting the poet with respect to expressibility and the paradoxical knot of motives therein.
22. Preston, *Four Quartets Rehearsed*, p. 12. Preston goes on to say that "the *rose* is the emblem of human love, becoming divine; the emblem of the martyr; the emblem of Christ's love (the Five Wounds were symbolized by a five-petalled red rose)" (p. 35).
23. Eliot, "Dante," *Selected Essays*, pp. 234–35. Cf. "Dans le Restaurant," *Collected Poems*, p. 53.

> It was there, in a downpour, that we took refuge.
> I was seven years old, she was very small.
> She was all wet, I gave her some primroses. . . .
> I tickled her to make her laugh.
> I experienced a moment of power and rapture.
> (translation)

24. Homer, *The Odyssey of Homer*, p. 139.
25. Tennyson, "The Lotos-Eaters," in *Tennyson's Poetry*, p. 48, ll. 24–27.
26. Tennyson, p. 50, ll. 110–11.
27. Eliot, "The *Pensées* of Pascal," *Selected Essays*, p. 358.
28. See Gardner, *The Art of T. S. Eliot*, and *The Composition of the Four Quartets*.
29. Bergsten, *Time and Eternity*, p. 113.
30. See Gardner, *The Composition of the Four Quartets*, p. 107.
31. Augustine, XI, 28, pp. 301–2.
32. Eliot, "Tradition and the Individual Talent," *Selected Essays*, p. 5.
33. Augustine, XI, 6, p. 282.
34. Augustine, XI, 7, pp. 282–83. There is also that incredibly lush passage where he and Monica are talking together. "And we sighed for it [wisdom], and we left behind, bound to it, 'the first fruits of the spirit,' and we turned

back again to the noise of our mouths, where a word both begins and ends. But what is there like your Word, our Lord, remaining in himself without growing old, and yet renewing all things?

"Therefore we said: If for any man the tumult of the flesh fell silent, silent the images of earth, and of the waters, and of the air; silent the heavens; silent for him the very soul itself, and he should pass beyond himself by not thinking upon himself; silent his dreams and all imagined appearances, and every tongue, and every sign; and if all things that come to be through change should become wholly silent to him—for if any man can hear, then all these things say to him, 'We did not make ourselves,' but he who endures forever made us—if when they have said these words, they then become silent, for they have raised up his ear to him who made them, and God alone speaks, not through such things but through himself, so that we hear his Word, not uttered by a tongue of flesh, nor by an angel's voice, 'nor by the sound of thunder,' nor by the riddle of a similitude, but by himself whom we love in these things, him- self we hear without their aid,—even as we then reached out and in swift thought attained to that eternal Wisdom which abides over all things—if this could be prolonged, and other visions of a far inferior kind could be withdrawn, and this one alone ravish, and absorb, and hide away its beholder within its deepest joys, so that sempiternal life might be such as was that moment of understanding for which we sighed, would it not be this: 'Enter into the joy of your Lord'? When shall this be? When 'we shall all rise again, but we shall not all be changed' " (IX, 10, p. 222). It takes a vast number of syllables in a dazzlingly periodic sentence for an inveterate wordman to arrive at the eternal Word in its silence.

POSTSCRIPT

1. Rueckert, *Kenneth Burke and the Drama of Human Relations*, p. 43.
2. Rueckert, pp. 27, 162.
3. Burke, cited by Rueckert, p. 162.
4. Weaver, "The Phaedrus and the Nature of Rhetoric," in *The Ethics of Rhetoric*, p. 5.
5. Weaver, p. 20.
6. Weaver, pp. 22–23, 25.

Bibliography

Abrams, M. H. "How to Do Things with Texts." *Partisan Review,* 46, No. 4 (1979), 566–87.

_____. *The Mirror and the Lamp.* London: Oxford University Press, 1953.

Augustine. *The Confessions of St. Augustine.* Trans. John Ryan. Garden City, N.Y.: Doubleday, 1960.

Austin, J. L. *How to Do Things with Words.* Ed. J. O. Urmson. New York: Oxford University Press, 1962.

Barthes, Roland. *A Barthes Reader.* Ed. Susan Sontag. New York: Hill and Wang, 1982.

_____. *Mythologies.* Trans. Annette Lavers. New York: Hill and Wang, 1972.

Bennett, Jonathan. *Linguistic Behaviour.* Cambridge: Cambridge University Press, 1976.

Bergsten, Staffan. *Time and Eternity.* Oslo: Berlingska Botryckeriet Lund, 1960.

Black, Max. *The Labyrinth of Language.* New York: Praeger, 1968.

_____. *Language and Philosophy.* Ithaca, N.Y.: Cornell University Press, 1949.

Booth, Wayne. *Critical Understanding: The Powers and Limits of Pluralism.* Chicago and London: University of Chicago Press, 1979.

_____. *The Rhetoric of Fiction.* 2nd ed. Chicago and London: University of Chicago Press, 1983.

Bradbury, Malcolm, and David Palmer, eds. *Contemporary Criticism.* London: Edward Arnold, 1970.

Bradley, F. H. *Appearance and Reality.* 2nd ed. [1897] 1930; rpt. London: Oxford University Press, 1969.

_____. *Essays on Truth and Reality.* Oxford: Clarendon Press, 1914.

Brecht, Bertolt. *Brecht on Theatre.* Trans. John Willett. London: Methuen, 1964.

Brooks, Cleanth. *The Well-Wrought Urn.* New York: Harcourt Brace and World, 1947.

Burke, Kenneth. *Attitudes Toward History.* 3rd ed. Berkeley, Los Angeles, and London: University of California Press, 1984. This edition has a new afterword by the author.

———. *Collected Poems, 1915–1967.* Berkeley and Los Angeles: University of California Press, 1968.

———. *Counter-Statement.* 2nd ed. 1953; rpt. Berkeley and Los Angeles: University of California Press, 1968. This reprint edition has a six-page addendum not found in the 1953 edition.

———. "Dancing with Tears in My Eyes." *Critical Inquiry,* 1, No. 1 (1974), 23–31.

———. "Dramatism." In *Communication: Concepts and Perspectives.* Ed. Lee Thayer. Washington, D.C.: Spartan Books, 1967, pp. 327–60.

———. *Dramatism and Development.* Barre, Mass.: Clark University Press, 1972.

———. "Fact, Inference, and Proof in the Analysis of Literary Symbolism." In *Symbols and Values: An Initial Study.* Thirteenth Symposium of the Conference on Science, Philosophy, and Religion. Ed. Lyman Bryson, et al. New York: Harper and Brothers, 1954, pp. 283–306. Rpt. in Burke's *Terms for Order* (q.v.), pp. 145–72.

———. *A Grammar of Motives.* Berkeley and Los Angeles: University of California Press, 1969.

———. "Kinds of Criticism." *Poetry,* 68 (August 1946), 272–82.

———. "King Lear: Its Form and Psychosis." *Shenandoah,* 21 (Autumn 1969), 3–18.

———. *Language as Symbolic Action: Essays on Life, Literature, and Method.* Berkeley and Los Angeles: University of California Press, 1966.

———. "The Language of Poetry, 'Dramatistically' Considered." *Chicago Review,* 8 (Fall 1954), 88–102.

———. "Methodological Repression and/or Strategies of Containment." *Critical Inquiry,* 5, No. 2 (Winter 1978), 411–15.

———. "Mysticism as a Solution to the Poet's Dilemma." In *Spiritual Problems in Contemporary Literature: A Series of Addresses and Discussions.* Ed. S. R. Hopper. New York: Institute for Religious and Social Studies, 1952, pp. 105–15.

———. "(Nonsymbolic) Motion/(Symbolic) Action." *Critical Inquiry,* 4, No. 4 (Summer 1978), 809–38.

———. "On Catharsis, Or Resolution." *Kenyon Review,* 21 (Spring 1959), 337–75.

———. *Permanence and Change: An Anatomy of Purpose.* 3rd ed. Berkeley,

Los Angeles, and London: University of California Press, 1984. This edition has a new afterword by the author.

_____. *Perspectives by Incongruity.* Ed. Stanley Edgar Hyman. Bloomington: Indiana University Press, 1964.

_____. *The Philosophy of Literary Form: Studies in Symbolic Action.* 3rd rev. ed., 1967; rpt. Berkeley and Los Angeles: University of California Press, 1973.

_____. "The Principle of Composition." *Poetry,* 99 (October 1961), 46–53. Rpt. in Burke's *Terms for Order* (*q.v.*), pp. 189–98.

_____. *A Rhetoric of Motives.* Berkeley and Los Angeles: University of California Press, 1969.

_____. *The Rhetoric of Religion: Studies in Logology.* Berkeley and Los Angeles: University of California Press, 1970.

_____. *Terms for Order.* Ed. Stanley Edgar Hyman. Bloomington: Indiana University Press, 1964.

_____. "Theology and Logology." *Kenyon Review,* New Series, I (1979), 151–85.

Chomsky, Noam. *Topics in the Theory of Generative Grammar.* The Hague: Mouton, 1966, pp. 7–24. Rpt. as "Topics in the Theory of Generative Grammar." In *The Philosophy of Language.* Ed. John Searle. London: Oxford University Press, 1971, pp. 51–75.

Copi, Irving. "The Growth of Concepts." In *Language, Thought, and Culture.* Ed. Paul Henle. Ann Arbor: University of Michigan Press, 1958, pp. 25–48.

Copleston, Frederick. *A History of Philosophy,* Volume VIII: *Modern Philosophy: Bentham to Russell,* Part 1: *British Empiricism and the Idealist Movement in Great Britain.* Garden City, N.Y.: Doubleday, 1967.

Crusius, Timothy. "A Case for Kenneth Burke's Dialectic and Rhetoric." *Philosophy and Rhetoric,* 19, No. 1 (1986), 23–37.

Culler, Jonathan. *The Pursuit of Signs: Semiotics, Literature, Deconstruction.* Ithaca, N.Y.: Cornell University Press, 1981.

_____. *On Deconstruction: Theory and Criticism after Structuralism.* Ithaca, N.Y.: Cornell University Press, 1982.

_____. *Structuralist Poetics.* Ithaca, N.Y.: Cornell University Press, 1975.

Danto, Arthur. *Nietzsche as Philosopher.* New York: Macmillan, 1965.

Dewey, John. *Experience and Nature.* La Salle, Ill.: Open Court, 1925.

Drew, Elizabeth. *T. S. Eliot: The Design of His Poetry.* London: Eyre and Spottiswoode, 1950.

Eliot, T. S. *Collected Poems 1909–1962.* London: Faber and Faber, 1963.

_____. *Knowledge and Experience in the Philosophy of F. H. Bradley.* London: Faber and Faber, 1964.

_____. *Selected Essays of T. S. Eliot.* New York: Harcourt Brace and World, 1960.

Empson, William. *Seven Types of Ambiguity.* 3rd ed. Harmondsworth: Penguin Books, 1961.

_____. *The Structure of Complex Words.* London: Chatto and Windus, 1952.

Fergusson, Francis. *The Idea of a Theater.* Garden City, New York: Doubleday, 1949.

Fowler, Roger. "The Structure of Criticism and the Languages of Poetry: An Approach through Language." In *Contemporary Criticism.* Ed. M. Bradbury and D. Palmer. London: Edward Arnold, 1970, pp. 172–94.

Frank, Armin Paul. *Kenneth Burke.* New York: Twayne, 1969.

Gardner, Helen. *The Art of T. S. Eliot.* New York: Dutton, 1959.

_____. *The Composition of the Four Quartets.* London: Faber and Faber, 1978.

Hawkes, Terence. *Structuralism and Semiotics.* Berkeley and Los Angeles: University of California Press, 1977.

Henle, Paul. "Language, Thought, and Culture." In *Language, Thought, and Culture.* Ed. Paul Henle. Ann Arbor: University of Michigan Press, 1958, pp. 1–24.

Hirsch, E. D. "Stylistics and Synonymity." *Critical Inquiry,* 1, No. 3 (March 1975), 559–81.

_____. *Validity in Interpretation.* New Haven and London: Yale University Press, 1967.

Holland, Norman. "The 'Unconscious' of Literature: The Psychoanalytic Approach." In *Contemporary Criticism.* Ed. M. Bradbury and D. Palmer. London: Edward Arnold, 1970, pp. 130–53.

Homer. *The Odyssey of Homer.* Trans. Richard Lattimore. New York: Harper and Row, 1965.

Hyman, Stanley Edgar. *The Armed Vision.* 2nd rev. ed. New York: Vintage, 1955.

James, Henry. *The Art of the Novel.* New York: Scribner's Sons, 1934.

Jameson, Fredric. *Marxism and Form.* Princeton: Princeton University Press, 1971.

_____. *The Prison-House of Language.* Princeton: Princeton University Press, 1972.

_____. "The Symbolic Inference; or, Kenneth Burke and Ideological Analysis." *Critical Inquiry,* 4, No. 3 (Spring 1978), 507–25.

Kant, Immanuel. *Critique of Pure Reason.* Trans. Norman Kemp Smith. New York: St. Martin's Press, 1965.

_____. *Foundations of the Metaphysics of Morals.* Trans. Lewis White Beck. New York: Bobbs Merrill, 1959.

Kenny, Anthony. *Wittgenstein*. Harmondsworth: Penguin Books, 1973.

Kuhn, Thomas. *The Structure of Scientific Revolutions*. 2nd ed. Chicago: University of Chicago Press, 1970.

Lane, Michael, ed. *Introduction to Structuralism*. New York: Basic Books, 1970.

Lentricchia, Frank. *After the New Criticism*. Chicago: University of Chicago Press, 1980.

———. *Criticism and Social Change*. Chicago: University of Chicago Press, 1983.

———. "Reading History with Kenneth Burke." In *Representing Kenneth Burke*. Ed. Hayden White and Margaret Brose. Baltimore and London: Johns Hopkins University Press, 1982, pp. 119–49.

Lowry, Malcolm. *Under the Volcano*. Philadelphia: Lippincott, 1965.

Malinowski, Bronislaw. "The Problem of Meaning in Primitive Languages." In *The Meaning of Meaning*. London: Routledge and Kegan Paul, 1923, pp. 296–336.

Nietzsche, Friedrich. *Basic Writings of Nietzsche*. Ed. and trans. Walter Kaufmann. New York: Random House, 1966.

———. *The Portable Nietzsche*. Ed. and trans. Walter Kaufmann. New York: Viking Press, 1954.

———. *The Will to Power*. Trans. Walter Kaufmann and R. J. Hollingdale. London: Weidenfeld and Nicolson, 1967.

Ogden, C. K., and I. A. Richards. *The Meaning of Meaning*. London: Routledge and Kegan Paul, 1923.

Olafson, Frederick. *Principles and Persons: An Ethical Interpretation of Existentialism*. Baltimore: Johns Hopkins University Press, 1967.

Pears, David. *Ludwig Wittgenstein*. New York: Viking Press, 1969.

Pratt, Marie Louise. *Toward a Speech Act Theory of Literary Discourse*. Bloomington: Indiana University Press, 1977.

Preston, Raymond. *Four Quartets Rehearsed*. London: Sheed and Ward, 1946.

Quine, W. V. O. *Ontological Relativity and Other Essays*. New York and London: Columbia University Press, 1969.

———. *Word and Object*. New York: MIT, 1960.

Ransom, John Crowe. *The New Criticism*. Norfolk: New Directions, 1941.

———. *The World's Body*. New York: Scribners, 1938.

Richards, I. A. *Interpretation in Teaching*. London: Kegan Paul, 1938.

———. *The Philosophy of Rhetoric*. London: Oxford University Press, 1936.

———. *Poetries and Sciences: A Re-issue of Science and Poetry (1926, 1935) with Commentary*. New York: Norton, 1970.

———. *Principles of Literary Criticism*. New York: Harcourt Brace and World, 1925.

Rorty, Richard. *Philosophy and the Mirror of Nature*. Princeton: Princeton University Press, 1979.

Rousseau, Jean-Jacques. *The Social Contract*. Trans. Maurice Cranston. Harmondsworth: Penguin Books, 1960.

Rueckert, William H., ed. *Critical Responses to Kenneth Burke, 1924–1966*. Minneapolis: University of Minnesota Press, 1969.

———. *Kenneth Burke and the Drama of Human Relations*. 2nd ed. Berkeley and Los Angeles: University of California Press, 1982.

Sapir, Edward. "Conceptual Categories of Primitive Languages." *Science*, 74 (1931), 578.

———. *Selected Writings of Edward Sapir in Language, Culture, and Personality*. Ed. David Mandelbaum. Berkeley and Los Angeles: University of California Press, 1949.

Sartre, Jean-Paul. *Being and Nothingness*. Trans. Hazel Barnes. New York: Washington Square Press, 1953.

Saussure, Ferdinand de. *Course in General Linguistics*. Ed. Charles Bally and Albert Sechehaye. Trans. Wade Baskin. London: Peter Owen, 1960.

———. "On the Nature of Language," in *Introduction to Structuralism*. Ed. Michael Lane. New York: Basic Books, 1970, p. 52.

Searle, John, ed. *The Philosophy of Language*. London: Oxford University Press, 1971.

———. *Speech Acts*. Cambridge: Cambridge University Press, 1969.

Sellars, Wilfrid. "The Myth of the Given." From "Empiricism and the Philosophy of Mind." In his *Science, Perception, and Reality*. New York: Humanities Press, 1963, pp. 164–70. Rpt. in *Phenomenology and Existentialism*. Ed. Robert Solomon. New York: Harper and Row, 1972, pp. 177–86.

Tussman, Joseph. *Obligation and the Body Politic*. London: Oxford University Press, 1960.

Tennyson, Alfred L. *Tennyson's Poetry*. Ed. Robert Hill. New York: Norton, 1971.

Weaver, Richard. *The Ethics of Rhetoric*. Chicago: Henry Regnery, 1953.

Wellek, Rene, and Austin Warren. *Theory of Literature*. 3rd rev. ed. New York: Harcourt Brace and World, 1962.

Whorf, Benjamin Lee. *Language, Thought, and Reality*. Ed. John Carroll. Cambridge: MIT, 1956.

Wimsatt, W. K. *The Verbal Icon*. Lexington: University of Kentucky Press, 1954.

———, and Monroe Beardsley. "The Affective Fallacy." In Wimsatt, *The Verbal Icon*. Lexington: University of Kentucky Press, 1954, pp. 21–39.

Winters, Yvor. *The Anatomy of Nonsense*. Norfolk: New Directions, 1943.

Wittgenstein, Ludwig. *Philosophical Investigations*. Trans. G. E. M. An-
scombe. Oxford: Basil Blackwell and Mott, 1958.
_____. *Tractatus Logico-Philosophicus*. Trans. D. F. Pears and B. F.
McGuinness. London: Routledge and Kegan Paul, 1961.
Wollheim, Richard. "Eliot and Bradley: An Account." In *Eliot in Perspective*.
Ed. Graham Martin. London: Macmillan, 1970, pp. 169–93.

Index